Taming Information Technology

Series in Human-Technology Interaction

Series Editor
Alex Kirlik, University of Illinois at Urbana-Champaign and the Beckman Institute

Adaptive Perspectives on Human-Technology Interaction: Methods and Models for Cognitive Engineering and Human-Computer Interaction
Edited by Alex Kirlik

Computers, Phones, and the Internet: Domesticating Information Technology
Edited by Robert Kraut, Malcolm Brynin, and Sara Kiesler

Attention: From Theory to Practice
Edited by Arthur F. Kramer, Douglas Wiegmann, and Alex Kirlik

Neuroergonomics: The Brain at Work
Edited by Raja Parasuraman and Matthew Rizzo

Information Foraging Theory: Adaptive Interaction with Information
Peter Pirolli

Human-Tech: Ethical and Scientific Foundations
Kim Vicente

Edited by Alex Kirlik

Being There Together: Social Interaction in Virtual Environments
Ralph Schroeder

Exposing the Magic of Design: A Practitioner's Guide to the Methods and Theory of Synthesis
Jon Kolko

Cross-Cultural Technology Design: Creating Culture-Sensitive Technology for Local Users
Huatong Sun

Taming Information Technology: Lessons from Studies of System Administrators
Eser Kandogan, Paul P. Maglio, Eben M. Haber, and John Bailey

Taming Information Technology

Lessons from Studies of System Administrators

ESER KANDOGAN
PAUL P. MAGLIO
EBEN M. HABER
JOHN BAILEY

OXFORD
UNIVERSITY PRESS

Oxford University Press is a department of the University of Oxford.
It furthers the University's objective of excellence in research,
scholarship, and education by publishing worldwide.

Oxford   New York
Auckland   Cape Town   Dar es Salaam   Hong Kong   Karachi
Kuala Lumpur   Madrid   Melbourne   Mexico City   Nairobi
New Delhi   Shanghai   Taipei   Toronto

With offices in
Argentina   Austria   Brazil   Chile   Czech Republic   France   Greece
Guatemala   Hungary   Italy   Japan   Poland   Portugal   Singapore
South Korea   Switzerland   Thailand   Turkey   Ukraine   Vietnam

Copyright © 2012 by Eser Kandogan, Paul P. Maglio, Eben M. Haber, and John Bailey

Published in the United States of America by
Oxford University Press
198 Madison Avenue, New York, NY 10016,
United States of America
www.oup.com

Oxford is a registered trademark of Oxford University Press
in the UK and in certain other countries

All rights reserved. No part of this publication may be reproduced,
stored in a retrieval system, or transmitted, in any form or by any means,
electronic, mechanical, photocopying, recording, or otherwise,
without the prior permission of Oxford University Press.

Library of Congress Cataloging-in-Publication Data
  Taming information technology : lessons from studies of system
  administrators/Eser Kandogan ...[et al.].
    p. cm.
  Includes bibliographical references and index.
  ISBN 978-0-19-537412-4 (pbk. : alk. paper)   1. Information resources management.
  2. Information technology—Management.   I. Kandogan, Eser.
  T58.64.T34 2012
  004.068—dc23
  2011053404

9 8 7 6 5 4 3 2 1
Printed in the United States of America
on acid-free paper

Contents

Acknowledgments   vii

Prologue: Why We Wrote This Book   ix

1. Motivations and Methods   1
2. People and Collaboration   19
3. Technologies and Complexity   51
4. Practices and Innovation   87
5. Tools and Automation   129
6. Organizations and Information   159
7. Communities and Trust   197
8. Findings and Lessons   229

Epilogue: Where are They Now?   247

References   263

Author Index   277

Subject Index   283

Acknowledgments

This book has been 10 years in the making, so there are a lot of people to thank. Because we may not remember them all, apologies to everyone we missed.

First, we thank our participants, the sysadmins and others who let us in to watch their activities and to talk about their jobs. Though we cannot name them, we are certainly indebted to them. We hope they find this book useful. It is for them, after all.

Second, we thank those who worked with us to collect and analyze data and to explore our conclusions through implementation, including Rob Barrett, Chris Campbell, Mike Chavoustie, Allen Cypher, Andrew Eberbach, Stephen Farrell, Peter Khooshabeh, Trevor Montgomery, Adam November, Madhu Prabaker, Joe Ryan, Suchi Saria, Leila Takayama, Josh Woods, Anna Zacchi, and Haixia Zhao.

Third, we thank those who supported the work over the years, including our managers, our funders, and others: Kathryn Britton, Jarir Chaar, Josephine Cheng, Steve Cousins, Mark Dean, Alan Ganek, Laura Haas, Anant Jhingran, Jeff Kephart, Robert Morris, Stefan Nusser, Dan Russell, Dan Shiffman, Barton Smith, Alfred Spector, Jim Spohrer, Ric Telford, Steve White, and Michelle Zhou.

Fourth, we thank those who read and gave comments on early drafts of this book and its parts, including Laura Anderson, Jim Barlow,

Rob Barrett, Terry Bleizeffer, Jeanette Blomberg, Melissa Cefkin, Susan Dray, Steve Greenspan, Laura Haas, Tom Limoncelli, Tom Moran, B. J. Scheid, and Ashish Sharma.

Fifth, we thank Oxford University Press, particularly Catharine Carlin and Joan Bossert, our editors, Jennifer Milton, who shepherded us through the production process, and Alex Kirlik, editor of the Human-Technology Interaction series, whose encouragement and subtle help over the last four years made this work possible.

Sixth, parts of chapters 2 and 3 were previously published in "Collaboration in System Administration" by Eben Haber, Eser Kandogan, and Paul Maglio in *ACM Queue*, volume 8, issue 12, December, 2010 (copyright the Association for Computing Machinery). It is reprinted here with permission.

Finally, we thank our families, who patiently supported us while we were not finishing this for so long. Thank you Elif and Eren Kandogan; Teenie Matlock; Sheri and Talia Byrne-Haber; Julie, Olivia, and Anika Bailey.

Prologue: Why We Wrote This Book

On a fall day in 2001, an executive took the stage in the auditorium at the Almaden Research Center to tell us about a bold new IBM initiative called autonomic computing. It was about how computer systems would soon be able to manage themselves using many of the same principles that an animal's autonomic nervous system uses to manage its bodily processes, whether breathing, beating, or repairing. It was a fascinating vision, and it was important because information technology (IT) customers were spending more money managing systems than they were spending buying the systems in the first place—and self-managing systems were expected to have lower total cost of ownership. This would be a win for IBM, with better differentiated technology, and it would be a win for customers, with lower costs in the long run.

As laid out at the time, autonomic computing aimed to make IT more self-managing, particularly, self-configuring, self-healing, self-optimizing, and self-protecting (see Kephart & Chess, 2003). It aimed to replace much of what was usually done by the people who managed IT systems with automation. So it was only natural when someone stood up at that presentation and asked, "Do you know what the people who manage systems actually spend their time doing?" The answer surprised us: no. IBM did not really know, and there was no literature on it (see Barrett, Chen & Maglio, 2003). So it was only natural for us to want to find an answer. That was the moment that launched us on a journey into the field to study IT system administrators. *What do they do?* How can we improve their tools and environments so that they are more effective and their systems run better?

And so we set out to observe computer system administrators in their natural environments. Equipped with camcorders, cameras, tapes, computers, and notebooks, we observed the activities, processes, and practices of real system administrators. Over 5 years, we made 16 visits to 6 different sites. We observed database administrators, Web administrators, system security experts, storage designers, infrastructure architects, and system operators. Whatever their specific titles, we refer to them all as *system administrators, sysadmins, administrators,* or *admins*.

At the start, our memories of computer support staff in college had left us with the image of a system administrator as a guy (and it was always a guy) in his 20s or 30s, with long hair and a ponytail, a T-shirt and jeans, working alone and able to answer any question and solve any problem, all facilitated by lots of caffeine. We soon discovered that the reality was much more complicated. We found that modern IT systems were so complex that no single individual could know everything. We found men and women, young and old, working together far more than we expected. Through e-mail, instant messages, phone, and face-to-face contacts, the work of system administration required extensive communication, collaboration, and coordination among various groups of highly skilled people, bringing together a variety of knowledge and expertise from different areas. In addition, we observed system administrators building their own tools, developing their own methods, and structuring their organizations so that, as a whole, the group could understand and manage systems that were beyond the capabilities of any single individual. We saw that tools, methods, and organizations were shared locally and more broadly in the sysadmin community. In the most successful cases, tools and methods evolved to become more useful, more robust, and more versatile. We saw best practices and tools mandated across organizations through standards, guidelines, and policies, which sometimes helped the organization be more effective through improved consistency and interoperability.

We now know what sysadmins do, and we know how to support their work. Sysadmins are critical and misunderstood. Their continual creativity and constant collaboration keeps systems running. By telling their stories in this book, we aim to make sysadmins and their work better understood by bringing to life the challenges they face and the complex environments in which they work.

I

Motivations and Methods

We were on an expedition. An expedition that led us into a huge unmarked building. An expedition that got us close to technical people who kept toys, puzzles, and a large coffee mug collection in their offices. It was an expedition that granted us passes to walk on the cold raised-floor that housed hundreds of supercomputers, and then to go below, down a steel ladder, where the draft pushed us up against a giant air conditioner.

We were doing ethnography. Not the kind that describes a foreign culture in some remote part of the world. We were studying the tribes of information technology (IT) specialists, database administrators, Web masters, storage designers, security administrators, infrastructure architects, and system operators. We were not cultural anthropologists. We were engineers, technologists, and computer scientists. Yet ethnographic research was exactly what we needed to do. Ethnographers conduct extended fieldwork, spending substantial time living and working among members of the culture they study. They are not just observers. They are participants. They contribute to daily work to develop a holistic understanding of a culture, experienced first hand by participating in the activities and traditions they study (Fetterman, 1998). Often the goal is to develop a "thick description," an understanding of practices, traditions, and ways of life within their social and historical context, by examining how tools, practices, processes, and organizations have evolved (Geertz, 1973).

Though we lacked the time and expertise to truly join the culture of system administrators, developing a deep understanding of the practices of system administrators was, in fact, our goal. We did our best to apply methods from anthropology to guide our studies (Bernard, 1998). First and foremost, we aimed to observe with a clear eye and an open mind, ready to see what was to be seen, discounting our preconceived notions of system administration. In this, we were inspired by ethnomethodology: We aimed not to prove or disprove any theories about administration work, but rather, we aimed to develop a clear description of that work and the social structures that arise from it (Sharrock, Anderson, & Anderson, 1986), and we aimed to interpret current practice in its social and historical context (Orlikowski & Baroudi, 1991). And it would be nice if we learned something practical along the way.

Why study IT management? Well, modern society depends heavily on IT. Consider the Y2K frenzy. Governments, corporations, and public were scared that at the turn of the 21st century, computer systems would simply stop working, with our commercial, economic, transportation, and defense infrastructures collapsing as a result. The potential risk was so great that hundreds of billions of dollars were spent updating computer software and systems to prevent the collapse of modern IT-based society (Manion & Evan, 2000). This feared collapse never came, and it is still debated whether it was averted by massive investment or whether the potential problems were never really that severe to begin with (Quiggin, 2005).

The point is that IT is pervasive, complicated, and practically invisible to the average person. When you click the "submit" button on your bank's Web site to transfer money to your son in college, or when you order groceries online to be delivered by a supermarket to your doorstep, IT and sysadmins make it all work. From banking to retail, consumer to business, government to nonprofit, every modern organization, process, practice, and tool is somehow affected or facilitated by IT. Having this technology work properly depends on every nut and bolt fitting together perfectly and every cog and chain running together smoothly. Nowadays, IT is so complex that no one has the complete picture of how it all fits together, not even those who manage it (Barrett, 2004). When parts of this machinery fail to work, even for a few hours or minutes, costs can add up to millions in lost revenue and the failure makes news headlines (e.g., Stone, 2008). Cost and complexity have led many enterprises to outsource their IT infrastructure to others. Though outsourcing to IT service-delivery companies may provide more certainty with respect to IT costs, all it really does is to shift the management burden to others.

So what makes IT work? To the end user, this amazing technology works like magic—except when it fails. Users get frustrated and complain. As we looked more deeply, we found that the technology is far from magic; it is the people and organizations behind the technology that are largely responsible for things working as well as they do. Simply put, people make all this work—24 hours a day, 7 days a week. They not only tighten the nuts on to the bolts, but also they are often the chains among the cogs of the disparate pieces of technology. They carefully monitor different parts of hugely complex systems: They know when things are working or are going wrong; they move data from one part of the system to the other; they interpret output of one part, transform, and feed it to another part; and they connect missing links between systems. Importantly, we saw them take the initiative, building their own tools, developing their own methods and practices, and structuring their organizations to better manage the problems of ever-more complex IT.

Trends

Our expeditions into the world of system administrators were inspired not only by the importance of IT management, but also by three important trends affecting the field. First, the work is increasingly done in the context of IT service delivery, in which IT management is done by a service provider for a client, based on a formal business agreement (Engardio, Arndt & Foust, 2006). Service providers have been very focused on understanding and improving practices to improve service and reduce costs. Second, human labor costs have grown to dominate the cost of IT management, more than hardware, software, and energy (Bozman & Perry, 2010; Cappuccio, Keyworth & Kirwin, 2002; Gartner, 1999; ITCentrix, 2001; Serenity Systems, 2005). Understanding how sysadmins work could give insights into how to stop or even reverse this trend. Third, automation has been proposed as an approach to reducing the human costs of IT management (IBM, 2001). Yet an understanding of the tasks to be automated is required to know whether automation is feasible, and if so, how to go about automating sysadmin tasks effectively (Brown & Hellerstein, 2005).

Business

What is IT service delivery? It is the practice of managing IT assets and services, typically in accordance with agreements between service provider and client. Client IT assets may include hardware such as computer systems (e.g., laptops, desktops, servers), networking equipment (e.g., routers, adapters, switches), and storage devices (e.g., disk drives, tapes, arrays), and software such as operating systems (e.g., Microsoft Windows, Apple OS X, Linux), database management software (e.g., MySQL, Microsoft SQL Server), Web application servers (e.g., IBM WebSphere, Apache Tomcat), and application software (e.g., PeopleSoft, SAP). Service providers may offer IT services including software license management, configuration management, procurement management, capacity management, availability management, and problem management. Agreements between provider and client are legally binding contracts, which include service-level agreements (SLAs) that define expected levels of availability, performance, serviceability, and delivery cost structure (and specify financial penalties when the promises are not fulfilled).

For example, a department store may outsource end-user services such as desk-side support to an IT service company with guarantees on availability and serviceability, and with a specific schedule of costs and penalties. Then, when the employees of the department store have technical problems, such as not being able to connect to an e-mail server, they would call the support team of the service provider to report the problem. The service provider would then open a problem ticket to track the issue and assign it a priority based on the severity of the problem. The goal of the service provider would then be to resolve the issue based on the priority assigned in accordance with the SLA. If the SLA specified that e-mail service problems would need to be resolved within two hours, the service provider would allocate the technical staff resources to troubleshoot and correct the problem quickly. If, somehow, the problem could not be resolved within the required time, the service provider would need to pay a penalty for not meeting serviceability requirements set forth in the SLA. There may be different levels of service defined for different divisions in the client company. For example, certain divisions that serve a critical function in the department store—such as online shopping—may need a high level of service, such as resolving problem tickets within an hour. Other secondary organizations, such as purchasing, may get a lower level of service, for instance, resolving tickets within a day.

Why would a department store outsource IT services to another company? Simply, because IT management is not one of the core competencies of a department store. A department store would rather focus on its customers, stores, and business model, leaving IT to others for cost and quality reasons. This is, in fact, a growing trend (Hirschheim, 2009). A lot of companies that previously had IT personnel on staff have shifted to outsourced services. As part of the service agreement, they may even have their existing IT personnel rebadged as staff of the service provider, having them continue to provide the same function but as employees of the service provider. This shift to an outsourced service model may, in and of itself, lead to productivity gains by formalizing the relationship between the parties and making explicit the cost structures that govern the interaction between them (Knittel & Stango, 2010).

Information-technology service delivery is big business. Gartner forecasts an annual growth rate of 7.3 percent with nearly $1 trillion expected to be spent worldwide in 2011 for hardware and software maintenance and support, consulting services, development and integration services, network and Internet services, solution development, staff augmentation, and outsourcing services (Gartner, 2007). This is reason alone to study IT service management.

Labor

People make up more than two-thirds of the overall cost of IT work, and that share continues to grow every year (Bozman & Perry, 2010; Gartner, 1999; ITCentrix, 2001), in large part because of disproportionate gains in computer speed and capacity compared to labor and productivity improvements. Computers get faster and cheaper every year, people do not. This is exacerbated by increasingly complex computer systems, with more components interacting in more ways, more configuration settings, and more things to go wrong for people to fix. Yet people are often blamed when things do go wrong. One survey of more than 100 technology, media, and communications companies listed human error as the leading cause of security failures by 75 percent of the companies: the majority of the threats were identified as resulting from human error (42 percent) and operational error (37 percent), rather than from malicious intent (Deloitte, 2006). Other research found that human operator error was the root cause of 20–50 percent of system outages (Oppenheimer, Ganapathi, & Patterson, 2003).

Fifty years ago, computers were huge, expensive, uncommon, self-contained, and used for fairly specific tasks. Over time, computers became smaller, cheaper, widely interconnected, and used for many more functions, from basic communications (e-mail, chat) to publicity and commerce (e.g., Web sites, e-commerce). With these trends, computer systems have become composed of many more hardware and software components, with ever-increasing numbers of configuration settings and interactions. The conceptually simple example of an e-commerce Web site may, behind the scenes, be composed of network load balancers, firewalls, multiple Web servers, application servers, and database servers, all carefully configured to work together.

This growing complexity of IT systems has inevitably led to specialization. For most sites, there is no one know-it-all system administrator any more. Today different groups specialize in different technologies. There are operating system administrators, who configure and manage low-level system software for computer hardware; database administrators, who manage database management software; storage administrators, who manage disk and tape systems; and so on. With responsibility for different system components distributed across different people and groups, communication and coordination are critical to effective management in IT service organizations.

Parallel to specialization based on technical expertise, there is also specialization based on the function and phase of service delivery. There are capacity planners, who determine the capacity requirements of an application during initial deployment; transition managers, who oversee the migration of an application from deployment to production; first-level support representatives, who respond to the client problem initially and propagate unresolved issues to a higher level; and so on. Though such specialization may emerge over time, it can also be the result of standardization of the practice. An example of standardization is the IT infrastructure library (ITIL), originally developed by the British Government in the 1980s (Office of Government Commerce, 2000, 2001, 2002a, 2002b, 2005a, 2005b). It is a standardized framework for describing IT service support and delivery activities to achieve effective operations. The ITIL covers IT service topics such as service strategy, design, transition, operation, and continual improvements. The activities of the ITIL include availability, security, deployment, change, and operations management, as well as financial management and the business perspective.

There is significant effort in sharing "best practices" among the communities of sysadmins. On numerous Web sites, such as www.sans.org (SysAdmin, Audit, Network, Security [SANS]), IT professionals share their experience through resources such as weekly digests, alerts, publications, and forums. IT companies also publish extensive documentation, such as IBM RedBooks, developed by the technical community, covering not only technical know-how information but also typical-use cases and best practices. Though this documentation can be very useful, it often assumes a much simpler world than the one sysadmins actually live in.

System administrators are embedded in complicated and dynamic social environments. So we are not just talking about the complexity of IT but we are also talking about the complexity of human relationships—relationships with one another, with technology, with organizations, and with whole business enterprises and communities of practice—and consequently, we must consider the complexity of socio-technical systems (Emery & Trist, 1965, 1972).

Automation

Given increasing labor costs in running IT systems and increasingly complex IT infrastructures, companies face a dilemma with almost every new software release: Should we continue to build on top of existing infrastructures? Or should we rethink the IT infrastructures with management in mind?

For instance, in IBM's autonomic computing vision, systems would configure, manage, and heal themselves according to high-level guidance provided by a system administrator (Kephart & Chess, 2003; see also HP, 2009). People would set policies, high-level statements of the scope, condition, utility, and goal of desired system behavior, and systems would interpret the policies in context to configure components, discover and correct errors, monitor and optimize resources, and proactively identify and protect systems from attacks.

Labor cost was the primary short-term motivation for IT service automation efforts—one delivery executive described to us how his department was seen as a cost center, and he was expected to reduce costs by 10 percent every year. Over the long term, however, the goal was to transform interaction between people and computing systems to empower people to communicate with computers at higher levels, in terms of business goals and trade-offs rather than in terms of low-level system configuration parameters. If achieved, this would be a fundamental shift in how IT systems are managed, transforming the role of people and their interaction with IT systems (see also Kandogan, Maglio, Haber & Bailey, 2011). Beyond technology, a fundamental issue here was adoption. Would people and organizations trust and adopt such disruptive technology? If they did, what would the adoption process be like? How would current tools, practices, and processes have to change?

Our studies

We began by asking whether IT service automation made sense—whether it was feasible and whether it could be adopted widely. Although that was the starting point, we soon realized that we first needed to learn the basics of existing IT system administration. Prior to our studies, little was known about the nature and practice of IT management work (Barrett, Chen & Maglio, 2003). Most previous research focused on practices in the initial design and implementation of IT, rather than on day-to-day management of systems. There were some ethnographic reports on design and innovation in engineering that discuss the interwoven nature of social and technical dimensions of engineering work (Vinck, 2003), and some on copier-repair technicians, whose values and objectives transcended the organization they reported to and united them beyond traditional boundaries to communities of practice with similar interests and expertise (Orr, 1996). Other ethnographies focused on the impact of technology on work itself, and on the structure of technical work and its organizational culture (Barley & Kunda, 2004; Barley & Orr, 1997).

Questions

We began with many questions. Given that IT management was very labor intensive, we needed to investigate the work of individuals involved. We needed to find out about their backgrounds, including their education, skills, and career paths. We also needed to understand more of the structure of the organizations they worked in. What sort of tasks did they perform and how was labor distributed and coordinated in IT organizations? How did people collaborate and communicate with each other? What were the processes, standards, and ad hoc practices in IT management? What was the nature of IT management work? Where was time spent? How was work measured? What was the nature of the social and business contexts work was conducted in? We also needed to understand more about IT systems and the tools used to manage them. What were the characteristics of the managed IT systems in service delivery centers? What made them easier or harder to manage? What sort of tools did administrators use to manage systems? How well did their management tools function? How were architectures and configurations managed over time? How were systems tuned for performance and reliability? How were systems protected from security threats? These were just some of the questions we had.

That was what our expedition was about: to learn how IT management really works—technologies, organizations, and people—and to try to figure out what could really improve IT management and, ultimately, IT service delivery.

Methods

Over five years, we studied service delivery at one of the largest IT service delivery organizations in the world. We also studied a large university computing center and a large government data center. In all, we made 16 field visits, observing and interviewing more than 30 administrators, operators, team leaders, and managers. This book is the result. It chronicles our experiences, our stories, and ultimately what we learned.

Our objective was to develop a deep understanding of IT service practice through detailed study of specific cases. Given the scale and variety of IT service operations, we knew from the start that we would not be able to cover all types of IT management jobs. We took a holistic approach in that we examined our participants at many levels, including skills, practices, and interactions within an organization and within communities of practice. In doing this, we used several methods, including naturalistic observation, contextual interviews, surveys, and diary studies. In this book, we present mainly data from naturalistic observations and contextual interviews, but our analysis is informed by surveys and diary studies as well (Barrett et al., 2004; Takayama & Kandogan, 2006).

Naturalistic observation is a method used by social scientists to observe participants in their normal environments (Preece, Rogers & Sharp, 2002). The objective is to minimize distractions, and observe as people interact and conduct their work. Contextual interviews, likewise, are conducted where work is done, so that participants can describe their work while being surrounded by the artifacts and tools of that work. Discussions focus on the work, but often expand in time and space to cover the social and historical context of work, tools, practices, and organizations.

In our observational studies, at least two researchers participated in each visit, which lasted between three and five days. In total, we spent about 50 days observing our participants. Typically, two researchers followed one participant per day as he or she worked in the office, attended meetings, and just went about his or her normal work. One of the researchers took notes and occasionally asked questions while the other videotaped interactions and other activities in the office. We asked participants to think aloud, which helped significantly in understanding the context of work. At the end of the day, we asked clarifying questions about the observations from that day. We collected artifacts—physical and electronic—created by and situated in the work environment of the people we observed.

We captured video and audio so that we could revisit details we might have missed. We found video to be essential because of the nature and dynamics of IT management. A lot happens within a few seconds. Because the terminology and tools were often unfamiliar to us, the video gave us a detailed account and also the time to research later what really occurred. We often found ourselves watching the same segment over and over to fully understand what happened.

Descriptions

To describe the various characteristics of system administrators, their work, and environment, we draw on examples from our field studies (e.g., Bailey, Kandogan, Maglio & Haber, 2007; Barrett, 2004; Barrett et al. 2004; Barrett, Maglio, Kandogan & Bailey, 2005; Haber, Kandogan & Maglio, 2011; Kandogan, Bailey, Maglio & Haber, 2008; Kandogan, Haber, Bailey & Maglio, 2009; Kandogan, Maglio, Bailey & Haber, 2009; Kandogan, Maglio, Haber & Bailey 2011; Maglio & Kandogan, 2004; Maglio, Kandogan & Haber, 2008). We organize our data by *episodes*, which we define loosely as situations involving a central individual or groups of individuals with a reasonably identifiable beginning and ending. Examples of episodes include identifying a problem, solving a problem, making a decision, and working with another person. Episodes will often be strung together into a longer story; for instance, we include an overall story comprised of several episodes revolving around George, a Web administrator struggling with the configuration details of a particular deployment (e.g., Barrett et al., 2004; chapter 2, this volume). In reporting details, we aim to preserve the anonymity of our participants by avoiding the use of real names and photographs, and by hiding other possible identifying characteristics. In all cases, participants gave us permission to observe them and to discuss our observations with others.

The episodes and stories include examples of planning, deployment, monitoring, and troubleshooting complex systems. They show social structure, historical context, interaction, collaboration, and communication among administrators. They expose the tremendous scale and complexity of modern IT systems, the practices that administrators adopt to cope, and the consequences when administrators fail to grasp how their systems really work. They demonstrate the use of various management tools—automated and manual, off-the-shelf and self-created. They show the proliferation of custom tools, which highlights the mismatch between many off-the-shelf tools and the needs of administrators. They provide evidence of how tools are shared and evolve over time. They describe both standard processes and ad hoc procedures, which many administrators develop and adapt over time to improve efficiency. They describe the organizations that IT staff work in, interactions and friction between groups, and informal roles and organizational structures people invent over time to get work done more effectively. They also describe broad communities and how system administrators work and collaborate beyond organizational boundaries.

Throughout, we found people coping with complex systems, and in most cases they coped effectively. That is what people do, after all. People are creative; they adapt to changes, build their own tools, discover ways to overcome problems, and organize themselves to be more effective. Yet the ever-increasing human cost of IT systems management suggests that they may not be managing well enough. We think real productivity gains could be achieved if this ecosystem of people and technology were more broadly understood by designers, managers, and others with an interest in IT, and we hope this book will help.

Analysis

To understand what was actually going on in our data, we analyzed the way people worked with technologies and with one another, framing these activities as coordination tasks that aid sense-making through building up common ground among participants. Common ground is the mutual knowledge, beliefs, and assumptions on which communication or any coordinated activity depends (Clark & Brennan, 1991). Common ground is developed over time through the basic cognitive process of *grounding* (Clark, 1996; Clark & Brennan, 1991). For example, in conversations, people try to establish whether what has been said has been understood, that is, whether it has been added to the common ground (Clark & Wilkes-Gibbs, 1986). They do this by watching for nods, listening for "uh-huh," asking clarifying questions, repeating phrases, and so on. Grounding depends critically on the purpose, the situation, the media, the participants, and many other factors (Clark, 1996). In many of the episodes described in this book, we discuss how different factors affect the fundamental process of building up common ground among sysadmins and others.

We saw organizations, methods, and tools put in place to simplify IT management and to make grounding easier and more effective (see also Klein, Feltovich, Bradshaw & Woods, 2005). For instance, sysadmins were often organized locally into teams of people with similar knowledge and skill (e.g., operating system teams or Web infrastructure teams), making communication among team members easy, given their common backgrounds and experience (see Bettenhausen, 1991; Gibson & Cohen, 2003; Hinds & Weisband, 2003). Of course, to maintain any complex system, members of different specialist teams must coordinate their activities, often supported by tools, practices, standards, and organizational structures that supported sharing of system state and other information (Jones, 1995; Lave, 1988; Malone, 1990; Rasmussen, 1986; Vygotsky, 1979; Woods & Roth, 1988). We describe many instances in which organizations, methods, and tools aim to support grounding and coordination of activities across individuals, teams, and technologies.

In fact, we think grounding is fundamental, the basic social and cognitive process driving *all* the activity we saw. Sysadmins work to understand their systems, and they work to understand one another, incrementally building up common ground through joint action. Whether interacting with others, tools, computer systems, or documentation, sysadmins engaged in grounding to make sense of situations and to share information (Brennan, 1998; Clark, 1996, 1999; Clark & Brennan, 1991). The way in which people build up knowledge, beliefs, and assumptions through conversation with others is the same way in which they build up knowledge, beliefs, and assumptions through interactions with systems, tools, and documents (Brennan, 1998; Clark, 1999). Nevertheless, we rarely saw individual administrators understand a system or a situation completely. Individuals relied on tools, practices, documentation, and other individuals and teams to do their jobs (see also Maglio, Kandogan & Haber, 2008; Wright, Fields & Harrison, 2000). In a sense, understanding and the ability to act did not reside within individuals but rather among individuals and artifacts in a kind of *distributed cognitive system* (Hutchins, 1995, 1996). In a number of stories in this book, we characterize information flow and action in terms of distributed cognitive processes.

Nearly all sysadmins we observed invented and used their own methods and tools for managing social and technical complexity. Such innovation is pervasive and constant; a natural outcome of sysadmins' interactions with their environments. Off-the-shelf tools are seldom well aligned with the needs of sysadmins (Barrett et al., 2004). The underlying technology is constantly changing, growing more elaborate, so the management tools and practices must change to keep up. Information technology systems are idiosyncratic, requiring system administrators to adapt tools and practices for their particular combinations of IT components (Fitzgerald, 2006).

We saw innovation occurring at many levels. Sysadmins frequently created tools and methods for their own use, optimized for their specific needs. Sometimes these tools and methods were shared informally among co-workers. Organizations, aiming to create consistency across people and time, formalize the creation, sharing, and adoption of tools and practices to improve standardization (Malone et al., 1999; Malone & Crowston, 1994; March & Olsen, 1989). Communities of practice (Wenger, 2001, 2006) develop broadly applicable tools and best practices for general cases (O'Dell & Grayson, 1998). Collaboration within communities, among practitioners, conferences, online forums, and open source projects are important in the distribution and spread of new tools and practices (Wenger & Snyder, 2000). Of course, there can be tension among the innovations at these different levels, with differing advantages in generality, flexibility, consistency, maturity, trustworthiness, and meeting specific needs. Throughout, we describe cases of the development of tools and practices from the perspectives of sysadmins, organizations, and communities.

We view the continual innovation we observed in IT management tools and practices as resulting from *evolutionary* processes (Arthur, 2009). On this view, technology evolves in four basic ways: (a) through standard engineering practice, as new and improved solutions are found to existing problems; (b) through structural deepening, as components are added to work around limitations, creating more complex mechanisms; (c) through invention, as radically new technologies are created based on new discoveries and novel combinations of existing technologies; and (d) through emergence over time, as environments and technologies encounter one another and are changed by one another over long periods (Arthur, 2009). We saw sysadmins develop their own tools and practices over time, adapted to their complex and idiosyncratic environments, often by combining existing tools and practices to fit new purposes or to work around problems. These processes implement a kind of hill-climbing search (Holland, 1992) based on deliberate exploration of the design space played out in individual situations and accumulated over time. The tools and practices that work effectively are shared with others, and they can evolve over time to embody best practices. Innovation is continual. As the underlying IT changes and as improved IT management tools and practices encounter the work, the work changes, which in turn demands new innovations. Throughout this book, we describe many examples of evolution of tools and practices.

Overall, our analyses are based on (a) how people work together and with technologies in grounding their understanding and in coordinating their actions and activities, (b) how constellations of people and technologies together comprise the cognitive systems capable of managing complex IT, and (c) how the tools and techniques people develop evolve incrementally to create structures that support effective and productive work in a complex and continually changing environment.

Roadmap

Each of the next six chapters highlights some aspect of IT management work by telling stories from what we observed, and by drawing out implications for design of tools and practices. These chapters can be read individually or together—or maybe even in any order. Each is meant to stand alone. Of course, we hope they do go together to tell a bigger story, and the last chapter aims to put it together.

We start with people, the critical actors in IT service, and then continue with information technologies, the substrate of IT service. For both, the fundamental issues are complexity and coordination in social, technical, and socio-technical systems. We next turn to innovation in methods and tools, and how people adapt their practices and their technologies as they try to cope with complexity. We then describe organizations and communities, and how they orchestrate the flow of information and work, both formally and informally. We finally weave the threads together into a set of fairly practical lessons that follow from our analyses of what we saw and what we heard in terms of grounding, that is, establishing common understanding among people and systems; distributed cognition, that is, creating effective work systems distributed across people, technologies, and time; and evolution, that is, making useful changes to tools, methods, and organizations that accumulate over time.

"People and Collaboration" (chapter 2) describes the social complexity of IT system administration through the story of George, a Web administrator who worked closely with many others in the course of debugging a new Web server. This story demonstrates the importance of collaboration, communication, coordination, and situational awareness as different people brought together their expertise in an attempt to solve a difficult problem. It also highlights the need for trust and understanding; we show how it was not sufficient to find a solution to the problem. In the end, George had to trust his collaborators to develop an understanding of the problem *and* of its solution.

"Technologies and Complexity" (chapter 3) examines technical complexity in more detail. First, the story of Dot examines the numerous steps and pitfalls involved in deploying a "simple" Web application in an enterprise environment, highlighting not only the complexity involved but also coping strategies used to integrate information from systems and other people. Second, we describe a *critical situation* in which a large group of experts was brought together in a single room to solve an intermittent, unpredictable Web application failure. This team spent many weeks together, trying to understand the subtle interactions between system components, collecting and exchanging information and ideas, and reconfiguring different components. This story demonstrates the heights of technical complexity, in which a problem could be so subtle as to require months of effort to solve it. It also shows many techniques people use to understand such problems, and provides some evidence about why the human cost of IT management keeps increasing.

"Practices and Innovation" (chapter 4) focuses on standard practices for accomplishing tasks through the story of database administrators Christine and Mike. They considered data loss the worst possible disaster, so their group developed a number of practices to avoid this, including keeping a central repository of step-by-step instruction documents for important operations, rehearsing all significant changes on a series of increasingly realistic test systems, and working side-by-side at the most critical moments to ensure a second pair of eyes oversaw those steps. The second story describes Patrick, a capacity planner who used standards developed in his organization as a starting point for allocating IT resources, but who relied mainly on experience. Overall, the chapter examines innovation in practices and methods, how such innovation is applied to new problems, and how it evolves.

"Tools and Automation" (chapter 5) provides examples of the wide range of tools we saw sysadmins develop to improve their productivity and effectiveness, including ad hoc tools for on-the-fly data processing and analysis, collections of small but useful tools that admins collect and pull out when needed like Swiss Army knives, and databases and shared repositories of reusable tools that perform significant tasks. We tell the story of Shawn, an operating system administrator responsible for keeping 120 Unix servers up-to-date with appropriate patches. He relied heavily on homegrown tools and methods for coordinating his team's activities and interacting with the client. We also tell the story of Diana and Mark, storage administrators at a large government facility, who created numerous custom tools as part of managing a massive robotic data-tape repository. Finally, we tell the story of Jimmy and his colleagues, database administrators working at a department store, who developed advanced automation to handle all their common tasks. The complexity and idiosyncratic nature of many IT systems mean that vendor-provided tools are often insufficient, and that administrators use their own creativity to fill the gaps.

"Organizations and Information" (chapter 6) discusses the importance of formally defined groups in IT management. System administration is more than just the work of individuals—it requires groups of individuals to work closely together and with other groups to effectively manage complex systems. It includes the story of Henry and Ryan from the operations and architecture groups in a managed storage service organization, and the story of Amy, a transition manager for a new service-delivery offering. These examine how the groups were organized internally and how their practices made for effective interaction with other groups and clients. They also show the importance of organizational bridges, people who translate and transform information between groups.

"Communities and Trust" (chapter 7) describes the importance of broader communities in IT management, such as informal groups of people who share a profession or specialty and engage in collective learning in their specific domain (e.g., Lave & Wenger, 1991). Through the story of Joe and Aaron, security administrators at a large university data center, we see formal and informal collaboration between departments in the university, ad hoc collaboration between different universities facing a widespread security incident, and global communities that collectively maintain information sites and open-source tools.

"Findings and Lessons" (chapter 8) tells what we learned overall. Through our focus on grounding, distributed cognition, and evolution, we develop a set of high-level lessons for IT management. We argue that effective management lies in supporting improved communication and grounding between individuals and organizations, and in establishing an ecosystem in which evolution of tools, practices, and organizations can flourish, where local innovations can grow into community standards, and where standards can be adapted to local needs. In the end, we see system administration depending on (a) collaboration among people, (b) adaptation of tools and practices, (c) orchestration of information and work across space and time, (d) communities of practice working together, and (e) automation that is appropriate to the human work of IT management.

Finally, in an epilogue, we present data from follow-up interviews done several years later with a number of our participants. Where are they now? What has changed for them? Does our story hold up? It seems to us that it does.

Summary

We were on an expedition. We went out to explore the world of systems administration, and this book documents what we found. We saw hugely complex IT infrastructures, valiantly tended by experts of every type, working together to tame that complexity. We saw real innovation, as administrator-created tools, practices, and organizations effectively simplified tasks. And we saw a kind of evolution, as innovations matured, were shared, and adapted across broader communities to create productive work systems. Society relies on sysadmins to keep its technological foundation solid, and so we should ensure their tools and environments support them effectively. In this book, we aim to provide some insight into the nature of sysadmins in particular and IT management in general—and we hope it will help lead the way to a future in which this important work is better appreciated and better supported.

2

People and Collaboration

> *"What're you talking about?"*
> —George, Web admin

George was in trouble. A seemingly simple task was taking all morning, and there seemed no end in sight. It was Friday and the customer was anxious to have the task done by Monday. George called in all kinds of help, working with people throughout the organization, but the problem remained intractable. He was supposed to go to a good-bye lunch for a departing co-worker; people kept sending him messages asking if he was ready to go yet. His manager kept coming in to check on his progress. He was really feeling the stress. And George was no novice. He had been working as a system administrator for several years, and he had a bachelor's degree in computer science. However, it seemed his expertise and experience were simply not enough. Part of the story was the complex technical environment—the servers and systems George managed—yet at least as important was the complex social and organizational environment in which he worked.

In this chapter, we illustrate the people factor in system management. We examine system administrators' complex social, organizational, and technical environments through the story of George (Barrett et al., 2004; Haber, Kandogan & Maglio, 2011; Maglio, Kandogan & Haber, 2008). We report on challenges George had in collaborating with remote partners, as they tried to understand system state through what George told them via phone, instant messages, and e-mail. The complexity of technical systems made collaboration difficult; George had to summarize, transform, and filter a large volume of information into a form that could be transmitted to others. Furthermore, George's reports were based on his observations and interactions with the system, which were influenced by his own understanding of the system. It turned out that George's mental model of the system was wrong, and as such, the information he conveyed to others was not always accurate. Social complexity and trust were also factors (Kanawattanachai & Yoo, 2002; Kramer, 1999; Kraut, Fussel, Brennan & Siegel, 2002; McAllister, 1995), because George had never previously met several of his collaborators, and it was often unclear to him what the others knew and what their priorities were (Cramton, 2001).

In showing administrators working in complex social, organizational, and technical environments, this story demonstrates how problems are worked through collaboratively, among individuals in diverse and distributed groups, among those who know each other well and those who do not, and among those who have similar skills and those who do not (Hinds & Kiesler, 2002). Much of this interaction involves efforts to establish mutual understanding or common ground about the state of the various systems (Brennan, 1998; Clark, 1996; Hutchins, Hollan & Norman, 1986). Grounding and collaborative action are needed because of unevenly distributed expertise and access to information (Hertzum, 2008; Klein et al, 2005): George did not know how to fix the problem and others could not help because they lacked critical information about what was happening in the system. In addition, formal and informal organizational arrangements, past experiences, and trust can strongly influence collaboration (Gibson & Cohen, 2003; Jarvenpaa, Knoll & Leidner, 1998; Jarvenpaa & Leidner, 1999; Tyler & Kramer, 1996).

The Story of George, Web Administrator

George was a Web application administrator for companies that outsourced their Web application management to George's employer, a large IT services company. He had been at the job for a bit more than a year, and before that he had worked for three years in technical support and general system administration. He had a technical background, having received a BSc in math/computer science. George worked on a team of other Web administrators at a sprawling 200-acre hilltop site that housed vast machine rooms and thousands of technical workers keeping the hardware and software running. This site was one of several such IT service delivery centers that George's employer had around the country.

We observed George at work over the course of two separate weeks, about six months apart. On the days described here, two of us were packed into George's office, along with George's office mate, Mark. They were at their desks next to each other, and we were situated behind George with a video camera, a laptop, and a note pad, trying to look unobtrusive. And strange as it may sound, it was working. They were talking, diving into their work, with colleagues frequently coming in to the office with questions or problems. Of course, they never completely forgot we were there, especially when one team member kept sending instant messages asking what it was like to be a movie star. Still, George and Mark were busy and needed to get their work done. We believe the impact of our presence was minor: At one very frustrating point, one of them exclaimed, "I hate this #$%&ing place...[long pause] Did you get that on tape? [laughter]"

As we watched, George worked with different colleagues on a variety of projects for different customers. In this story, we concentrate on one particular project that led to a tense troubleshooting session. Though most projects were not as fraught as this one, it brings out important aspects of administration work, particularly its human side.

Complex Technical Environment

George described the project one Tuesday morning as he was getting up to speed, researching the steps involved:

> **George:** What I'm working on, there's a new environment that the customer is setting up. They're going to have WebSEAL on a front-end server, and basically WebSEAL is going to have junctions to back-end Domino servers where the employees are going to go in and access their mail over secure Web interface. So basically we're creating...we're waiting on a new IP address for the WebSEAL server, and we need firewall ports open between the WebSEAL server and the back-end Domino servers so they can talk to each other, and right now I was told

that the IP address for the WebSEAL server is in place, so they want me to try creating the new WebSEAL instance on the server. So that's what I'm doing.

George mentioned that his colleague Ted was working at the same time on a related problem with the WebSEAL server. As George spoke, instant messages flashed on his screen from Ted, with information about his progress. This was typical: The system had lots of moving parts and people worked on different parts in parallel.

At the time, we were unsure about what George's description meant, exactly, and even George appeared to be learning the details of his task. We watched as he then went through e-mailed instructions, and researched online documentation describing the commands and configuration steps required. By researching these sources ourselves, and by carefully examining our video recordings, we eventually understood the task.

George was working to fulfill a customer request: they wanted Web access to their e-mail. Conceptually, this is straightforward idea, yet behind the scenes numerous software systems on multiple computers had to be configured to make this happen. He needed to install and configure a new instance of Web server software (WebSEAL) to communicate through a network firewall to a middleware server (Policy Director), which in turn allowed communication with a back-end e-mail server (Domino) via a junction. (See Boxes 2.1 and 2.2 for more details on networks and Web applications.) The customer had an existing Web server, so George had a working example to follow.

The system configuration before George started work is shown in Figure 2.1, though George never constructed such diagrams himself. As shown, communication across a firewall is directional: There was a specific opening (on port 7135) for communication from the original WebSEAL instance to the Policy Director (PD) server, and another (port 7234) for the opposite direction.

An e-mail that was sent to George described four high-level steps that were necessary to provide e-mail access via the Web:

1. Ask the network team to allocate an IP address for a new WebSEAL instance.
2. Ask the firewall team to open ports on the firewall to allow the new instance to communicate with the PD server.

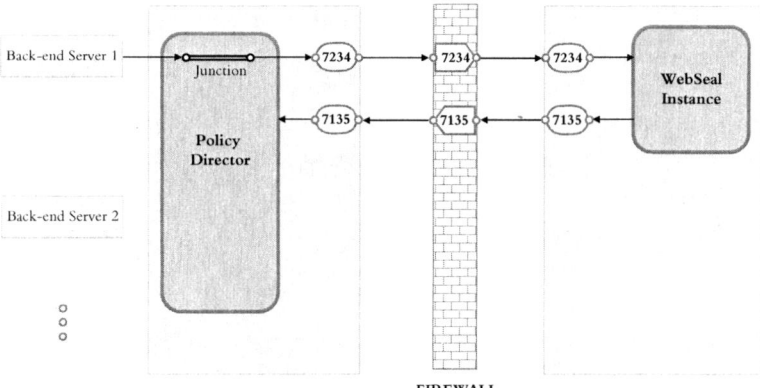

FIGURE 2.1 Initial configuration of the system before George started work. The customer had an existing Web server, communicating with the Policy Director server via specific firewall openings.

Box 2.1 Computer Networks

Computer networks are ubiquitous in modern society, as integral as telephones and highways. They rely on the work of many Web and network administrators who configure, deploy, and troubleshoot the underlying infrastructure. The foundation of the World Wide Web is the Internet, a globe-spanning network that permits computers to exchange information with one another. When discussing the Internet in our stories, key concepts include:

Servers. A server is a computer connected to a network that provides some service, for example, a file server stores and retrieves files. Maintenance for file, Web, database, and e-mail servers is a significant part of enterprise system administration.

IP address. An Internet Protocol (IP) address, like a phone number, is a unique identifier for a computer that enables other computers to connect with it over the Internet (for example, as of this writing, www.whitehouse.gov had the IP address 92.122.208.131).

(continued)

24   Taming Information Technology

> **Box 2.1 (Continued)**
>
> **Network ports.** Because computers often have multiple programs communicating over a network, each program must have its own port number (e.g., Web servers usually listen for requests from Web browsers on port 80). If IP addresses are like phone numbers, network ports are like telephone extensions, with an additional number required to reach a specific party. For two machines to exchange data, each must know the IP address of the other as well as which ports to use to send and receive messages. Administrators need to configure each piece of software with the correct IP addresses and port numbers.
>
> **Firewalls.** To provide data security, most corporate computers are not connected directly with the Internet. Of course, this presents a problem for corporate Web servers, whose very job is to deliver data to the outside world. A firewall is often used to manage the flow of data between computers inside an organization and the outside world. A firewall regulates network traffic, preventing all communication except that between explicitly permitted IP addresses/port numbers. For two machines to talk to one another across a firewall, the firewall must be set up to allow messages to flow on those ports. Network administrators spend time establishing and verifying the rules defining permitted traffic.

3. Create a new instance of WebSEAL, specifying the IP address and ports to use.
4. Create the necessary junctions by configuring the PD server to allow the new WebSEAL instance to access the Domino e-mail servers.

George had already completed the first two steps. He had received an IP address from the network team, and requested two port openings from the Firewall team: port 7137 to the PD server, and 7236 from the PD server. For Step 3, George had found online documentation that described the task in great detail. It included sample commands and configuration settings to change the existing WebSEAL instance and to create the new instance.

With these instructions handy, George started his task as early as Tuesday morning but ran into a series of problems that were not resolved until Friday. The software that Ted was re-installing needed to be running before George could make his changes. So George was blocked by Ted's problem, and Ted in turn was blocked by some changes from the customer side. This was typical. When they tried to fix one problem, another would often appear. Over the next few days, Ted got the PD server running, the network team created the firewall openings, and finally George could proceed.

Mysterious Errors

It was Friday morning, and George was ready to create the new WebSEAL instance and configure the PD server. He copied the command needed to create the new instance from online instructions:

```
PDWeb_config -i {instance} -m {internal port}
```

He pasted this on the command line for the WebSEAL server machine, and filled in values for instance and internal port:

```
PDWeb_config -i instance2 -m 7137
```

The online documentation defined *internal port* as "Unique port number for inter-Access Manager server communication. Value must be greater than 1023. (Values less than or equal to 1023 are reserved.)" Quite precise, but not very clear.

Commands like this were the bread-and-butter of George's work. Whether creating new instances of software systems or monitoring and managing their operation, George used combinations of keywords on the command line (which were pretty cryptic to us). Such commands have the advantage of being compact and precise representations of an action, yet they offer little guidance if you do not know the exact meaning of options such as "-i," or "internal port." In this case, the `PDWeb_config` command was used to create the new WebSEAL instance, named `instance2`. George specified port 7137, which, given the ports he requested the firewall team to open, he seemed to believe

Box 2.2 The World Wide Web

The World Wide Web defines a set of protocols that use the Internet to let people view and navigate a wide variety of information in a consistent and easy way. Web browsers receive information encoded in a standard language (HTML); in the early years of the Web, this information was primarily static text or pictures, but soon thereafter Web applications were developed to support more dynamic browsing. Any time a Web page accepts information from the user or performs processing to display new information, a Web application is involved. Web applications and the software that supports them form a major part of the infrastructure of modern enterprises, allowing Web pages to work with database information and to act as front ends for business applications and other software. Though a variety of technologies have been used to create Web applications, the most common architecture for Web applications at the time of our observations included:

Web servers. When you type a URL (e.g., http://www.white house.gov) into a Web browser, the browser software on your computer communicates over the Internet with a Web server program, usually running on some far away machine. That server then sends the contents of static Web pages, or data from a Web application server.

Web application servers. These execute computer programs when certain URLs or portions of Web pages are requested by the browser.

Web application. This is a program that is launched by the Web application server to process information and return data to be displayed in the user's browser. For example, e-commerce Web sites are frequently implemented using a Web application in which the application logic supports functions such as listing products, adding or removing products from a "shopping cart," computing shopping cart totals, validating payment, and so forth.

Database management systems (DBMS). Database management systems store data used by the Web application. Following the e-commerce example, databases would keep track of catalog

(*continued*)

> **Box 2.2 (Continued)**
>
> information (items for sale, their descriptions, prices, inventory, etc.), client information (name, address, past purchase history), current shopping carts, and so on. Some Web applications also rely on back-end e-mail, document, or media servers to provide dynamic content to the user.
>
> This multilayered approach had several advantages: Each component is optimized for its own function, components can be mixed and matched from different vendors and run on the same or different hardware as performance and security requirements dictate, and components can be replicated if they prove to be a bottleneck. This flexibility comes at a price; each of the components must be carefully configured to work properly with the others. In addition, these architectures can be considerably more complex than this simple example, for increased scalability, flexibility, and security.

was the port for *sending* communication from the WebSEAL instance through the firewall to the PD server (see Figure 2.2).

The command executed without error. So at this point, it appeared to George that the new WebSEAL instance was created and configured properly. It was not. George did not realize that although each WebSEAL instance needed a unique port to receive communications from the PD server, the PD server shared a single port (7135) for all incoming WebSEAL communication. In this way, network ports are similar to phone extensions: You only need one to receive calls from multiple other parties. The `internal port` parameter in the `PDWeb_config` command referred to the port on which a WebSEAL instance *received* communication from the PD server. George thought it was the other way around: The way he set it up, the new WebSEAL instance could talk to the PD server (via the already existing firewall opening for 7135), but if the PD server tried to communicate back using port 7137, the firewall blocked it (see Figure 2.3). However, the system only tested communication in one direction when the new instance was created. The problem remained hidden.

George saw the first sign of trouble when he tried to create the PD server junction to permit the new WebSEAL instance to access the

28 Taming Information Technology

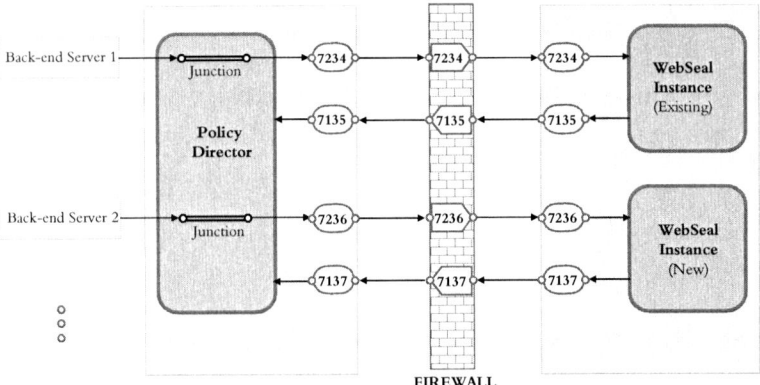

FIGURE 2.2 The configuration that George thought (incorrectly) he had created for the new WebSEAL instance. George believed he needed two new ports, one in each direction, opened on the firewall to allow communication between the new WebSEAL instance and the Policy Director. He also defined a new junction on the Policy Director to allow access to another back-end server.

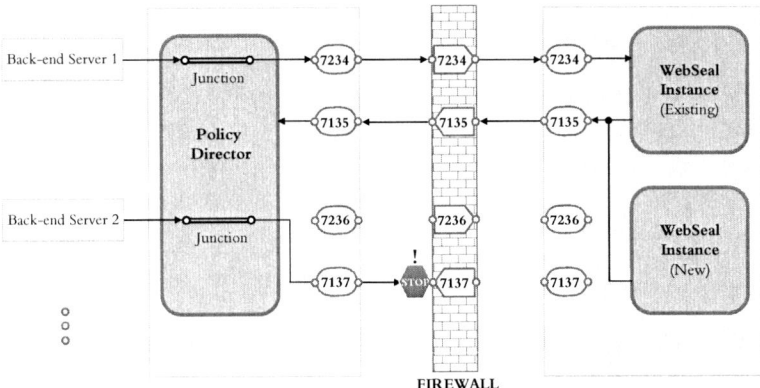

FIGURE 2.3 Actual configuration after George created the new WebSEAL instance and defined a junction on the Policy Director. Policy Director tried to communicate to the new WebSEAL instance over port 7137 but the firewall rules did not allow communication in that direction. Moreover, the new WebSEAL instance used the default port 7135 (not port 7236) to communicate to the Policy Director.

new back-end server, a Domino server giving e-mail access to the customer. His instructions contained the following command for configuring junctions:

```
server task webseald-(server name) create -t tcp -h
(hostname) -i -s -b ignore
```

He filled in the address of a back-end server for hostname, and "instance2" for server name, and then received an error message in response:

```
Could not perform the administration request. Error:
Could not connect to server (status: 0x1354a424)
```

Given that there were at least three servers in George's environment—WebSEAL server, Policy Director server, and Domino e-mail server—the meaning of this error was not at all clear. George then ran a command (iv_status) to list the servers known to the PD server, and the list showed the new instance ("instance2-webseald-webhost") as well as the original instance ("webseald-webhost").

Because "instance2" was on the list, it appeared to George that the new WebSEAL instance had been created correctly. However, because the PD server reported the new instance name in a slightly different syntax ("instance2-webseald-webhost" instead of just "instance2"), George tried his junction command using a number of permutations of the server name and command syntax, but to no avail. Finally, he tried configuring the PD server to permit the original WebSEAL instance—not the new one he created, but the one that was running when he started all this—to access the back-end e-mail server. This worked correctly, suggesting to him that the problem was related to the new instance. In addition, this gave the customer Web access to e-mail using the original WebSEAL instance. So George told his manager via an instant message that the customer could start testing the set-up using the old WebSEAL instance, and the manager said he would inform the customer. George then went back to debugging the problem with the new instance.

George worked alone for most of the morning. This was not unusual, sometimes he would work closely with others, sometimes he would not. George's main challenge so far seemed to be technical, a problem with the configuration of the system. The documentation and the error messages provided little information. It was 10:30 AM, and he had made little progress. He really wanted to finish by lunchtime for his colleague's going-away party. What was George to do? He needed help.

Remote Troubleshooting

At his manager's suggestion, George called Adam, the architect for this particular customer solution. He described the problem to Adam on the phone:

> **George**: I created the second instance in the same server as the original instance. No trouble there. When I went to create the junction to the back-end server from that instance it gives me a message something like, "could not find server" or "could not connect to server." I made sure it was running. I am not sure why it won't accept the junction. It is not a problem with the server. It is a problem with the additional instance.

George then did a Web search to get further information on the error and read to Adam what he found:

```
Error: 0x1354a424 (324314148) Could not connect to
server
Explanation: see message.
Action: Make sure the server is running and accepting
connections.
Name: iv_s_socket_connectnot
```

There was little useful information here, but it did suggest a problem with the network connections. Adam told George that it might be a connection problem. George agreed.

At this point, we see George's mental model of the problem begin to affect what he told others: in this case, inadvertently directing Adam to think the wrong way about the how the system was set up. George believed the instance creation was successful because the `PDWeb_config` command had produced no error messages and because the PD server's list command showed the new instance. The apparent success of the instance creation and the ambiguity of the error message led George to believe that the connection problem might have had something to do with the different names for the instance shown by the various tools. In the `PDwebWeb_config` command, he specified "instance2" as the name of the new instance. Yet output of the server list command showed "instance2-webseald-webhost" as the instance name. When he ran the `iv_status` command, the same server name appeared as "webseald-instance2." Examining the WebSEAL configuration file, he saw yet another variation on the instance name. George raised his concerns about these differences to Adam:

> **George**: I am just a little confused. I think the problem may be in the discrepancies with the naming conventions. You know, I see different names in different places.

George and Adam spent the next 40 minutes investigating the apparent discrepancies in the server names. They tried to force the names to match by tweaking the WebSEAL configuration file, but to no avail. Outside of the command line, the main way George would manage software systems was by modifying their configuration files. WebSEAL's configuration file contained several hundred option-name/value pairs, including one specifying the instance name. Had George looked all the way through the file, he might have discovered the problem when he saw the entries describing port numbers for PD server communication in each direction, but with so many entries in the file, he was not likely to do so.

Next, Adam and George examined the log files. Most software systems create log files, which contain time-stamped events or errors in the operation of the system. Log files can provide information about why a system is exhibiting certain behavior. George started with the file "webseald.log," carefully scanning through the entries there, even though entries were time stamped the day before (i.e., before anything related to the problem could have occurred). He e-mailed a copy of the log file to Adam, who noticed some errors and asked George to explain.

> **George**: Failed recovered, failed recovered. We see that in all our WebSEAL instances in our environment. It has something to do with the firewall timeout. It is not what is causing this problem though.

At that point, George realized that they were looking at the log file for the original WebSEAL instance, and that there was a different log file for the new instance. George then checked the new log file, though not as thoroughly this time around, and saw the same "failed recovered" messages. Among all other errors, George did not notice unusual network socket failures that were also in the file (we noticed them in our video analysis later on):

```
The 'ssl_writechunk' routine failed for 'gsk_secure_
soc_write', errno = 406
```

These messages appeared among the many "failed recovered" errors that George was used to seeing. They indicated a network problem, yet looked very much like the "usual" errors. Had he noticed it, he would have had a very good clue that the problem was related to sockets. However, it was overlooked by George, and not reported to Adam.

George certainly worked in a complex technical environment: Different programs used different naming conventions, error messages were unhelpful, configuration files and log files were long and difficult to look through. All this made George even more confused about how the system worked (as we will see throughout). Yet, here, we also see some of the social and organizational aspects of George's environment. Faced with a substantial problem, George sought the help of his manager, who in turn sought the help of the system architect, Adam. George engaged in deep problem solving with Adam, interacting by telephone and sharing error messages and documents by instant message and e-mail. And as we saw, this kind of remote collaboration was difficult (Cramton, 2001; Kraut, Fussell, Brennan & Siegel, 2002; Larrson, 2003).

Organizationally, George and Adam worked in different groups and had very different responsibilities. George was responsible for day-to-day delivery, whereas Adam was responsible for the way the overall system worked, and he had been responsible for designing the overall system in the first place. Adam was more senior than George in that his job role had greater scope and responsibility. At many times, George deferred to Adam, and George seemed to expect Adam to just know what was going on and how to fix the problem. Adam had more responsibility than George but was completely dependent on George for information about the system. George selectively picked what to communicate with Adam because there was so much information available from the system. For his part, Adam was not deeply embedded in the details of the applications, and he was really starting with the same kind of understanding of the system and its details as George. Adam was, in fact, dependent on George for almost all information about the system and its state. Adam was not grounding his understanding *in* the state of the system, because he could not interrogate the system directly; rather, he was grounding his understanding in George's model of the system through his interaction with George. This made a big difference, of course.

These barriers to grounding between Adam and George are examples of a broader problem. Expertise, authority, and access are not evenly distributed among sysadmins. Adam had expertise, but only George had access to the system. George's model of the system's port configuration was just plain wrong, meaning it would be very difficult—perhaps even impossible—for him to help Adam build a correct model of the system state. Furthermore, George and Adam communicated and interacted through very limited channels of phone, instant message, and e-mail, which led to additional complications. We saw that information sharing was difficult, especially given the size and format of the log files. George filtered information, sharing the wrong file with Adam; if he had shared the right file, Adam might have noticed the telling error messages amid the usual "failed, recovered" messages. Overall, we see that establishing common ground can be especially difficult in an environment with unequal access and limited communications channels.

Obstacles to Collaboration

Near the beginning of their phone conversation, Adam asked if George had called technical support. George was dubious, saying that, in his experience, technical support's solution to most problems was to "reinstall, reinstall" the software. However, running out of options to try, George made the call to get official technical support for the WebSEAL product. Well, actually, he asked Mark to call tech support on *his* phone because he had Adam on his own phone. To get the information needed for this, George rummaged through old e-mail to find the phone number and his customer number, and then he sent them by instant messaging to Mark, who dialed his phone and handed it to George. George read his customer number and then summarized the problem and hung up to wait for the call from tech support:

George: We created a second WebSEAL instance on a WebSEAL server, and when we try to create a junction from that second instance, we get an error code indicating that it couldn't find the server....

Almost an hour later, Danny from technical support returned George's call (on Mark's phone).

George's working situation was a bit more complicated than simply one-on-one interactions with Adam and then with Danny: George also worked with his office mate, Mark, and George's manager sent Ted into the office to help George in person. In fact, Ted arrived in George's office at about the same time Danny from technical support called. On entering the office, Ted said simply, "A junction problem?"

George had Danny on the speakerphone on Mark's phone and he had Adam on the speakerphone on his own phone.

George: I've got Adam on this line and support on that line.

And they both laughed. This laughter—and Ted's simple greeting, "A junction problem?"—tells us something important: George and Ted shared a lot of common ground already. They had been working together on the task all week, and the greeting reinforced the point to George: Ted already knew about the problem and he was there to help. Moreover, when George explained what was going on at exactly that moment—multiple phone calls on multiple phones—shared laughter indicated they both understood the intensity and gravity of the situation. It simply was not normal to be on two phones at once. It was funny.

Danny, the tech support rep, quickly switched from phone to instant messaging, as that freed up Mark's phone and made it easier for George to share error messages by cutting-and-pasting them from the command line into the messaging window. Ted watched George and Danny exchange messages and chatted with George and Adam about the problem for the next few minutes.

Ted: I'm going to go back to my office, we'll just work on [an instant messaging tool]. Or do we have a conference call going here?

George: I'm just calling Adam, we're trying to work through it.
Ted: We'll go through [an instant messaging tool]. I'll look on my box and see if we can get through to it and then see what I can find.
Mark: If you want to plug in down here you can...
Ted: Well, it looks a little crowded, so...

Ted was obviously referring to the two of us, crowded along with George and Mark, their desks, books, computers, and our video camera into a small office. We did not blame him for getting out of there and getting to work on the problem himself.

For the next 10 minutes, George worked in parallel with Danny, Adam, and Ted, and maintained an ongoing conversation with Mark about the weather. Really!

A little later, Danny asked George via instant message:

```
Danny: Can you verify listen port 7234 or 7237 is
listening?
```

Now, this was exactly the right question, the one that could point George to the source of the problem (as shown in Figure 2.3): 7234 was the listen port for the default instance, and 7137 was the listen port for the new instance (although Danny wrote "7237," it seems likely to us that he, in fact, meant "7137," though the typo might have confused the issue). George ran a command to list all incoming network ports in use on the WebSEAL machine. The resulting list included ports 7137 and 7234 and about 20 others. George muttered to himself, "7137 and 7234. This is the problem! [pause] Huh. Oh, no wait! Hmm, that should be fine."

In fact, here, George spotted one symptom of the underlying problem: the new instance was *listening* for traffic on the port that he thought it used to *send* traffic. However, he focused instead only on 7234. Why? It seems George incorrectly assumed that both new and old instances were listening on the same port. He said to Danny:

```
George: It is listening 7234...is it ok that it
listens on the same port as the default instance?
```

It turns out that it is simply not possible for two processes (in this case, the new instance and the default instance) to listen on the same port. That would be like two different houses having the same phone number. It just does not make sense. It seems likely that this question was confusing to Danny, who after about a minute responded:

```
Danny: Don't think so.
Danny: Do you have the WebSEAL admin guide?
George: Yes.
```

At this point, George spoke aloud to no one in particular, "You've got to be kidding me." And then directed himself to Adam on the phone:

George: Just to keep you updated, the guy from support, he made me check to ensure that it was listening on the 7234 port, and it is. My question to him is, Do you need to listen on a different port for the second because the first instance listens on the 7234, so does the second instance...?

At that point, another message from Danny arrived:

```
Danny: one sec trying to find it...working from home today.
```

George stopped his train of thought:

George: Oh God, this support guy is asking me for the WebSEAL admin guide.
Adam: No!
George: I swear!

George did not expect much from tech support to begin with, but this last question about the admin guide made him completely lose respect for tech support. Yet just before asking about the manual, Danny had asked a question that could have quickly led to resolving the problem. Adam told George that he knew someone else who could help, and eventually brought one of the software developers who wrote the WebSEAL software itself into the discussion. Among all this, Adam missed the obvious issue too: that the two instances of WebSEAL needed to listen on two different ports. It seems Adam was not really following the situation too closely.

Danny continued to send a few messages, but George replied only twice and then ceased communicating for a while. Later, one of Danny's messages pointed out that George had to change the listening port for the new instance in the webseald.conf file—the correct fix for the problem—but on seeing that, George said to Adam:

George: This guy doesn't know what he's talking about.

From that point on, George ignored Danny completely. The instant message windows that contained the exchange with Danny became covered over with other windows. Danny's last message arrived about 15 minutes later:

Danny: What is happening?

Well, what was happening? Some aspects of this seem straightforward: George began with little confidence in technical support, and when Danny implied that he did not know the answer (by asking for the manual), George simply wrote him off, as did Adam (it seems). But there is something more complicated going on here, and we have hinted at it. George's incorrect understanding of the way the ports connect the servers led him to miss critical information displayed on his screen. In fact, Danny seemed to know very well what he was doing. He asked the critical question ("Can you verify the listen port?"), gave the correct information ("Don't think [two processes can listen on the same port]"), and provided instructions on how to actually fix the problem (change the listening port for the new instance). The problem was not Danny. The problem was George.

It is worth considering the effects of the communications medium. Danny and George were conversing using instant messages, which lack nuance and are relatively slow compared to voice (Connell, Mendelsohn, Robins & Canny, 2001; Isaacs, Walendowski, Whittaker, Schiano & Kamm, 2002; Nardi, Whittaker & Bradner, 2000). If Danny and George had been using the phone, there might have been time for more back-and-forth and clarification of the issues, avoiding the misunderstanding in both directions (Voida, Mynatt, Erickson & Kellogg, 2004).

George's problems were likely confounded by the complex set of parallel conversations he was engaged in. He was working with Adam, keeping him up to date, and trying various ideas together. He was working with Ted, bringing him up to speed and interacting through instant messages. He was working with Mark, who seemed always aware of what was going on in George's world, and who had his own problems. Of course, he was working with Danny. And though we did not mention it, during these same 15–20 minutes, he also interacted with his girlfriend, the people he was planning to go to lunch with, and his manager.

Debugging George

After communication with Danny stopped, a series of exchanges between George and Ted eventually led to the resolution of the problem. Ted discovered that the PD server was trying to communicate with the new instance over port 7137, and Ted tried to explain the situation via instant message:

```
Ted: We were supposed to use 7236. Unconfigure that
instance and...
George: Can't specify a return port...you only
specify one port
```

George knew that the original command only permitted him to specify one port. George's response suggests that he thought the specified port went the other way, and did not know how to specify the port connecting the PD server to WebSEAL.

Ted explained how he came to this conclusion (to use 7236 rather than 7137) by pasting into instant messages the commands he ran to test communication from the WebSEAL server to the PD server, attempting to persuade George that he had the correct diagnosis. The exchange became more heated:

```
Ted: You specified the wrong port.
George: No, I didn't.
Ted: You did it wrong. Yes, you did. You need to put
in 7236.
George: We just didn't tell to go both ways. The other
port has nothing to do with this.
Ted: Well, all I know is what I see in the conf file.
George: We thought that was the return port. That is
not a return port.
```

```
Ted: There currently is no listener on [PD server] on
7137. So use 7236. DO IT!
```

By this point, Ted had found the problem and knew how to solve it, but he had to convince George of the problem and the solution. Because George was responsible for the system, Ted also had to get George to execute the solution to the problem himself. In many ways, the exchange here is comical, but it is also telling. Ted tried to convince George of the problem with the port settings by making a logical argument, demonstrating command results via messages. When that did not work, Ted tried to simply tell George what to do with little explanation, resulting in this "you did it wrong, no I didn't" series of exchanges.

A key point came when Ted said, "all I know is what I see in the conf file." Here, we see that because Ted—unlike Adam and Danny—had direct access to the configuration file, he could discover himself that the ports were misconfigured. Unlike Danny and Adam, Ted did not have to rely on George relaying information accurately (see also Maglio, Kandogan & Haber, 2008). As we saw previously, George did not accurately relay the port information with Danny, and he misdirected Adam with the error messages as well.

In terms of grounding, Ted and George each interacted independently with the various systems, and each could establish mental models of the systems independently. Ted and George interacted with one another to establish common ground in several areas: (a) the way the systems actually worked, which depended on how they presented their state through responses to commands and information squirreled away in configuration files; (b) the mental model of the systems that Ted constructed through his interactions with the systems; and (c) the mental model that George constructed.

Apparently frustrated with the instant message conversation, George said to Mark, "Can you please call him?" Recall that George's phone was tied up with Adam, so Mark put his phone on speaker to call Ted.

Ted: Ted speaking.
George: What are you talking about? 7236?

There was no greeting. George picked up the conversation where they left off on instant messaging. He asked specifically about the port number, 7236, that Ted had been telling him to use. Through instant messages, Ted had been trying to establish some common ground over the port numbers associated with the different directions to and from the servers, but that did not work. Over the phone, George asked again about the same port. There was something he did not understand, but Ted's logical explanation was not helping either.

> **Ted**: Yeah?
> **George**: We thought that it came in on 7137 and went back on 7236, but we were wrong, that 7236 is like an HTTPS listener port or something?
> **Ted**: It will still come in on 7135 to talk to PD server apparently…
> **George**: Right?
> **Ted**: What's happening is it's actually trying to make a request back, um, through the 72…well, actually trying to make it back through the 7137 to the instance…and it's not happening.

George carefully explained his understanding of how the port numbers were used by the WebSEAL server to communicate with the PD server: 7137 was the port used for communication *to* WebSEAL and 7236 was the port used for communication *from* WebSEAL. Ted tried to explain what the configuration actually was, but not very clearly.

> **George**: I know. I know that. But I can't tell it to…
> **Ted**:…just create it with the 7236. Trust me.

It seems to us that Ted gave up explaining with "Trust me." No more grounding about the cause of the problem, really, just the solution.

> **George**: Why? That port's not, that's going the wrong, that's only one way, too.
> **Ted**: Trust me.
> **George**: It's only one way. Do you understand what I am saying?

George was not convinced. He wanted to understand. What was it about 7236 that agitated Ted so much?

> **Ted**: Cause it's the PD server talking back to the WebSEAL instance.

Ted explained that 7236 was the port the PD server could use to talk to WebSEAL.

George: Yeah, but how does WebSEAL talk to the PD server to make some kind of request?

George thought it was the other way around.

Ted: 7135 is the standard port it uses in all cases. So we had it wrong. Our assumption on how it works was incorrect.
George: All right, all right.

Ted got through to George, finally: "Our assumption…was incorrect," meaning "we were both wrong about the port numbers." But it still was not quite enough. Ted sensed George was uneasy, and so he lightened the mood:

Ted: If it doesn't work you can beat me up after.
George: I want to right now. [Laughter on both sides]

This episode represents the dramatic climax to our story of George. All that has come before has built to this point, and all that comes afterward was simply mopping up. What exactly happened? It seems Ted eventually realized that George did not have an accurate understanding of the way the communication between the servers worked, and so rather than simply having to debug the system, Ted, in fact, had to debug George. The switch from instant message to phone was probably critical to Ted's realization; voice communication carries much more nuance and the quick back and forth is better for finding out what another person understands (Connell, Mendelsohn, Robins & Canny, 2001). When he realized George's misunderstanding, Ted's key statement was "We had it wrong. Our assumption on how it works was incorrect." It was not just George who misunderstood, Ted misunderstood, too. Of course, maybe Ted did understand, but saying it this way helped solve the problem. Everyone had to be debugged. The reality of the system's configuration—as determined by Ted through his interaction with the system itself—bumped up against George's (and maybe Ted's) understanding of the system's configuration. So it was Ted's job to tell George—to convince George—how the system actually worked. When that failed, it was Ted's job to convince George that he had the solution, and to trust him. He did this mainly by relying on their friendship—and laughter.

Ted had discovered the underlying problem, and proposed a workable solution, but he still was not sure if George understood. The phone conversation continued.

> **Ted**: Actually, you can create a new one.
> **George**: Yeah, that's what I'm gonna do [sighs].
> **Ted**: I'm telling you man, this is what's happening. You can see by the connection it's trying to make. There is no 7137 listener on PD server right now, so what is it going to try to connect to?
> **George**: Yeah, I understand what you're saying.
> **Ted**: You know sure, we can see this in the logs, but I think we're already there where we've found out what the issue is.
> **George**: All right, all right.
> **Ted**: It's trying to make a return port.
> **George**: All right! [shouting]
> **Ted**: I verified in the other Web server log that the…
> **George**: Can you hang on please!
> **Ted:** that the SSL port is actually the the…
> **George:** hang on please…
> **Ted**: is the '234 port
> **George**: cause I understand what you're saying. Just relax. I need a minute to do it.
> **Ted**: Very good.

Once Ted got George to accept the general idea of the problem, he tried to explain again exactly what the problem was. George did not really care. He was frustrated. He wanted to fix the problem. At this point, Ted and George had different interests. Ted still aimed to establish mutual understanding, and George aimed to get the problem fixed. He had gone from denial to acceptance. He was simply not interested in these explanations. It irritated him that Ted kept on about it.

Ted was on hold, Adam started talking, others started instant messaging, and George was working to change the port settings. After a few minutes, he said:

> **George:** I can't, I can't think because I've got too many [expletive] people annoying me…There's too many people. I hate when

there's too many people involved, and everyone's telling me to do something different and it's like you can only do one thing at a time, you know.

At this point George began isolating himself to focus on the fix. He hung up the phones, closed all eight of the blinking instant message windows, and re-created the WebSEAL instance as suggested by Ted, using port 7236. This time the PD server junction configuration worked correctly (resulting in the configuration shown in Figure 2.4).

George then called Adam back and attempted to explain the process that had solved the problem:

> **George:** All right I think we got it. What we did was, uh what did we do? The, uh, rather than specifying the 7137 port, that, cause...What happened was we had opened a port going to... We were under the impression for some reason that the port that WebSEAL instance talks to PD server over is 7137 and then PD server returns on 7236, or 7135 and 7234, whatever. That was the impression we were under, so we opened the firewall ports with, um, and we opened it for 7137 to go from WebSEAL to PD server and then 7236 to go PD server to WebSEAL, so we only needed to open one port because, uh, and the port we needed to open was

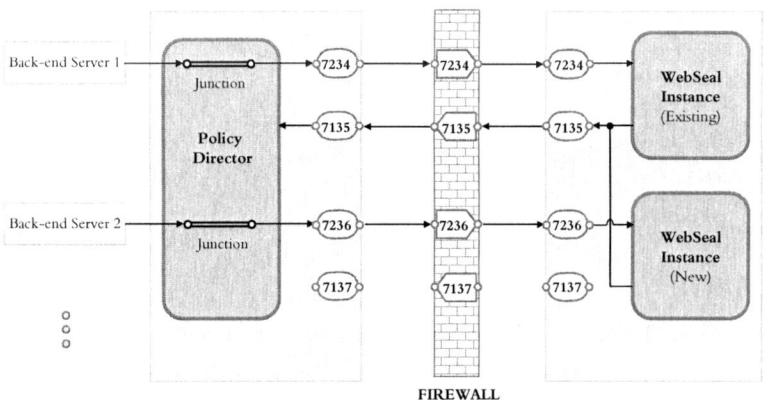

FIGURE 2.4 Final configuration after George's fix per Ted's suggestion. George specified port 7236 for the Policy Director to communicate with the new WebSEAL instance. The new WebSEAL instance used the default port 7135 to communicate back to the Policy Director. Port 7137 was not used.

the one that PD server goes back to WebSEAL on, so we already had that open, but it was the 7236 port so we just, I created the new instance specifying that as the port, so in the -m option I specified 7236 and I created all the junctions and everything looks cool at this point.

Though he had solved the problem with Ted's help, it seems George still had not internalized an understanding of it. His explanation of how the ports connected to the servers was incomplete at best. So in the end, Ted had not really debugged George's model of the system, but he had somehow convinced him to follow his directions for solving the problem.

No one person—not George, Ted, Adam, Mike, or anyone else—could accomplish the task alone. No one person knew enough. In a very real sense, it was the entire set of people, tools, and technologies that knew enough and that could accomplish the task—a kind of distributed cognitive system that operated effectively only as a whole (Hutchins, 1996; see also Maglio, Kandogan & Haber, 2008). In this case, the representational state in the form of system settings flowed via instant messages and phone between George and Ted. Each conveyed state found inside the system, and each interpreted state in the context of his individual understanding of the system. They each made up only part of the overall cognitive computation that ultimately solved the problem.

With everything working correctly, George rejoined the instant-message conversation:

George: all junctions are done. u r da man!
Ted: it worked???
Ted: just kidding ;)
Ted: sorry to be so rude then, I still love you.
George: I will never question you again.
Ted: You are the policy director king. that was fast man.
George: No prob.
George: I've got to run out for a few.
Ted: OK. Punch me later?
George: No, kiss you.

Need we say more?

System Administration as Collaboration

Overall, George's world was pretty complex—technologically, organizationally, and socially. He had to understand and work with large technical systems, and, at the same time, he had to navigate and work with large organizational and social systems.

Consider the organization. First, George worked in a group devoted to maintaining Web-related systems. There were about 15 people in this group, most of whom worked in the same building. George's manager was also located in the same building. George shared an office with Mark, another system administrator in the same group. Second, George had responsibility only for a small part of the overall operation of the systems he worked with. He shared responsibility with many others who were physically distributed around the country, such as Adam, the system architect. However, there were many others, including database, network, and operating-system administrators responsible for other aspects of the systems George worked on. Support personnel for individual applications and software were also available to help George, as we saw with Danny from technical support. Third, George's organizational environment also included clients, none of whom directly appeared in the episodes described here, but who had substantial influence over the activities described (including requesting the changes that resulted in George's problem in the first place). Throughout the session, George interacted with as many as seven people over the three hours of troubleshooting we observed. He used phones and instant messaging as well as face-to-face conversations and e-mail. At times, he interacted with multiple people at once through multiple different channels, as when he was speaking to Adam over the speakerphone while communicating by instant messaging with Danny.

Now consider the social environment. George had personal relationships with several of the people in this story. He was friends with Mark, his office mate. During this episode, we saw Mark not only facilitating George's work by making phone calls on his behalf but also supporting him emotionally, chatting about weather, sharing laughter. George was also friends with Ted, and they worked closely on various projects during our observations. Ted's presence gave him emotional support, and they

Box 2.3 Observations for Design—George

In the story of George, we saw several aspects of system administration work that were relevant to the design of administration tools and practices. First, we saw systems comprised of multiple components, sometimes coming from different vendors. Sysadmins spent considerable time and effort configuring components to work together and establishing an understanding of the system as a whole. Second, system administration is inherently collaborative. With access and expertise distributed across people and organizations, troubleshooting with remote participants is common and sharing system state is important. Third, solving a problem may require debugging a person as well as debugging a system.

We also observed a number of situations in which existing administration tools did a poor job supporting the needs of sysadmins. For one thing, divergence between system components was an issue: George found three different components reporting the same information using different syntax, and he wasted 40 minutes trying to reconcile them. For another, the communications tools George used did not work well enough to enable his remote collaborators to understand the actual state of the system because they relied on George to process and transmit all information. At many points, error messages were a problem. For instance, one error, "Could not connect to server," lacked detail—Which server? Which port?—and was reported well after the configuration step that caused it. Moreover, configuration itself was a problem, with George's misunderstanding perpetuated by a poorly documented command-line option ("internal port" was too vague to indicate communication direction), and a configuration file containing hundreds of options spread out over many pages (so that the port specifications for the two directions were not visible at the same time).

trusted each other. George felt free to shout and get angry when Ted's suggestions did not make sense, and Ted was willing to admit he was wrong to help things move forward. George also interacted with people he had never met before, such as Adam and Danny, and those collaborations were less successful.

Finally, consider the technical environment, particularly as it relates to communication and to people. As described, the systems themselves were technically complicated and interconnected in complex ways—generating unhelpful error messages, creating long configuration and log files, and more. George relied on multiple methods of communication, often using different methods in parallel to communicate with the same people at the same time. George and other participants also used tools and systems to affect the technical systems and to uncover and share system state. Most of the time, George was the only one with access to the system he was configuring and troubleshooting, meaning that all requests for information and all requests to take action had to go through him. At several points, we saw George provide others with incorrect or incomplete information. Only when Ted began working with the same systems did somebody other than George have direct access to critical information in the systems, and only then was the problem solved. But the systems themselves were not too cooperative in that they often provided misleading or incomplete information, as with the error messages and documentation (see also Maglio & Kandogan, 2004).

In some sense, George was responsible for orchestrating a diverse group to solve his problem. After all, he coordinated the activities of many others, activities that ultimately led to a solution. However, we might just as easily think that Ted was responsible for solving the problem; he was the one who discovered the configuration error and what to do about it. Or we might also think that George's manager was responsible, because the manager sent Ted to help. Maybe all of these are right. But we think it is better to see the overall system as responsible for finding and fixing the problem (Hutchins, 1996). Here, we saw a kind of distributed cognitive system in which information flowed across multiple technologies and people, each computing only part of the overall result. These episodes demonstrate how complex coordinated activity can emerge from everyday organizational and social interactions. If we focus simply on an individual or on a single technology, we will miss much of what happened, and much of what makes managing complexity possible (Woods, 1988).

We saw George multitasking throughout, doing many different things at once. He worked with Mark on Mark's problem, he kept his manager updated on the status; he worked simultaneously with Adam, Danny, Ted, and others on the port issue. At one point, George had active conversations going in eight instant messaging windows. He had verbal conversations on two phones and with people in the office at the same time. This is typical of knowledge-work (Czerwinski, Horvitz & Wilhite, 2004; Mark, Gonzáles & Harris, 2005). For much of it, George seemed unaware of how many threads he was managing, right up until he said, "I can't think because I've got too many [expletive] people annoying me..."

Was all that multitasking necessary? Maybe. George simply had to solve the problem, and he had to solve it quickly. It was a kind of shotgun approach—ask lots of folks for help, maybe one will pan out. Of course, one did. However, this approach had a cost. Each person had to be brought up to speed on the basic issue. Each person had to ask for information, sometimes requiring George to send them parts of configuration and log files or command output via e-mail, instant message, or read aloud over the phone. He shifted focus constantly, as when he was working with Danny by instant messaging and talking to Ted in the office, or when he was updating Adam by phone and sending instant messages to Danny. One might argue that all this attention shifting actually made things more difficult (Hudson, Christensen, Kellogg & Erickson, 2002).

George's interactions with others followed a pattern we found throughout our data. As the person responsible for the system, George served as a kind of hub, sometimes coordinating the activity of others, such as the network team allocating IP addresses or the firewall team opening up ports, and sometimes exchanging information from others, such as Adam and Danny. As the hub, George aimed to establish common ground through one-on-one interactions with the system and with other people. All common ground established among the firewall team, the network team, Adam, and Danny depended on George, who was the only one of them who could interact with the system. Ted was different. He could access the system independently, and so his understanding did not depend on George.

Building common ground means aligning mental models. In getting help, George was trying to help align his mental model of his situation with those of others by providing information on system state and explanations of system workings. The problem was that George's mental model of the situation was incorrect (as shown in Figures 2.2 and 2.3), making it just about impossible for him to create a correct mental model in the minds of others, especially in people with whom he did not share much common ground to begin with. Consider what happened when he was working with Danny from technical support. He transmitted incomplete information about which ports were open because what he saw on the screen did not fit his model of the world, and so in trying to create the appropriate mental model for Danny, it was completely reasonable to leave out information that did not make sense. Consider what happened when Ted had found the problem and the solution. He could not convince George what the problem was because George could not fit the explanation into his model. Only when Ted suggested that George effectively throw out his model, saying "our assumption on how it works was incorrect," did they make progress.

In short, George's story has many facets, but the most critical is that system administrators work in complex technical *and* complex social environments. System administration work is inherently collaborative.

3

Technologies and Complexity

"...even though it says it's failed, it did work."
—Dot, Web admin

Dot was trying to deploy a new Web application but she was having trouble with the automated configuration and deployment tool. Fortunately, she had done this before. She was following instructions from the application development team, which described how to configure this particular application, and another set of instructions for complying with local Web application practices at her site. Still, it was not easy. The two sets of instructions conflicted. Sometimes a step in the process would succeed despite the appearance of error messages, and sometimes error messages simply gave insufficient information to determine what had gone wrong. In the end, Dot got the job done, but it took much longer than she expected.

In this chapter, we present episodes that illustrate the technical complexity that sysadmins face when trying to understand complex systems. First, we tell the story of Dot's difficult deployment. She ran into trouble resulting from inconsistent instructions, mysterious errors, and a user interface that did a poor job supporting her tasks. This story provides examples of the limitations of automated configuration tools, the ways that sysadmins fall back to manual processes when automation fails, how sysadmins can arbitrate between conflicting instructions, and the problems of certain user interface approaches for complex tasks (Hertzum, Andersen, Andersen & Hansen, 2002; Parasuraman, Sheridan & Wickens, 2000; Sheridan, 2002; Spool & Synder, 1995; Woods, 1988). In the second story, we describe episodes from a critical situation, or crit-sit, in which a large group of sysadmins worked closely together for many weeks to solve a critical customer problem caused by a subtle interaction between system components (Haber, Kandogan & Maglio, 2011; Heath & Luff, 1992; Mark, 2002; Woods, 1996). This story provides an excellent example of collaborative troubleshooting in a large group (Rogers, 1992; Rogers & Ellis, 1994; Roschelle & Teasley, 1995; Teasley et al., 2000), made necessary by the extreme complexity of the underlying system. In both stories, we examine communication and coordination processes among systems and people, particularly grounding as a central process in understanding and managing systems and coordinating not only with other people but also with technology and documentation (Brennan, 1998; Clark, 1999; Clark & Brennan, 1991; Edmondson & Beale, 2008).

Modern IT systems are so complex that, often, no single person understands the whole in detail (Barrett, 2004). As a result, teams of different specialists must manage systems. As technical complexity leads to social complexity, specialization occurs in expertise, function, and phase of service delivery (Dewar & Hage, 1978; Lawrence & Lorsch, 1967; Whalley & Barley, 1997). These specialists must work together: people in different parts of the organization, people who report to different managers, and people who have different goals and different measures of success. This makes communication, coordination, and grounding all the more difficult (Becker & Murphy, 1992; Fussell et al., 1998).

The Story of Dot, Web Administrator

Just east of Boulder, Colorado, against the foothills of the Rocky Mountains, there is a huge site, with 24 buildings and more than 2.5 million square feet of space. Once the home of significant computer hardware manufacturing, the site now is a large data center with a vast army of IT workers designing, configuring, monitoring, and maintaining the computer infrastructure on which modern enterprises rely, such as corporate Web sites, instant messaging infrastructures, networked computer storage, and help desk services. We made five visits to the Boulder site over three years, observing people managing Web, storage, operating systems, instant messaging, and system provisioning. This is where we met Dot.

Dot was a junior Web administrator, with experience in several areas of system administration. After working on mail servers for five years, she had grown tired of that and moved to Web management to do something new. One morning we observed her as she prepared to install a new version of a corporate sales-support Web application. (See chapter 2 Box 2.2 for details on Web applications.)

Dot's primary role was deployment, monitoring, and troubleshooting internal Web applications and application servers. The Web applications she deployed were developed by various teams within the organization. Each application was then tested by another team in Georgia. Once applications were tested and approved, the application files were delivered to Dot, who would then install them in the appropriate Web application servers. This would often entail working with various configuration files, and adjusting settings in the application server administration console. Dot worked with many different applications running on many different Web application servers.

Given the business-critical nature of Web applications, there were many restrictions in place to ensure smooth operation. For this, they instituted "change windows," specific periods in which all maintenance work was to be completed to limit application downtime to non-business hours. We found such change windows in virtually every area of system administration (see also Frisch, 2002; Limoncelli, Hogan & Chalup, 2007). As Dot described it, her site's main change window was:

> **Dot:** ...on the weekend from 9 PM on Saturday to 7 AM on Sunday, and then we have what we call tower-specific windows during the week where some limited things can be done Monday to Friday from 8 PM to 11 PM.

The complexity of the deployment process, combined with the limited and inconvenient times for these windows, meant that Dot and other administrators spent considerable time preparing for changes well in advance, ensuring that all necessary information was collected ahead of time, that all steps of the process were well understood, and that any required computer files were preconfigured and immediately available and on hand during the change.

In addition, to ensure reliability of Web applications, Dot's site used a staged deployment approach, with different regions of the distributed file system set aside for test, staging, and production. Each application was first deployed to test servers to verify that it worked correctly. Once tested, the application was then promoted to a staging area to test the deployment process, and finally onto the production area for real use. Once files were in the production area they could not be modified manually, ensuring that a running, production application could not be changed except through an atomic copy operation from the tested and verified application in the staging area. The network was also partitioned: Development and testing occurred on computers in the "blue zone," a region of the network separated by a firewall from the client-accessible "green zone," where production applications ran. Dot's command-line windows were colored blue or green, depending on which type of machine she was connected to.

Coordinating Information

One morning we observed Dot preparing for an application deployment. As deployments went, Dot described this one as relatively simple: upgrading an existing sales-support Web application to the latest version. To achieve better performance and reliability, the application was to be deployed onto three different application servers.

The process of installing and configuring the application seemed pretty complicated to us. Dot had to install the appropriate application files in specific directories on the staging area, set configuration parameters (including, for example, server names and network port numbers) in several different files, ensure that all settings were correct for the new application and did not conflict with existing applications, transfer the files from staging to production areas, make the application server itself aware of the new application and start it up, and then replicate all these settings across three different application servers to ensure redundancy (in case of failure) and higher capacity. There were lots of details, for instance, in the steps of the process (order of steps, parameters), configuration settings, and file locations and the like. Dot had to perform the deployment during an evening change window, so she wanted to make sure that she had all the details to get through the process in a reasonable time.

To help her in this job, Dot acquired two different sets of instructions. One set came from the application developers. These instructions took eight pages to describe the overall process, with details such as version and configuration information for software components used by the application, such as WebSphere Application Server (WAS), the DB2 database, and utilities including JavaMail and Log4J. Dot was only concerned with the WebSphere application server configuration; even so, that part of the instructions was still lengthy (see Figure 3.1).

Many of these configuration steps involved manually editing configuration files and running various command-line programs (for an example, see Figure 3.2). To follow the instructions, Dot had to fill in the application-specific values of the several parameters used in the commands, such as node name, port number, and XML file location. This required Dot to have a variety of detailed configuration information at hand.

Dot told us the developer-provided instructions for this deployment were better than average:

Dot: It depends on the app. If it's a brand new app, a lot of the developers don't know a lot about administration, so they just assume that we know what they want, they don't fill it out. Some apps that have been around, they know what we're looking for. This is one of the better ones I've seen, though a few things seem to be missing, but it's not that serious.

- Check for all components (verify all files present)
- Expand the EAR file (all the files for an application come packaged as a single "EAR" file, this step expands the files to form an appropriate directory structure)
- Edit the XML Objects (used for automatic configuration information, which may need to be customized for the local site)
- Import the XML (for automatic configuration of deployed application in WebSphere)
- Add to the WAS Application Classpath (let WebSphere know where this application stores its files)
- Make sure session Manager is configured (configuring WebSphere to allow this application to access a DB2 database)
- Prepare for Cloning (get ready to replicate this application across multiple servers)
- Create Clones (do the replication)
- Transport Property (make each clone listen on the appropriate network port)
- Regen Plug-in (update WebSphere to use the new configuration)
- Verify (test to make sure the application is working correctly)

FIGURE 3.1. High-level sections (with explanations) of Dot's instructions concerning WebSphere Application Server. Each section was composed of more detailed instructions.

> **Import the XML**
> Import each XML object in the following order:
> 1. Server Group or Application Server (depending on what has been delivered)
> 2. Enterprise Application
>
> The following command will import any of the XML files:
> **/usr/WebSphere/AppServer/bin/XMLConfig.sh**
> **-adminNodeName <actual_node_name>**
> **-import <XML_file>**
> **-generatePluginCfg true**
> **-nameServiceHost <actual_node_name>**
> **-nameServicePort <actual_port_number>**
>
> **<actual_node_name>** the name of the WebSphere node that you are importing the applications into,
> **<actual_port_number>** the number of the port on which WebSphere admin server is running, and
> **<XML_file>** the full path to the XML file that you are importing.

FIGURE 3.2. Details of the "Import XML" step used for application deployment by Dot.

One common problem with developer instructions was omissions that resulted from the simpler environment that the application developers worked in—there were many "real world" things the developers simply never encountered:

Dot: Usually it's proxy information, since most developers don't have [network] proxies, they just hit their test environment directly, they aren't using it, so they don't think of what it needs to be, and they assume that we know what they want.

In this case, the application developer environment was directly connected to the network, but the client environment was not, meaning that network settings and related instructions given by the developers could be incorrect.

Because of omissions and environment differences in the developer-provided instructions, Dot also consulted various local on-line documentation repositories that contained detailed descriptions of how to configure each piece of software at her site. One set of instructions, describing all the steps needed to configure WebSphere Application Servers at the local site, was sufficiently important that Dot printed it out and kept it close at hand as she deployed the application. These instructions contained no details specific to the application itself, but they contained many configuration details relevant to all the WebSphere applications at Dot's site, such as information on the distributed file system accessible from the blue or green zone computers, and instructions on how to expand files in a staging area and "promote" them to the production area.

To successfully deploy an application that adhered both to its specific application needs and to local site standards, Dot had to coordinate information from both developer instructions and site-specific instructions. Abstractly, we can imagine she was engaged in the process of establishing a shared mental model with the application developers (via application instructions), local administrators (via the site instructions), and her systems (Brennan, 1998; Clark, 1999). The developers specified application-specific requirements, the local documentation provided site-specific requirements, and the systems themselves embodied a model of the way they worked. Dot had to interact with the systems and the instructions to uncover the clues and fit them together with her existing model of the systems to discover what the configuration settings should be and what sequence of steps she should follow to put it all together. Grounding was not always straightforward, and it was often made more difficult by the distributed nature of the information sources Dot had to bring to bear (Birnholtz, Finholt, Horn & Bae 2005; Hertzum, 2008).

Grounding System State

On the day leading up to the evening of deployment, Dot spent two-and-a-half hours going over the instruction sets, annotating the printed instructions (highlighting important sections, adding host names and ports numbers and so on), reading additional online documentation, examining lists of application files, preconfiguring various settings, and consulting co-workers via instant messages when the instructions were not clear. For example, Dot spent 10 minutes examining the configuration of every existing Web application on the server to find an unused network port for the new application. As she worked, she created a text file and wrote down all the commands to run for the deployment. Several were more than 100 characters long, with numerous parameter values specific to the particular application and environment (as seen in the XML import instructions; see Figure 3.2). This file permitted Dot to gather all the information ahead of time and to keep it ready in an executable form. It also reduced the chance of errors when entering these very long commands, as the text editor allowed Dot to see the entire command whereas her command line showed only about 70 characters at a time.

Dot expected the deployment to take 20 minutes or less. She thought she was quite well prepared with the annotated instructions, all the necessary configuration information, and her file containing commands ready to be copied and pasted onto the command line. However, she was working from both developer-provided and local instructions, and with the different levels of detail between the two instruction sets, there was some ambiguity about the order of certain steps. The first steps were clear, and she got as far as "Edit the XML objects" without error. The next step from the developer instructions was "Import the XML," which used XML configuration files provided by the developers and customized by Dot to automatically configure all settings for the new application. When she executed this step, it produced several pages of error output that included text such as,

```
Failure to initialize the Node configuration, XMLC0032E:
Naming Exception: The JNDI operation "lookup" on the
context "domainRoots/UnspecifieddomainName/..." with
the name "ejsadmin/homes/NodeHome" failed. Please
get the root id cause Throwable contained in this
NamingException for more information.
```

This text contained some clues as to a possible problem: It talked about "naming" and "domain names" and "naming exceptions," all of which might mean an incorrect host name was specified in the configuration file. In fact, Dot said that she might have overspecified one of the host names, using a fully qualified name (e.g., "server1.com") rather than an unqualified name (e.g., "server1"):

Dot: The only reason I did it that way was because I was working on this other project, thinking that I should have been doing it that way all along. It's probably not the case.

To test her theory, she changed the server names. However, when she tried to load the XML configuration file again, the same error appeared.

In troubleshooting this error, Dot engaged with instructions, error messages, output on the computer system's command line, contents of configuration files, and instant message interactions with colleagues to try to understand what the problem was. Dot interpreted the "naming" error message in the context of recent interactions she had with naming issues in a different system, and then performed a little experiment to test her understanding (Brennan, 1998; Hutchins, Hollan & Norman, 1986). Unfortunately, her hypothesis about fully qualified names being the problem proved to be wrong.

This kind of experimentation is like the joint activity of an ordinary conversation in which agents test their understanding of each other by trading words and sentences (Clark, 1996). The difference in Dot's case is that the other agent (WebSphere Application Server) was not trying to test its understanding too (cf. Brennan, 1998; Clark, 1999), but merely responding to Dot's request. Dot was certainly engaged in the process of grounding her understanding of the state of and operation of her systems *by interacting with her systems*. This type of interactive, improvisational approach to figuring out systems was common across the different sysadmins we observed. Understanding human–computer interaction as a kind of conversation is not a new idea (see Brennan, 1998; Hutchins, Hollan & Norman, 1986). Of course, we do not suppose that sysadmins are working to develop common ground with their systems exactly as they would with one another, but we do suppose it is a similar kind of process of grounding that underlies human–human interaction (Brennan, 1998). It is important to note, however, that systems vary considerably in their level of "cooperativeness"—some give up information fairly easily (with regard to details in system logs, output, errors), whereas others, whether because of the design of individual tools or the convoluted complexity of the whole system, make obtaining an accurate understanding very difficult.

At this point, Dot was not certain whether the error message prevented the application from deploying, saying, "I'm getting an error, but I don't know if it's an actual error or not." In her case, the system was indeed cooperative in the sense of giving her lots of information, but the information was not in a usable form. She was not clear whether the error was in fact preventing successful deployment. To test whether the application had deployed, she brought up the application server's graphical user interface (GUI) management console to see if the application she was trying to configure was listed (which would mean it had been created). The console showed about 20 applications, but not the new one. Dot refreshed the view several times over a few minutes in case the application was slow to appear in the list. There were a number of errors messages in the log window, but Dot told us that those were associated with a different application.

Dot looked again at the configuration file and instruction printouts and could find no obvious problems. She was concerned that the two sets of instructions—the local instructions associated with all applications at her site and the application-specific instructions provided by the application developers—left some ambiguity, particularly about the order of operations. Specifically, the local instructions mentioned promoting the code to the production area before configuration, whereas the developers (lacking separate staging and production file systems) did not mention anything about this. Because she could not resolve the ambiguity in the two sets of instructions, Dot decided simply to hold off the "Import the XML" step, and, instead, to try the next step in the local instructions first. That is, when faced with a conflict between developer instructions and local instructions, she needed to interact with the system itself more closely to establish how it operated. In the next step, she encountered a different problem: The command she needed to execute the next step apparently did not exist on the computer she was using. With the help of local documentation, Dot discovered that she had been using the wrong version of the command because she was connected to the green-zone (production) system rather than the blue-zone (development/test) system. Apparently, the zone difference did not matter for the first step of the process, but file movement required different commands in different zones, something Dot did not know.

Manual Interactions

Armed with the correct version of the command for the green-zone system, Dot successfully completed the next step. At this point, she tried once more to use the automatic configuration from the XML files, but again hit the same error. Finally, giving up on this course entirely, Dot configured the application manually using the GUI console. The console included a wizard that allowed the user to configure new Web applications step by step, each on a different user interface panel. Although the wizard could theoretically allow the user to easily perform a complex operation one step at a time in the correct order, in practice it also meant there were more opportunities for disruptions, because the wizard might require information the user did not have. She studied the wizard and looked through the developer-provided XML file to decide which information in the file needed to be transferred to the wizard.

Dot started the eight-step Web-application creation wizard, and got hung up on the first step because the package of Web-application files did not appear in the wizard display. After three minutes switching back and forth between the wizard and the command line checking various directories, she discovered that the wizard had selected the wrong server by default. Selecting the right server manually, she was able to proceed, and she made it to the seventh step, which involved choosing the application server in which the Web application would run. At this point, Dot realized that she had not yet created the application server, so she canceled the wizard to do that. Creating the application server required a single screen with seven tabs, which Dot filled in using information gathered from the printed instructions and the command line. She specified one field incorrectly, making a typo in the name of the directory for log file output, but she did not realize it at the time and no error was reported until later. The final step was to create a "server group" that would coordinate multiple instances of the application running on different servers. At this point, she was able to run the application-creation wizard to completion successfully.

All these steps were Dot's attempts to overcome the failure of the automatic configuration based on XML configuration files provided by the application developer. Each Web application needed to run in an instance of the application server software, which in turn needed to be coordinated for reliability as part of a server group. The XML import step was supposed to automatically create all these components in the appropriate order, but when that failed, Dot was left to work out the details herself by interacting with the system, documentation, and files.

Before moving on, let us examine the interaction with the wizard from the grounding perspective. Use of the wizard can be considered a joint activity between system and user (in this case the system administrator). At each step, the system would ask a set of questions to be answered by the user. Yet this joint activity is driven only by the system, because each step is predetermined by the system and is unknown to inexperienced users; the user has little opportunity to interrupt or ask a question. Problems can occur, as they did in Dot's case, when the user is not prepared for and has no way to hold off the current joint activity (to engage in another activity to perform the missing step or to find the missing information). This happened when Dot realized she failed to create an application server on the seventh step of the wizard and had to cancel the wizard to perform this missing step, and then redo all the wizard steps again.

Once the application, application server, and server group were created, Dot returned to the developer instructions. She used a "clone" command to expand the server group to include copies of both the application and application server on other servers to provide increased reliability and performance. Next came a command called "regen Webserver plug-ins," a step that Dot could not explain but was certain was necessary. She wanted to make sure all versions used the network port she had determined earlier. The correct way to do this was to change the value once for the server group, then "ripple" the change to update the configuration of each clone. The ripple command failed, so Dot tried the "regen Webserver plug-ins" command again just in case that might fix the problem. It did not. She was even uncertain if the error message really indicated a failure, saying, "Sometimes I've noticed that even though it says it's failed, it did work." Manually checking the port numbers for each clone revealed that the ripple had not worked correctly, so Dot changed the port for each clone by hand.

Finally, Dot tried starting up the server group, but got yet another error message, "No such file or directory" (though which file was not named in the error message). She tried the step again, just to make sure, and got the same error. She then looked through various configuration panels in the graphical user interface, and discovered the log file path typo she had made when creating the application server. She fixed the typo, and the application finally started.

Solving the Puzzle of Complexity

Overall, this story captures many aspects of technical complexity faced by administrators we observed across our studies. A Web site appears simple to the user, but much goes on behind the scenes to make it work. To provide enterprise-level reliability and resiliency, Web sites are actually comprised of many different parts including Web servers, application servers, and server groups operating across different computer servers (not to mention the network firewalls, authentication servers, and content servers we saw in chapter 2). Each of these components needs to be configured properly to work with all the others, and the

---

Box 3.1 Observations for Design—Dot

The story of Dot highlights two important aspects of the administration environment: (a) sysadmins often perform complex, multistep operations during limited change windows, usually with significant preparation; and (b) sysadmins may face divergent requirements from development and deployment organizations, requiring ingenuity and experimentation to resolve differences.

It also shows several instances in which administration tools did not effectively support administration work. For one, there was no tooling support to help prepare for complex, multistep, change window operations—Dot gathered information and created scripts manually. For another, error messages were a problem: When automated configuration failed, the errors were too voluminous to comprehend, with page after page of Java stack dumps. Later, when configuring the server log file, the error was reported well after the configuration step that caused it. At several points, Dot noted that error messages do not always indicate errors. Finally, the wizard that Dot invoked as part of the configuration process did not provide visibility about the prerequisites for every step, and it did not permit her to pause the wizard when she realized she had not yet created one of those prerequisites, forcing her to cancel and start again from scratch.

configuration often requires multiple steps with multiple places where things could go wrong.

Moreover, Web applications were created by one team, tested by another, and deployed and managed by a third. The developers and testers for Dot's application had different environments, a likely cause for the failure of the automatic configuration step. Environment differences also led to the different instruction sets that Dot used, because the local environment had constraints and requirements unknown to the developers. The differences in coverage and detail between the sets of instructions left certain steps ambiguous, with Dot unsure about exactly how to proceed when errors occurred.

Technical complexity also reduced Dot's ability to understand what was really going on with the system. Twice, when faced with an error message, she was unsure whether the error meant that the operation had truly failed. As with George (in chapter 2), the error messages were often insufficiently specific and reported too late. Dot later faced a message saying "No such file or directory" with no indication of the file in question. The lengthy error after the automatic configuration step provided no clue about the cause; in fact, Dot never did determine why that step failed. Errors were also reported too late: In Dot's case the "No such file" message occurred when the server was started rather than when she typed the wrong file name in the first place.

In the end, these problems did not prevent Dot from completing her task, though they certainly slowed her down. When faced with obscure error messages or ambiguous instructions, she did her best to adapt, gather more information, figure out the problem, and find a way forward by trial and error, solving the puzzle one piece at a time. Obviously, the technical complexity of modern IT systems has a profound impact on the complexity of the human labor required to configure, deploy, manage, and troubleshoot them. Thus, we see Dot's job as a kind of information coordinator, ferreting out scraps of information from various sources—instructions, documentation, error messages, architecture diagrams, experience—and putting them together to build a working IT system (Carlile, 2002; Paepcke, 1996; Star, 1989). In our observations, her interactions with other people were often mediated by the documents she received. She interacted with her system to try to determine how to proceed when the documents proved insufficient. She had to align her mental model of the situation with the actual situation, and what is more, she had to align her mental model of the to-be-installed application with that of its developers and then adapt that model to her actual environment.

The Story of the Crit Sit

On a hot July day, in a windowless conference room, in a huge IT delivery center in Boulder, Colorado, 8 sysadmins from all over the country worked together and with many others on the phone and in chat rooms, all troubleshooting a stubborn and intermittent failure in a sales-support Web application that was critical to an important customer. No one had any idea what was wrong. They huddled together over their laptops, discussing theories, conjectures, and ideas—hoping they could discover the problem, fix it, and go home. We were there, watching this group tackle a critical situation, or crit-sit, an all-hands-on-deck process for solving a difficult customer problem.

System administrators live in fear of crit-sits, the formal process invoked when a client is extremely unhappy with the behavior of an IT system (Haber, Kandogan & Maglio, 2011). Experts on all components of the system, as well as client-facing technical people, are brought together into a single room to work until the problem is solved. Crit-sits were usually invoked because of subtle, emergent problems in highly complex systems (Oleson, Hagan & DeMoss, 2009; Woods, 1996). Crit-sits were not particularly common at the Boulder site—one administrator estimated being part of maybe four per year—and their duration was more often on the order of weeks rather than months. Sometimes they were the only way to fix problems.

We spent a day observing a crit-sit that had just gotten underway to address the intermittent failure of a Web application. Given that Web applications are comprised of many components (Web server, application server, application, and often other components such as databases and e-mail servers) created by different teams, and often different vendors, it was not surprising that a very subtle problem could emerge. We watched 8 experts in various areas work together in a big conference room—what they called a *war room* (Mark, 2002)—to debug a problem (see Figure 3.3). Other people kept coming and going, but the core team remained the same:

- Roger—Web application server expert
- Karen—Web service delivery team lead
- Serena—Web service delivery
- Pablo—lead developer for the Web application
- Ray—application developer
- Jim—Web infrastructure expert
- Tom—database service delivery
- Eli—general sysadmin

We were able to identify 4 others on a speaker-phone conference call, and 12 more joining in via instant-messaging, including project managers, database administrators, service delivery executives, and technical support representatives for the software products involved. After our day of observation, we followed progress on the problem by staying in contact with several of those involved. We even obtained the entire technical

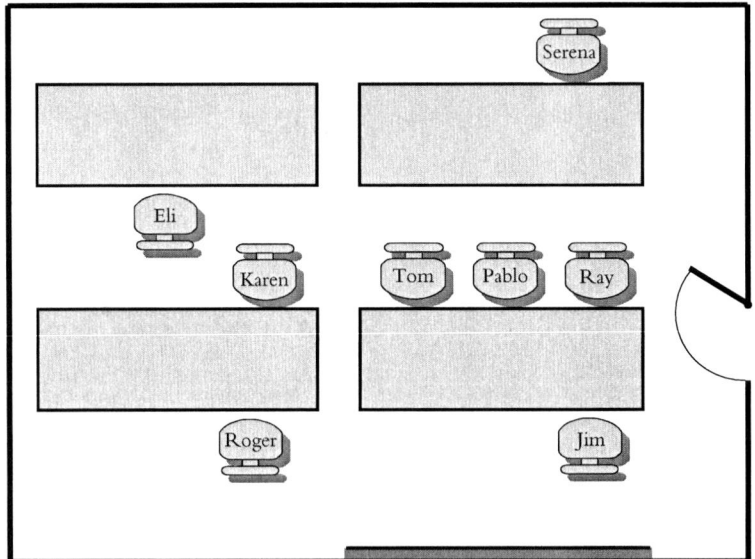

FIGURE 3.3. Configuration of the crit-sit war room showing where the technical and business people involved normally sat—though they would often move around to talk to each other, work together on their computers, or discuss ideas on the whiteboard.

support problem log, which documented the first report of trouble, the establishment of the crit-sit, more than 200 formal interactions between the system administrators and various technical support teams, and the final resolution 83 days after the problem first occurred.

At first, it seemed amazing to us that this many people had been instructed to sit together in a single room, dedicating all their time to work on a single problem until it was solved. Indeed, one of the people in the room complained via an instant message to a colleague off site,

```
we're doing lots of PD [problem determination], but
nothing that I couldn't have done from home ☺
```

Box 3.2 Technical Support

Most computer users have experience with technical support, those people we call when we cannot get our computers to do what we want. It turns out that system administrators, despite their expertise, also make use of technical support when they face problems they cannot solve.

At the sites we observed, support teams were arranged in a tiered structure, with each level dealing with progressively more difficult problems. The help-desk team—the first point of contact for clients when they had a problem—was often referred to as level-one support. Level-one support specialists were typically junior-level employees. They dealt with common and frequent problems for which there was a well-known solution or recovery action. If level-one support could not solve a problem, they would open a problem ticket to escalate to level-two support.

Level-two support analysts were more experienced than level-one, had access to more diagnostic tools and information, and were authorized to take more aggressive action to solve client problems. The level-two support team was, among other things, expected to check log files for errors. For example, if there was a potential connection problem between a Web application server and a database—the two were not "talking"

(continued)

> **Box 3.2 (Continued)**
>
> to each other—level-two support could find the logs, open them, and search for entries that might confirm or elaborate the hypothesis. They also *recycled* applications and servers (a shutdown followed immediately by a start-up), which would often "clear" the system and allow it to return to normal operation. One support analyst told us that the established policy was for level two to try to recycle twice before escalating the problem to the level-three team. If level two could not get the system up and running, the team would have to perform a root-cause analysis (RCA), an arduous process that could take days or weeks to complete.
>
> If level-two support could not fix the problem, they would escalate to the most highly skilled, level-three support analysts. It was imperative that the level-three team fix the problem, as they were the last line of defense. However, in some cases, even level-three support needed help, and this usually came in the form of product-level support, which had a similar tiered structure. Product support usually involved help working through tricky configuration settings, operational commands, or interpreting complex error conditions—but occasionally, there was a bug in the product that required a code fix to be developed and applied. In such cases, standard operating procedures dictated that the IT data center level-three support team and the product level-three support team would be engaged, as well as senior- or executive-level management on both sides.

Yet after watching the people at work, there seemed to be real value in having all of them together in one place. The room was alive with different conversations, usually many at once diverging and rejoining, and with different experts exchanging ideas or asking questions. People would use the whiteboard to diagram theories, and others could see and contribute to the discussion. When something important occurred, the attention of everybody in the room was instantly focused. In addition, the group chat room was used as a historical record for system status, error messages, and ideas. Individual chat was also used for private

Technologies and Complexity 69

conversations within the room and beyond, either exchanging technical information, such as,

```
if I'm not closing prepared stmt in WAS 4.x and
I do close result set and connection but I still
get CL1012SE error...will this still result with
the connection open?
```

or complaints, such as,

```
they have code of FLINTSTONES era and want to run it
in 21st century ☺
```

In what follows, we give a low-level view of crit-sit activities based on our observations of the administrators at work in the war-room. This story provides a clear example of the complexity of modern systems, and of the huge efforts that must sometimes be brought to bear to identify and fix problems. This crit-sit required a variety of technical specialists to monitor and observe the different parts of the system and to work together to understand what was going wrong.

Transient Problem

The critical system was a Web application comprised of a Web server (IBM HTTP Server or IHS), a pair of Web application servers (WebSphere Application Server or WAS), and a database management system (DBMS) supporting several local databases (DB2-local) and also acting as a gateway to a database on a remote mainframe DBMS (DB2-remote) (see Figure 3.4.).

As a whole, the system had worked well for some time, but after a major software upgrade to WAS and a minor upgrade to DB2-local, the system started failing in an intermittent and unpredictable fashion. Surprisingly, the symptoms appeared in IHS—a component that had not been upgraded—rather than in the upgraded components.

As a Web server, IHS would accept connections from Web browsers up to a set maximum number of connections. Each IHS connection would in turn connect to WAS, and a specific application running on WAS would then connect to one or more of the databases in DB2-local or DB2-remote. The problem would manifest when the number of IHS connections rose suddenly to the maximum number allowed, at which point IHS would crash (i.e., shut down without warning).

70 Taming Information Technology

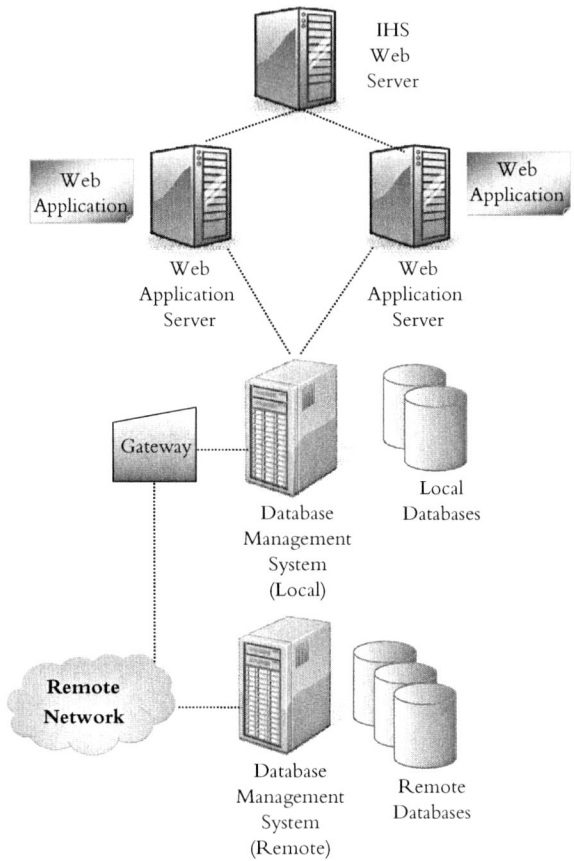

FIGURE 3.4. Basic system configuration in the crit-sit: HTTP Server (IHS) serves Web pages for Web applications on the Web application server, accessing data from local and remote database management systems.

Of course, it was the client that originally detected the problem, which was that the Web application would intermittently stop working. When the IT service delivery team in Boulder could not determine the cause quickly, they contacted technical support for the software products (IHS, WAS, and DB2), according to the official problem record. There were different support representatives for IHS, WAS, and DB2, and different levels of expertise, from the frontline people who answered the phone and collected information to the high-level developers familiar with the finest details of the products (see Box 3.2 for more details on technical support). There were major technical contributions from seven DB2 support representatives and from three WAS support representatives.

According to the problem log, troubleshooting started with IHS/WAS (given that was where the symptom first appeared), but moved to DB2 in the second week; then to troubleshooting both IHS/WAS and DB2 together for several weeks; and finally troubleshooting settled on DB2, as evidence accumulated that it was the cause of the problem. Because DB2 and WAS were both developed by IBM, the technical support representatives for both products worked together and coordinated their efforts, though one of the participants commented that such cooperation probably would not have occurred had the products come from different vendors.

The crit-sit was established at the beginning of the third week after the team first contacted technical support, and ramped up day-by-day after that to bring in additional experts in IHS, DB2, WAS, and the specific client application. We observed the team a week later. The crit-sit continued through week 10, at which point an acceptable solution was found, and was closed in week 11 after a sufficient period with no application outages.

There were a number of reasons it took so much time and so many people to solve the problem. The multiple system components and many possible interactions among them required extensive monitoring and experimentation, modification to configuration settings, use of special tracing and logging modes, and observation to see if the problem re-occurred. The failure was intermittent, making it necessary to run the system for hours or days to see if each change had any effect. At certain points, the admins tried installing new hardware and special versions of software to better monitor the problem. Possible problems were found and fixed along the way, but the true root cause was hard to find.

In the end, they found that the problem originated in a very subtle interaction between the Web application and the way it used WAS to connect to DB2. More specifically, the application used an undocumented, unofficial function to connect from WAS to DB2—it worked in older versions of DB2 but did not work as expected in newer versions. In fact, the upgrade of DB2 had triggered the problem. So, in fact, DB2 was working correctly (that is, working as it was documented to work), and WAS was working correctly too. The application itself was using

DB2 incorrectly. This kind of problem turned out to be very difficult to isolate.

Summarizing System State

The war room, where everybody worked together physically, certainly lowered the barriers of communication. For example, at one point when Karen, a delivery manager, said that she needed to brief management about the state of problem, people all over the room started adding their ideas and opinions, clarifying issues, and finishing each other's sentences. Because Karen was in the same room with all the other technical people, she was already aware of the situation and could ask a very specific technical question regarding the ongoing work.

> **Karen**: So, can you give me, before I go into this meeting with <executive>, for the max-appls being set at 40, is it basically because they don't match? The application is set at 40, and the thread limit is not set at a different level? I need a very English, down level, you're talking to a kindergartener…

Karen was capable of understanding the technical issues herself, but she needed as simple an explanation as possible for management. She was concerned with whether configuration settings in different parts of the system matched, particularly settings concerning the number of threads that a process could run.

> **Ray**: You'll have to ask Pete [on the phone], I haven't seen his files, I want to ask him if he's had another CLI trace.
> **Jim**: [Starts drawing diagram on the whiteboard] I think the max-appls here is 40 [on the DB]…
> **Karen**: But on the application side?
> **Jim**: …but the app running here [inside WAS]…
> **Ray**: The app side hasn't set it, because there's no connection pool…
> **Jim**: [writes symbol for infinity]
> **Tom**: WebSphere has no control over it, since they [the app] are using their own connections…if this is the problem, then it's overloading, it's flooding…

At this point, the working theory was that the settings of the maximum number of threads did not match in different parts of the system (DB2 versus the application, which was running inside WebSphere Application Server or WAS), and particularly that one part had a limit set and another part did not. In this case, it might be possible for one to overwhelm the other by trying to make more connections to it than it can handle. At least, that was the thinking at that moment.

> **Roger**: Could there be a chance that a couple of connections didn't get closed? Or is it assuming all 30 are going and all 30 are getting closed? Or there could be chances that the resources are not being...
> **Ray**: I have to research more into what the SQL error...what the program flow during an SQL error as opposed to just a normal exception.

However, other explanations seemed possible: Closing the connections might be the problem. It might be that when an error happened (e.g., an error in the database system), the connection it was associated with might not be closed properly, leading to a kind of leakage of connection resources and, ultimately, to failure (when the system ran out of resources).

> **Karen**: So there's no connection pool whatsoever? Or no connection pool outside of the application?
> **Jim**: There's really no connection pooling implemented at all for this particular app. The connections are getting closed, but I don't think they're getting closed fast enough, so the number of connections grows beyond 40, and that's when he starts seeing errors on the 41st on the WAS side.
> **Ray**: He's looking at the CLI trace. That's from DB2, right? It has nothing to do with WAS. The question is, is there another CLI trace that shows that it happened simultaneously?

Ideas were offered and discussed, and theories changed quickly. It was brainstorming, people sharing ideas, facts, evidence, working toward a common ground of what was really happening with the system. That is why the crit-sit was necessary: Information needed to be collected and correlated from many parts of a complex system. The co-location seemed to help that process by lowering the barrier to communication and to getting the attention of others. The interaction between people in the room was much more lively than with those on the phone—the people on the phone would occasionally speak up with a question or theory, but there was not the same kind of back-and-forth as in the room.

Yet they were not making much progress toward answering Karen's particular question; they got distracted by the flow of ideas. The only thing they were sure about was that they did not know why the connections would suddenly grow and cause IHS to crash.

The conversation continued at a rapid-fire pace for the next five minutes, only winding down when one of them noticed the level of connections rising again, and everybody went to their computers to gather more clues. Karen never got a good, simple description of the problem. Their working theory related to a mismatch in the number of allowed connections between the application and DB2, and whether the application needed to implement "connection pooling."

Let us consider part of this exchange in more detail. Establishing a common understanding among such a large team was difficult, in good part because of the complexity of the underlying system that they were attempting to understand. With different experts for different parts of the system, there were several conversations going on in parallel. First, there was Karen's quest to get a kindergarten-level explanation of the current theory that she could share with the executives. Second, there was conversation among the other participants over details of the connection pooling theories. Third, there was a conversation about what information could be gained from tracing data extracted from the running system. These conversational threads were all related, of course, but they did not all help Karen, exactly.

In the exchange, Karen started with a question about a specific parameter setting and its relation to other parameter settings. Tom replied that Karen would have to ask someone named Pete, and Jim offered that the parameter setting for DB2 was 40. Neither addressed Karen's question. Karen was trying to ground her understanding of how the system worked by understanding how particular settings related to one another. It seems to us that she had an implicit mental model in which WAS and DB2 could communicate over a (potentially) maximum number of connections at any one time. If the two sides did not agree on what that maximum number was, there could be trouble. At this point, Jim and Greg took turns to tell her that, in fact, WAS (and more specifically, the application itself) did not use a setting for the maximum number of threads or connections. Karen's question did not make sense; her assumption of how the system worked was incorrect. She inquired further about connection pools, to start to repair her mental model of the system. Jim told her that there was no connection pool at all.

As observers, it is, of course, not possible to know for certain what Karen's mental model actually was, and what she was actually going to tell the executives. Karen appeared to be trying to understand the system by establishing common ground with those in the war room around the connection and thread settings. Several conversations were going on, but Karen aimed specifically at these issues. These were factual issues about the settings embodied in the running computer system. One complication was that Karen needed only a very basic description to report back, but most of those in the war room had much more detailed knowledge of the system. The mental model that Karen needed to convey to the executives needed to be simpler than the mental models of those in the room, making harder her job of grounding the current working theory.

Karen's process was to gather information about system state by interacting with the people responsible for different parts of the system: Tom, Jim, Ray, and others. This was similar to the process Adam went through (chapter 2) when he tried to ascertain the system state by asking George to run commands, send log files, examine configuration files, and so on. In both cases, the process was only partially successful: In Adam's case, George's misunderstanding distorted the information he sent, and in Karen's case, the others in the room kept getting distracted by their own process of establishing common ground on the state of the system. The systems and situations were both technically and socially complex, and so the process of coming to the correct understanding about how things worked—correct enough to do the job, anyway—was not easy. In Karen's case, sense making was so complicated that it required not one person but many people, which in turn required more coordination.

Making Sense of Chaos

Sysadmins in the war room and on the phone spent considerable time monitoring system components, and collecting, analyzing, and correlating information from several sources. We saw what seemed an endless stream of traces generated and analyzed, and log files searched for clues. Data from different components were pasted into the common chat room so everyone could look for patterns. A sysadmin would walk across the room, look at another's code and discuss scripting syntax. Discussions would grow and shrink—when people overheard questions or issues where they could contribute, they would speak up.

Sometimes there would be nothing of interest happening, and people would start doing miscellaneous work related to the problem while they waited for any signs of failure. During one of these quiet times, we observed a few of the sysadmins working together on a script to better monitor the number of IHS connections. Because the overall problem seemed related to a high number of IHS connections, continually monitoring this number was important, yet there was no built-in tool to do this. On the WebSphere side though, there was a nice graphical chart recording the number of connections over time. To complement this, Roger started to write a script that counted IHS processes regularly. The script would query the number of processes every two seconds and print it out with the current time. However, he could not get the output formatted the way he wanted, with the number of connections and the time stamp on the same line. Roger recruited Jim and Ray, resulting in a lengthy discussion of the various scripting languages available and of the best way to capture and format the output of commands. Spoken comments went back and forth, as did code snippets via instant messages and e-mail. Eventually it evolved into a kind of competition, with Roger and Jim recruiting further help from outside the room, and three of them arriving at different solutions at about the same time.

Once the script was written, Roger executed his script, and put it on a common server so that others connected to the server would see the number of IHS connections at the same time. Not everyone was connected to the server, so occasionally Roger would shout out the values as they grew higher, and sometimes copied and pasted the time-stamped numbers into the common chat-room.

As we watched this seemingly routine chaos of human conversations and system interactions, the system started heading toward yet another failure. All through the day, there was increased activity in the room whenever the number of IHS connections started to rise—everyone would focus on their parts of the system in case some new clue appeared. When the IHS failure occurred, they investigated all the different components, trying to understand the state of each to see how it might be contributing to the failure. There was considerable discussion in the room and many theories about what might be wrong and how to fix it.

Moreover, even coming to the conclusion that the system had, in fact, failed was not straightforward. Various parts of the system kept functioning or looked like they were functioning even though others looked like they had failed. It was critical for the sysadmins to discover indications that the system was *about to fail*, because that would enable them to activate their internal tracing and monitoring to capture more information about the system state. Once the system failed, it would be too late to retroactively collect data about system state preceding the crash. Because they could not reliably reproduce the problem, they had to wait for it to happen, hope they would catch it just before it was going to happen, collect data about what was going on inside the system at the time it happened, and discover something in the data that would point to the problem.

Serena: Connections are 116, so we need to decide what we're going to do.

The number of connections to IHS was rising, and so they needed to decide exactly what data they were going to collect. People around the room tried to connect to the system, and for many there was no indication that the system was slowing down and about to fail:

Pablo: Yeah, but it's working fine.
Serena: You're right.

A few seconds later, though, Serena suggested that things were not working fine.

Serena: No, mine's still thinking.
Pablo: Well, mine was thinking just now, but I stopped it, did it again, and it went fine.
...
Serena: It's not letting me in.
Pablo: It's working fine, but not very consistently, I think.

When Serena said, "mine's still thinking," she meant that she had used her Web browser to request a Web page from the system and the system had not yet delivered it. Pablo confirmed that that had just happened to him, but he went on to say that when he tried it a second time, the system had delivered the page. Serena was not convinced, and Pablo offered the explanation that things were "fine but not very consistent."

> **Kathy**: So are they in there o.k., or is it just getting signed in?
> **Pablo**: Well, the time I had a problem was signing in, but…

Because Pablo suggested that there some kind of inconsistent behavior—sometimes it delivered the Web page and sometimes it did not—Kathy asked which Web pages were being delivered. Pablo clarified that he had tried the page for "signing in," which would invoke the "entitlement" process behind the scenes (that is, verifying who was entitled to use the application):

> **Pablo**: It does almost look like there's some sort of problem related to sign-in, that may be related to the entitlement. Very often when you look at what's running, there's an awful lot of authentication service, which is the thing that gets called when you hit enter on the sign-in page. And that goes off to IR and it's…something tied to the database. There's also another survey called check cookie survey, which is part of the whole thing too. And that's the one thing that was slow for me, but whether it's the second problem or not, I don't know. But I keep running sys, and it's working fine.

Here, Pablo tried to elaborate the computational process that went on behind the scenes when someone signed on to the system. The explanation seemed unclear to us, yet no one in the room asked for clarification, so perhaps his statement reflected the ambiguity of the underlying situation. There might be a problem with the entitlement or authentication part, which was somehow related to the database. There might be a problem in some "check cookie" process as well. In any event, it was not clear whether the system was actually failing or not.

To be fair, they really did not know very much about the problem at this point, and Pablo was not the only one with incomplete theories. The whole point of the crit-sit—of bringing everyone together—was to gather data and discuss, to brainstorm. Several conversations were going on at once. Interleaved with the conversation among Pablo, Serena, and Kathy about whether the system had indeed failed, Jim and Roger were still discussing the connection and thread settings.

> **Ray**: Yeah, but from what I understand it was right around 45 threads being used for ServOps, so why did it crash when there should be 150 threads...
> **Roger**: You've got IHS maxed out, right, WAS has got [garbled] but IHS has got capped at 256, and if you try to increase IHS, then you're playing with CPU utilization.
> **Ray**: I'm not saying increase IHS, but if there's worker threads available, then why would IHS have a problem handing it off to WebSphere?
> **Roger**: IHS does not have handing off to the WebSphere, that's why IHS, at some stage IHS maxes out, WAS doesn't max out.
> **Ray**: Yes, but why is that?
> **Roger**: Because WAS is taking too many times to process one request, it's basically stuck on one process, and IHS keeps on accepting requests, and does not get an appropriate feedback from the WAS.

In the previous conversation with Karen, the question of the number of threads or number of connections revolved around possible differences between WAS and DB2, yet here it revolved around differences between WAS and IHS. The idea was that if WAS was limited in the number of things it could do but IHS was not, WAS could become a bottleneck.

Seconds later, Roger, who had been monitoring the number of connections on IHS and posting them to the chat room, announced that the system had indeed failed.

> **Roger**: And we got maxed out. Yep, we're maxed out. Taking a core dump again, let's see what it shows.

This was not enough to convince everyone that the system had, in fact, failed. Serena was still sure that she could access the system through the Web.

> **Serena**: And we have connections maxed out and I'm on the site just fine. What's going on? Are you sure we didn't change anything?

…

Serena: How is this happening? That makes absolutely no sense. [jumble of voices] Yeah, the connections are maxed.

….

Serena: Maybe I was working off a cached copy. But I closed my browser!

It took a while for Serena to convince herself that the system failed in the usual way. It had. But she kept on retrieving Web pages through her browser, something she should not have been able to do if the system was in its failed state. Perhaps the Web browser stored (or cached) previous versions of the Web pages it retrieved. So Serena kept seeing those previous versions rather than new versions when she tried to access the site—on the face of it, there was no way to tell when the pages had actually been retrieved. She incorrectly thought that stopping and restarting the Web browser cleared its cache of old pages.

Roger: I think it's dead. ServOps, no it's something to do with…
Ray: It's entitlement. No, wait, ServOps, No wait,…[laughter]
Roger: It is ServOps.
Greg: Why don't you guys make your mind up, either one or the other.
Pablo: If we could make our minds up, we wouldn't be sitting here. [laughter] That's the whole problem.

It was dead. But why? What was the problem? Roger, Greg, Jim, and Pablo just had to laugh—laugh, and dive back in. What else could they do?

Within a few minutes, the evidence for a real outage was unambiguous: None of them could connect to the system. They began to pick apart the different components, trying to determine the state for each during a failure in hopes of understanding what was going on when the system stopped responding. One component called "ServOps" had a number of threads that were not responding, which had been discussed earlier as a possible cause.

Greg: How about it, we address something that was discussed 10 days ago about redirecting ServOps?

Pablo: Well, that occurred to me this morning as well, because otherwise that thing is going to come back and haunt us every few days, and some one will say, "ServOps, ServOps."
Ray: They have the instructions to do it. I've given it to them.

Another person noticed that a certain file on one of the two WAS servers appeared to have an incorrect size, suggesting it might be corrupted, so they copied a known-correct version before restarting. Then they debated whether to increase the number of allowed database connections, and who could do that task. Although the failure this time did not appear to be related to database connections, in previous cases it had, and this seemed like a good time to make the change:

Roger: Should we increase 40 to 80? Who can do the increase? Karen? Or Chris?
Ray: Whoever replaced Chris, who's backing him up today.
Greg: Amber?
Amber: I'm on the phone. This is Amber, I'm Chris's backup.
Roger: Amber, we want to increase the max application...
Ray:...whatever the max connections is on the database...
Roger:...on the [database name] from 40 to 80.
Amber: O.K., we didn't reach max connections...
Ray:...but we have before...
Roger: This time we didn't reach because ServOps created the magic this time.
Amber: O.K., you want to increase it from 40 to 80?
Roger: Yes please.
Amber: O.K., and that will require a recycle [restarting the database].
Roger: And WAS is currently down.
Amber: O.K..... Is that o.k. that it's [the database is] used by [another application] as well? Is that o.k.?
Unknown voice on the phone: We'll live with that.

Not only did they need to decide the course of action, they had to find the person responsible for taking the action, ground her in the need to take the action, and then she needed to make sure that side effects from the action were acceptable. Having all the appropriate people within earshot allowed this process to proceed quickly.

Once IHS, WAS, and DB2 were restarted, the room calmed down noticeably. The participants had gathered what data they could, made a few changes that might help the problem, and only time would tell if the failure would re-occur. Nothing dramatic occurred during the remainder of our observations; indeed, Roger appeared to be catching up on non-crit-sit work while waiting for new clues to appear.

The crit-sit remained open for six weeks after our visit. We do not know how long the participants continued to work together in that conference room, but the client support data records extensive work including the addition of new hardware to improve WAS performance, tracing, configuration changes, software updates to DB2, and analysis of the network between the WAS and DB2 machines. Finding the solution took longer in part because client support personnel were unable to reproduce the problem on their own systems, and turning on database tracing often slowed the production database to the point where the system was unusable. Only through careful monitoring and turning on tracing at just the right time was the problem eventually pinpointed.

We initially found it astonishing that a problem could take so many people and so much time to resolve. Yet the underlying system and its subtly interacting components were so complex that only a team of specialists working with one another closely could pull together the information needed to determine the cause of the failure and the appropriate solution. They needed to share ideas, data, and theories, and run countless experiments, all aimed at helping them to develop an understanding of the system and why it was failing. Only through close cooperative work could they do all this. At first the crit-sit seemed crazy, wasteful, and heavyweight, but after close examination, it appears to be a necessary and logical outcome of the technical complexity of the problems it is used to solve.

Complex Interactions

Simply put, the crit-sit was a prime example of how technical complexity increases as the number of connections between parts of a system increases, and of how a group of different experts was required to work together to understand the system. The problem was not attributed to any one part; the problem emerged only because of a peculiar interaction between several parts. In highly coupled systems, a change in one part can have unexpected consequences for the whole (Rasmussen, 1986; Woods, 1996). That made troubleshooting such problems all the more difficult. In this story, we saw that dealing with such situations meant balancing that increase in technical complexity with an increase in human complexity, coupling human resources to create more and more channels through which people can monitor, share, and discuss their situation openly and easily. The war room facilitated unlimited conversations between any number of people simultaneously. Ideas were shared freely. Anybody who heard an interesting lead could contribute to it or refute it. This was a distributed pattern of collaboration, where each person was responsible

---

Box 3.3 Observations for Design—The Crit-Sit

The story of the crit-sit demonstrates the extreme complexity of modern IT systems and the practices that sysadmins adopt to manage subtle and intermittent problems. Modern IT systems are aggregations of many components, each with many configuration settings, and each managed by different experts. Subtle problems can arise when a change in one component causes problems in another. However, the crit-sit process itself—bringing many experts to a single place to concentrate on a single problem—can foster brainstorming and collaborative debugging to help solve these subtle problems.

The sysadmins told us that the crit-sit was expensive and incredibly disruptive to their normal work. Those assembled together in the crit-sit used the same communications tools as everybody else: instant messaging, e-mail, and face-to-face meetings. They had no special tools to help brainstorm or collect and integrate data. They had no tools to create the rich experience of face-to-face interactions without the cost and disruption of gathering people from across the country and putting them together in a single room.

for his or her own system component, and engaged with various others to establish common ground about how the components interacted. There appeared to be a broadly shared, high-level common ground on the overall state of the system, but also disjoint, lower-level common ground on the details of component interaction, held by subsets of the crit-sit personnel. This chaotic environment facilitated idea generation and establishing common ground at different levels, though it was not always effective in solving specific issues (as we saw in the case of Karen's question). On the whole, however, the crit-sit appeared to work to determine what was happening to the system and engage collective reasoning to fix the problem (Orlikowski, 2002; Drury et al., 2010).

Grounding in a Complex Environment

Today, IT is critical for almost all aspects of modern business—and perhaps all aspects of modern life. Yet IT systems are growing increasingly more complex, comprised of layers of components interacting with each other in intricate ways. The stories of Dot and the crit-sit show many of the issues that arise with such technical complexity. There are so many ways to connect components in modern IT systems—so many systems, so many configuration parameters, and so many potential unexpected interactions—it is difficult for an individual or even a group to understand the overall system. The components are complex even in isolation, as evidenced by the verbose commands, obscure errors, and the need for extensive technical support.

Complexity increases when multiple components are connected together. Each component must be correctly configured with respect to the others, and, frequently, expertise on different components is distributed across people and organizations (Sandusky, 1997). At the simpler end of the spectrum were Dot's struggles to get the application clones on different machines to use the same network port, and her problems of different environments between staging and production. The crit-sit shows a kind of worst case of intercomponent complexity, in which a problem arose out of a very subtle interaction between parts of the system—one that took weeks of full-time work by a large team to determine what component was at fault and how to fix it. Too often, system design does not take into account the complex environment in which systems are actually deployed (Velasquez & Wiesband, 2008; Verdoes, 1997). Error handling is a striking example of this: Messages are simply not specific enough (e.g., "Could not connect to server," or "No such file or directory"), and errors are sometimes reported long after the action that caused them (Maglio & Kandogan, 2004).

How do system administrators deal with all the technical complexity? By trying to ground their mental models of the systems with reality—relying on documentation, experimentation, and conversation. They engage in joint activity, exchanging words with each other or interacting with systems to achieve a common ground, an understanding of their systems (Clark, 1996). Dot grounded her understanding of the state and operation of her systems by interacting with developers and other sysadmins via the instructions they produced, and engaging directly with her systems (Brennan, 1998). Dot had her own experience and understanding of how her systems worked, and she needed to reconcile this with the developer instructions, which did not take into account the practices and constraints of Dot's environment. Dot also engaged with the system to collect information and gain understanding of system state after each step of the process. Dot's interactions with the wizard were especially interesting: Because the wizard's steps did not match her usual practice, Dot was required to stop and restart the wizard.

Karen's process of pulling information about system state out of Tom, Jim, Greg, and others was a collaborative effort, with people interacting with each other, and multiple people interacting with different parts of the IT system. This approach was necessary because the systems and situations both Dot and Karen dealt with were technically complex. Understanding how things worked was difficult. Relevant information was hard to find, and the system behavior required interpretation. For Karen, interpretation required many people, which in turn required more coordination.

In sum, we observed the key to successful sense making in complex, highly interconnected technical environments is balancing technical complexity with increased coordination among participants to ground understanding of the overall system state and system behavior (Brennan

1998; Clark, 1996; Hertzum, 2008; Klein, Feltovich, Bradshaw & Woods, 2005). That joint activity can occur between people, mediated by documentation, instructions, messages, and conversations. It can also occur between people and systems, mediated by interactions with wizards, command lines, or configuration files. Technical complexity and coordination complexity go hand-in-hand (Bystrom & Jarvelin, 1995).

4

Practices and Innovation

> *"This whole thing we do is a dress rehearsal."*
> —*database administrator*

Indeed it was just like a theatrical dress rehearsal. Christine was preparing for a lengthy and complex database operation on a customer's machine. In doing this, she rehearsed the operation on a series of increasingly realistic test systems. She even had a "script" from a colleague who had performed a similar procedure in the past to guide her. Christine studied the script carefully, gathered information specific to her task, and began rehearsing the whole procedure using test systems the week before the "performance" on the customer's machine. The final day was a dress rehearsal—doing the entire operation on a machine that replicated the customer's environment. During this rehearsal, she hit several unanticipated obstacles, but this was par for the course. It was good that she shook out all the problems during the rehearsal; otherwise the customer could have been hit with an extended outage. Rehearsal was an invaluable practice to deal with scale, complexity, and risk in managing systems.

In this chapter, we describe several episodes from the work of Christine and her colleague Mike, whom we observed over several days as they rehearsed a database operation on a series of test systems. The lesson from these episodes is that administrators innovate, improving their practices and methods in response to the pressures of the business and work environment (Cargill, 1999). We illustrate several kinds of practices. Some were institutionalized, such as rehearsal of lengthy and complex operations to reduce risk and to ensure completion within short change windows. Institutionalized practices were well established, well documented, and required significant infrastructure support (Goh, 2002;

Gupta, Iyer & Aronson, 2000). This did not mean, however, that such methods did not change over time. In fact, as we will see in Christine's story, administrators improved their practices based on their experiences. Other practices were less formal, such as the practice of "peer reviewing" commands and scripts *before* they were executed to reduce chances of introducing errors. These appeared to be local innovations, informally developed, evolved, and shared over time to meet the needs of administrators on the front lines. We also discuss episodes from our interviews with Patrick, a capacity planner, who used standards developed in his organization as a starting point for allocating IT resources, but who relied mainly on his own experience to make decisions.

In examining the practice of system administrators within their complex social, organizational, and technical environments, we found constant innovation in practices in response to pressures in the environment. We also found those best practices being shared through interactions among people and through artifacts, such as documents in shared repositories. Shared artifacts allow users to refine practices based on their experiences, and to add their improvements back into the organization's commons.

Standard practices offer many benefits, including consistency and predictability, but their stability can be a problem if they do not change quickly enough for the fast-changing domain of IT (Rada, 2000; March & Olsen, 1989). Of course, individual innovations can cause problems by introducing unchecked change into the system. We will compare and contrast standards and individual innovation. We think that a reasonable balance can be achieved when individual innovation, driven by the system administrators in the field, is slowly disseminated to broader groups or communities, and ultimately evolves into standards after many applications and refinements.

The Story of Christine and Mike, Database Administrators

Christine and Mike worked at a large IT service delivery center that hosted numerous large-scale computer systems for Fortune-500 companies. They were part of a team of database administrators (DBAs) delivering database management services for several customers. We observed them during rehearsal of a large table-space-move operation (see Box 4.1 on databases).

Why rehearsal? The database administration work we observed often involved lengthy, multistep operations that took hours or even days to complete, and which had to be done during limited periods called *change windows*. To ensure that such operations were done correctly and within the allotted time, administrators often practiced operations on

---

Box 4.1 Databases

Data are crucial for modern enterprises. From accounting to human resources, sales, and customer information, critical data are stored as databases within database management systems (DBMSs). With the broad adoption of e-commerce, databases are an important part of business transactions, and as such, they are expected to be available 24/7 so that business can be conducted around the clock. Unscheduled outages—or worse, loss of data—have significant cost. On the whole, DBAs focus on maintaining the availability, security, and recoverability of data.

The responsibilities of database administrators vary, depending on experience and specialty, but they include optimization or tuning (improving database query performance by making changes to the design or to how the data are stored on disk), installation and configuration of DBMSs, monitoring DBMS performance and capacity to ensure correct operation, planning for new or expanded databases, and maintenance (e.g., updates to DBMS software, or making more disk space available if capacity is running out, and moving data around to make use of that space).

All the databases we observed were relational databases, in which data are stored as tables with rows and columns. Each table is stored in a table space, a region of disk set aside for exclusive use by the DBMS for storing a particular set of database tables. When table spaces become too full, it is necessary to create one or more new table spaces, and move some tables from full to empty table spaces.

test machines before performing them on a customer's *production* machines. One of the administrators we talked to described the process:

> If I have three development systems, I start off with an educational system, make sure it works there, do it in another development system, make sure it works there, and then do it in the QA [quality assurance] system, and once those three are complete—no problems, we have our steps now, we have our timing and we roll it into production.

Another DBA said, simply, "This whole thing we do is dress rehearsal." Indeed, what they did was very much like a dress rehearsal, as operations were repeated on test servers of increasing complexity before being performed on the real production servers. The DBAs described four levels of systems. At the low end, there were sandbox or education servers. These contained the system software—in the case of database administrators, database management software—but no data. Often, database administrators used sandbox servers to learn, to test specific commands, and to try out options. Next, there were development servers. These contained some sample data in addition to the system software. Then, there were consolidation or QA servers. These were exact replicas of the production servers. Typically, every change that went to production servers first had to go through consolidation servers to be verified, and only then were they performed on production servers (either automatically or manually).

Staging operations through multiple levels of systems was not unique to database administrators. We saw this method practiced in other domains, such as Web and storage administration (see the story of Dot in chapter 3). Staging was a good method in that it reduced—and in some cases eliminated—human error by verifying tools and processes before using them on client data. We saw installations in which propagation of changes to production systems was performed automatically, reducing system down time to a minimum and greatly reducing the possibility of error.

Rehearsal was an institutionalized practice requiring technical support from the organization in the form of dedicated computer systems for development, testing, and quality assurance. The IT organization not only provided such infrastructure but also devised tools and processes for promotion of change from one system to the other. The roles of the people involved in rehearsal were clearly defined, such as change managers, who were responsible for identifying risks, planning change schedules, coordinating system changes, and monitoring progress. In many cases, there were also change management tools developed to help coordinate this work.

At the time of our observations, Mike was mentoring Christine as she was getting up to speed on a new account. Christine was an experienced DBA. This was an important customer account and both Mike and Christine wanted the transition to be as smooth as possible. Mike spent much of the time in Christine's office providing advice and double-checking her actions. When he was not there, he was almost always available by phone or by instant messaging.

Copy, Test, Document, Revise

Christine and Mike managed databases that were part of SAP, an enterprise resource management system. As they described it, SAP databases were challenging to manage because of their huge scale and variation from installation to installation—a typical SAP installation had 25,000 database tables. Most tables in SAP grow over time, and they may eventually exceed the available storage space. Christine told us that one of the table spaces was near its capacity of 64GB, and it included two very large tables of about 15GB each. Her job was to create a new table space and move these two tables into it.

This was a fairly involved process; during the course of the table-move rehearsal, we observed Christine and Mike work side-by-side for hours planning, executing, and checking the results. At the beginning, Christine had received a 20-page document with detailed instructions and sample scripts from Hillary, who had performed the same operation recently. This document was stored in a shared repository containing similar documentation about many common operations, and was available to all DBAs at the site.

For the table move, the documentation was detailed (see Table 4.1). It included 16 major steps, including backing up the database, dropping old indexes and creating new ones, dropping old views, renaming new tables, and updating statistics. The documentation also included template

TABLE 4.1   One-page instructions for the table-move operation created Hillary and used by Christine: For each step, it shows details of the action, who is responsible for performing the action, when it starts, how long it takes. While performing the operation, Christine annotated this sheet with her times for each step.

```
Sample Implementation Plan (checklist)***
Use this on day of change with MOVE TABLE section

DBA to create two new tablespaces ZSAPBTAB1D/ZSAPBTAB1 and
run db2look and create all scripts for the move of tables
VBFA, VBRP, VBPA, LIPS, NAST
Basis to create new SAP data classes for the new tablespaces.

Implementation plan for Moving tables to new tablespaces.
```

Step	Who	Action (directory dba/work/tblmove)	Start	Dura.	Day	actual
1	Hillary	Offline backup with SAP down after	6:00	5 hr	Sat	
2	Hillary	Create new tables (prefixed with QCM) and insert data db2 + c -tvf crttables. ddt -z crttables.out	11:30	3.5 hr	Sat	
3	Hillary	Drop indexes and constraints on original tables db2 -tvf dropindexes. ddl -z dropindexes.out	15:30	2.5 hr	Sat	
4	Hillary	Create-indexed and constraints on new tables db2 -tvf crtindexes.ddl -z crtindexes.out	18:30	3.5 hr	Sat	
5	Hillary	Drop the old views associated with the original tables db2 -tvf dropviews. ddl -z dropviews.out	22:30	1 min	Sat	
6	Hillary	Rename original tales with a QCMT prefix db2 -tvf rentables1.ddl -z rentables1.out	22:40	1 min	Sat	
7	Hillary	Rename new tables to use original table's names db2 -tvf rentables2. ddl—z rentables2.out	22:50	1 min	Sat	
	Hillary	Page/call Patrick2				

8	Patrick	Test access to the table by listing its contents in transaction SE16	23:00	4 hrs	Sat
9	Patrick	Check whether the table has been accessed (ST04, detailed analysis, snapshot structures, tablespace snapshot)			Sat
10	Patrick/ Hillary	Update table statistics Runstats.sh > runstats.out			Sat
11	Patrick	Check consistency of the tables (Se14, Edit, extras, runtime object, check)			Sat
12	Patrick/ Hillary	Execute script to recreate views associated with tables db2 -tvf crtviews.dll -z crtviews.out			Sat
13	Patrick	Change the data class of the table to the new class for to the new tablespace	3:00		Sat/ Sun
	Patrick	Page Lotus to notify 'ok to start testing'			
14	Lotus	Perform application tests to make sure the moved tables are working properly.	3:30		Sun
15	Hillary	Drop the old tables prefixed with QCMT	4:30		Sun
16	Hillary	Offline backup Finish	4:45 10:00	5hr	Sun

scripts that could be filled in to automate parts of the process. Christine also kept a single-page summary of the implementation plan close by throughout the procedure, and she carefully annotated it during rehearsals with the time required for each step to help in scheduling the real operation on the production systems.

In preparing for the rehearsal, Christine went over all the templates and created scripts that were specific for her task, making sure proper table space, table, and column names were filled in (see Figure 4.1). When

```
connect to lc0 user sapr3 using xxxxxx
-------------------------------------------------
-- DDL Statements for table "SAPR3 "."VBEP"
-------------------------------------------------
CREATE TABLE "SAPR3 "."QCMVBEP" (
"MANDT" CHAR(3) NOT NUL WITH DEFAULT '000',
"VBELN" VARCHAR(10) NOT NULL WITH DEFAULT ' ',
"POSNA" CHAR(6) NOT NULL WITH DEFAULT '000000',
...
...)
IN "ZSAPBTAB4D" INDEX IN "ZSAPBTAB4I" NOT LOGGED INITIALLY;
insert into SAPR3.QCMVBEP
select * from SAPR3.VBEP;
commit;
-------------------------------------------------
-- DDL Statements for table "SAPR3 "."VBAP"
-------------------------------------------------
CREATE TABLE "SAPR3 "."QCMVBAP" (
"MANDT" CHAR(3) NOT NUL WITH DEFAULT '000',
"VBELN" VARCHAR(10) NOT NULL WITH DEFAULT ' ',
"POSNA" CHAR(6) NOT NULL WITH DEFAULT '000000',
...
...)
IN "ZSAPBTAB4D" INDEX IN "ZSAPBTAB4I" NOT LOGGED INITIALLY;
insert into SAPR3.QCMVBAP
select * from SAPR3.VBAP;
commit;
```

FIGURE 4.1 One of the scripts edited by Christine for the create-table step of the table-move operation. The scripts were edited by Christine to add information specific to the tables being created, such as field names and types.

creating scripts, she often copied and pasted the sample script template from the documentation into a new file and substituted specific values she gathered, also by copying and pasting from output of commands she ran. She was very meticulous.

> **Christine**: You get this information [pointing to the table columns on the screen] from the output of the db2look command so I just made sure that I had all of the information that I needed. And I am making sure that I have the proper table space. No typo there, which it shouldn't. I copied and pasted. And I am also checking it against our Web page ... That one looks good.

Over time, Christine's group had embodied certain best practices within the sample scripts to prevent common mistakes. Mike explained that, by inheriting these (sample) scripts, they essentially inherited these practices:

> **Mike**: If the index has special characters, then index name has to be in double quotes. If not, it fails. What the heck? We ran into a problem in the past. Now, it is better to put the index in double-quotes, just for the heck of it. It doesn't hurt. Some of the headaches that we ran into before, it is [now] in the procedures for the script.

As she modified scripts, Christine also changed the file suffix to put her name on the script filename. She explained that this practice helped her easily identify her scripts among others in the script repository. Christine created all her scripts in the directory /sapdbawork/dbawork/tbmove/move2002. The file structure was arranged such that all the SAP-related database admin work was in /sapdbawork/dbawork/, and from there, they created subdirectories for specific tasks, such as the table move (e.g., tbmove), and the specific implementations of these tasks (e.g., move2002). Along with the scripts, database administrators also kept the output log files from execution of the scripts for future reference.

In all, Christine created 7 scripts to complete parts of the whole 16-step procedure. Rather than create a single script that did it all, the practice was to use multiple scripts and have the administrator manually check the results in between:

> **Christine**: You have to check the output after each step in case there is any error. It is easier to back out if you catch it early on. So, if we add it all together and say at the first step there is actually an error and but ... I guess you could put error checking in the script, too.

This was a good approach because building error checking into scripts is difficult (Brown & Patterson, 2003; Weimer & Necula, 2004). Particularly, in the case of database administration, the number and type of errors to be handled is large because of the sheer complexity of the tasks and systems. The practice we observed was that, after each script was run, the DBA would check the output and system state to make sure the script had functioned correctly, and if not, would determine what had gone wrong. Some of this relied on human judgment. In addition, it can be quite difficult to programmatically test that an operation succeeded, and that not all errors indicate failure. Assessing the severity of errors and what an error actually means was the kind of knowledge administrators build up as they gained experience. Often, it is easier to have a human-readable instruction asking the DBA to ensure that a table was created with a given name and structure than to write a script to do it.

Christine was ready to start the rehearsal. She created all the scripts she needed. She told us that once scripts were validated on consolidation servers, doing the table move on production servers was fairly straightforward. All they needed to change were the system names in the scripts so that consolidation server names were replaced by production server names. This usually meant changing a single line in each of the scripts so they could do a global change on all scripts at once to limit potential human error. Using the same scripts for testing and production seemed a good practice:

> **Christine**: Usually by the time you go to production [systems] everything is pretty smooth. The development [systems]? Yeah, you might miss . . . You may make a parameter too large, which uses too much RAM to cause it to crash, too small, or a typo somewhere. By the time it gets to production, if you do it three other times, your scripts are pretty much set, you just run them.

What have we seen so far? Well, clearly Christine's practices were aimed at addressing the constraints of her technical, social, and organizational environment. Given complex operations to be performed, high demands for reliability and availability, and low tolerance for failure, she and other database administrators innovated in several ways. One was the sort of error avoidance that Christine demonstrated by not typing commands or database table names—preferring to copy them from scripts, instructions, and command output. The SAP database had more than 25,000 tables, so a typo in one table name could easily be another table name, and mistakes could have disastrous consequences.

An institutionalized practice for dealing with risk was rehearsal of complex operations on test machines before trying them on the production machines. Given the length and complexity of the table-move process, and the limited time window permitted, it was critical that the scripts and instructions be worked out completely before running them on the production machines. As Christine said, the expectation was that by the time it got to production, everything would run smoothly.

Another organizational practice was the documenting of procedures and experiences. The shared repositories for scripts and instructions allowed system administrators to create organizational knowledge of how to do their tasks, knowledge that could be shared from person to person and improved over time. The script repository was carefully organized by database type, task, type of operation, and year. If needed, administrators could easily examine past scripts, output, and errors encountered. The document repository contained several versions of the instructions and allowed easy feedback. Instructions were stored as high-level narratives when necessary, leaving much to be interpreted by the administrator. Instructions could include low-level details when necessary, with specific commands and sample scripts. In addition, some documentation also contained instructions on how to produce new scripts, serving as a kind of human-readable template.

Formal and Informal Organizational Support

Christine was not alone in the table-move rehearsal. There were many others involved from her immediate group and her larger organization. These included the change manager who oversaw the whole process, the SAP support team, and Mike, who sat next to her most of the time. This was a coordinated effort, with clearly defined roles and responsibilities. There were many checks and balances throughout, including getting proper approvals, monitoring and verifying system state, and more. Though the actual execution of the table-move on the production machine might take as long as a day, the formal process of preparation and approval could take far longer:

> **Christine**: Usually, the customer will contact the service manager, who would put it in a plan. The plan is discussed at our weekly technical meeting. That is one day. We will discuss it, we will map out, figure out how long it is going to take, if it is feasible. And the next time we meet the customer that week, we present

our plan [about] how long that is going to take, and we try scheduling a date for downtime with the customer. And once the customer gives the OK, a change request gets put into place by the availability or service manager, or by myself, if it is something I am going to do myself. And the availability or service manager would OK that. Once it gets OK'ed we do our work.

In addition to the formal coordination process, we saw a lot of informal discussion through e-mail, instant messaging, and phone. Because multiple teams were involved, each detail needed to be validated and approved by several parties. For example, Christine exchanged e-mail with her colleagues in the SAP basis support team, which provided application support for SAP. In one such e-mail, Sriram from the basis team asked Christine to verify the table-space names, and it turned out that she had a typo: Her scripts listed the servers as `ZPAPBTA4D` and `ZPAPBTA4I` when they were supposed to be `ZSAPBTA4D` and `ZSAPBTA4I`. She had to be very meticulous. There was no room for error. But she was not alone. She had the whole organization behind her, keeping its collective eye on her progress.

After Christine submitted a change request for the table-move operation, the availability managers approved the change on the consolidation servers to begin at 9 AM Friday. She had a window of 10 hours to complete the dress rehearsal. Assuming that went well, the production work—the actual changes to the customer systems—was scheduled for the following day, Saturday. In the meantime, she started preparing for the rehearsal.

Earlier that week, Christine had created the two new table spaces. She wrote a short, single-line script to create the table spaces. In fact, she reused an existing script so that she did not have to reinvent the particular syntax. We observed script reuse, even for single-line scripts, several times—another practice that aimed to limit chances of error.

On Friday, the day of the rehearsal, Christine was also on-call, meaning that, if urgent issues came up with other databases, she would have to be available to handle them. As it turned out, throughout the procedure, we observed her being called in to phone meetings, responding to issues on other accounts, and consulting other database administrators. As we will see, this had substantial impact on her ability to focus, resulting in confusion and a close brush with disaster.

As 9 AM Friday approached, Christine went over the documentation once again to see if there was anything she might have missed. She would start at 9 AM sharp:

Christine: So, we will have to wait till nine since that is what we put the change for. I don't want to bring anything down until then.

Bringing systems down automatically triggered alerts for the 24/7 team, and she did not want them to panic. When the clock struck 9, she said, "Okay, it is 9 o'clock" and then updated her instant messaging status to "do not disturb." Clearly, when she was doing her work, she did not want to be bothered. This was a time for focus, and she needed to limit distractions. However, because she was also on-call, she kept her beeper on as an alternative channel for people who really needed to get in touch with her. And there was always the phone too.

So just before 9 AM, she called the 24/7 team:

Christine: I am just going to give them a call and tell them that I am doing this change, as kind of a heads up.

This seemed like a good practice, giving a heads up to various interested parties before starting an operation, even when they were officially supposed to be aware of it. Christine had the whole organization supporting her work, but the organization also needed Christine to keep them aware of how things were going. This gave a sense of awareness to others who might have different concerns and priorities. Besides, these conversation opportunities offer people a chance to reprioritize tasks, discuss future plans, and reduce misunderstandings (Isaacs, Walendowski, Whittaker, Schiano & Kamm, 2002; Nardi, Whittaker & Bradner, 2000; Whittaker, Frohich & Daly-Jones, 1994).

Finally, Christine was ready to begin. She was seated at her desk with her laptop in front of her, its screen filled with terminal windows showing command-line connections to the remote machines where she would do her work. To execute the first script, Christine carefully typed the following command into a terminal window, as documented in the implementation plan:

```
nohup db2 +c -tvf crttable.ddl.christine -z crttables.
out.christine
```

This command would create new tables using the instructions in the file "crttable.ddl.christine," sending any status or error messages to the file "crttables.out.christine." In typing this on the command line, she, in fact, copied and pasted the script name from the directory listing. As mentioned, we saw her use copy and paste extensively for server names, scripts names, database names, table names, and so forth. She practiced this method deliberately and rigorously, which helped reduce the chances of introducing typos into commands that could take hours to complete.

Just before hitting "enter" to submit the command, she held back for a couple of minutes to survey what she was about to do:

Christine: OK, Here we go . . . Uhh, let me double-check.

As she said this, Mike walked in to check on her:

Mike: Almost ready here?
Christine: I am starting . . . I brought down SAP and I am going to do this one.
Mike: [looking at the screen] You need an ampersand at the end.
Christine: Oh, in the background?
Mike: Yeah. Cause it will lock up your screen.

She made the change on the command line, and also made a note of it on the paper instructions. As soon as Mike walked in, he began helping—for the most part just being another set of eyes to make sure commands were written correctly.

Mike: Let me see . . . . nohup + c, . . . You go for it.

Mike had explained that the command should "run in the background," meaning that her terminal window would be available to run other commands immediately after the command was submitted—thus she would not be waiting for this one to finish. To run commands in the background, she had to place an ampersand at the end of the line. After another minute or so examining the command, Christine finally hit "enter." Because the script was running in the background, all output from the script went to a file. She immediately received notification that the script had finished, which was so quick that she thought that there could be a problem. She brought up the output file, and each command was marked with the same error:

```
SQL0900N The application state is in error. A database
connection does not exist. SQLSTATE=00003
```

Looking over her shoulder, Mike quickly identified the issue:

Mike: DB2 started, or . . . ? I know you said you stopped SAP but did you start DB2?

Christine was unaware that the script to bring down SAP had also stopped DB2. This was not part of the documentation, though she quickly added it to her notes to update the documentation for future operations. Having Mike there helped her to easily understand the system state, clearing any confusion, and quickly getting her back on track. So it was not just formal organizational support, it was also informal peer-to-peer interaction that supported her work. Throughout the rehearsal, Mike's informal mentoring helped Christine many times, providing technical guidance, emotional support, and another pair of eyes.

Rehearsing Procedures

After restarting DB2, Christine reran the script (Figure 4.1), which was supposed to connect to the appropriate database, create a new table QCMVBEP (in a new table space), and insert data from the old table (the one in the nearly full table space) into the new table, commit the data, making the new table permanent, and then repeat the process with a second table QCMVBAP.

This time around, the script did not finish right away. So she opened another screen on Mike's suggestion to monitor the output file. Again, something did not look right. There was no error, but the script quickly moved on to the second step. What happened to the first step, the first table?

Mike: In less than a minute it builds the new table?
Christine: This is the second table though that I have in my script [pointing to output from the script]
Mike: Is the first one running?
Christine: That is what I am going to check . . .
Mike: Let's go down [as Christine scrolled the output file]
Christine: Nope.

102   Taming Information Technology

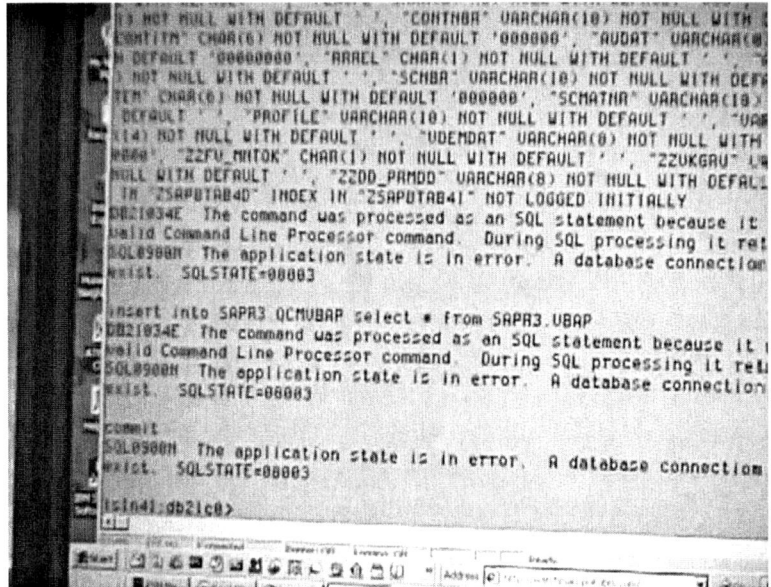

FIGURE 4.2   Christine looked at the errors after running her table-create script. Several errors occurred because of a typo: The first complained about an unexpected token in the script, a syntax error; the second complained about there being no database connection.

There were error messages in the first few lines of output, yet the second table creation seemed to be progressing normally (Figure 4.2). Something was strange. Christine was puzzled. As soon as Christine opened an editor to look at the script (see Figure 4.1) Mike noticed the problem:

Mike: Your "connect" needs a semicolon at the end.

Christine tried to make sense of this. She reasoned that there was only one *connect*, so how could the second table-create command execute before the first one? Mike explained that because of the missing semicolon between the *connect* and *create table* statements, the database parsed the two statements as one big erroneous statement and simply ignored it. The system then continued to the second *create table* statement, but because the *connect* command failed, the second table was actually being created using incorrect, default credentials.

Christine fixed the script by putting in the missing semicolon, but she had to let the script continue to execute. Mike suggested she open yet another screen and "drop" the table that was being created under Christine's ID (the default in this case) rather than SAPR3 (the correct credentials). Christine tried to verify the name of the new table that was being created, but all her attempts failed because her script was in a critical section that prevented other database commands from executing. This also prevented her from safely stopping the script, so she had to wait for it to complete. Christine worried that she was wasting time:

> **Christine**: How long does that usually take?
> **Mike**: The question is how big is the table ... I would say about half hour.
> **Christine**: Arggh!
> **Mike**: That is why we do it on the nonproduction first.

He was right. It was a dress rehearsal and they were uncovering problems in their procedures and scripts. The following day, they were scheduled to do the real work with the customer's production systems.

For half an hour, they discussed the problem, dealt with other issues, and when finally it became clear that the critical portion of the script had finished and they could get another command through the system, they issued a command to stop the script, and moved on to deleting the table that the script had created. However, now the "drop table" command returned an error:

```
> db2 DROP TABLE SAPR3.QCMTVBAP
DB2034E The command was processed as an SQL statement
because it was an invalid Command Line Processor
command. During SQL processing it returned the
following error:
SQL0204N 'SAPR3.QCMVBAP' is an undefined name.
SQLSTATE=42704
```

Once again we see an error message with many details but not much information. Christine and Mike thought the problem might be related to syntax—the way in which they typed the command and its parameters—so they tried putting quotes around the parameters, but got the same error. Mike asked Christine to verify that she was properly connected to the database, and she was. They discussed whether the table name needed "SAPR3" in front of it. Finally, after consulting the manual and many failed attempts to delete the table, Mike realized what was going on:

> **Mike**: It backed out the whole thing, cause we never committed it. It is not going to find anything. That is why the command didn't work because it couldn't find the stupid thing. Sometimes you think too much into it.

They had aborted the script before the second *commit* statement, so the table had not been made permanent. They were both surprised but also relieved. They had solved the problem, but were back to where they started. This diversion had cost them 45 minutes.

Christine fixed the script quickly and executed it again—again carefully noting the start time. This time, she changed the way she ran the script by adding the -s option to abort script execution in case of errors:

```
nohup db2 +c -stvf crttable.ddl.christine -z
crttables.out.christine
```

Another 30 minutes passed and the first table in the script was created. Christine noted the time on her paper instructions:

> **Christine**: I will put that in the notebook. So, if someone else does this in six months or a year, they will have some basis to go by.

As the second table was being created, she received an e-mail notice about one of the production database table spaces being 93 percent full. This was a bit of a concern. She told Mike that she already had a single-line script to add space to table spaces, but was reluctant to execute this script herself. She was uncomfortable working on both consolidation and production servers at the same time, as that opened up the possibility of errors should she type a command into the wrong window:

> **Christine**: I would do it, but I don't want having a production screen up when I am doing something else. Because they are all the same color [terminal window background color] and you could accidentally type in the command in.

This separation of concerns was, as far as we could tell, a locally developed practice to manage the complexity of duplicate databases on test and production systems. Avoiding simultaneous work on both systems was the best way to prevent an operation intended for one system from being executed on another, with potentially disastrous results.

Mike offered to make the change himself and left for his office. Christine decided that, based on past experience, the second table would take a while to finish, so she spent time updating the documentation based on her experience thus far. She made a note that DB2 needed to be restarted after bringing down SAP, and also changed the sample scripts to add the -s option, which would stop script execution after the first error, eliminating the problem that had resulted from the missing semicolon.

Throughout the whole day, we observed Christine going back to the documentation and making updates with lessons learned whenever she was waiting for an operation to finish. This was useful for future reference for her and also for any of her colleagues who might be doing the same task in the future. Her notes would become organizational knowledge, solidifying the processes and procedures of her organization (Carlile, 2002; Ackerman, Wulf & Pipek, 2002).

In this episode, we saw several methods for avoiding errors. First, Christine and Mike often followed a practice similar to pair programming (Williams & Kessler, 2002). Both would sit side by side and Christine would have Mike examine a command she was about to run, using a second set of eyes to spot potential mistakes before they occurred. Related to this was the approach of running relatively short scripts, followed by human validation of results. These permitted Christine to catch and fix errors before too much time had elapsed. It was also a reasonable response to the difficulty of programmatically describing and validating the expected system state after a script had run—not all error messages really indicated errors, and checking the system state sometimes required human judgment.

Organizational Awareness

The table-create script finished at 1:30 PM. Christine noted the time on the implementation plan and continued with the next couple of steps, executing scripts for dropping and creating indexes. Mike kept an eye on her even though he was now back in his office. He sent her an instant message noting a possible error in the "create-index" script.

> **Mike:** `before you run the dropviews.ddl, please stop by. you need to run primarykey.ddl script.`

Later, he came by and talked about this with Christine. She had been pulled into a conference call as part of her on-call responsibility. While she listened to the phone meeting, she still worked on the rehearsal and discussed her progress with Mike, who told her about the error he saw:

> **Mike**: You see, I have never seen the message. When you create the index you get the message about the primary key. I remember seeing the primary key when you create the index . . .

Mike noticed that some statements were missing from the create-index script and he prepared another script to be executed before the next step. He must have realized this because the script output did not contain the "usual error message" that they always got when they altered primary keys. Christine agreed to execute the script before the next step.

While Mike was in her office, Christine asked him about involving the SAP basis team later in the procedure. Earlier she had sent a note to the team but had not yet received a response. She sent another instant message to Sasha, her SAP basis team contact:

> **Christine:** `fyi we are running create-indexes for an hour.`

Later, she got a reply.

> **Sasha:** `oh ok.`
> **Sasha:** `It seems like lc0 took about 8 hours. LP0 may be faster than this.`

Sasha was apparently also keeping track of how long things were taking. He gave her his contact information. In the meantime, Mike left for home but promised to be online as soon as he got there. Sure enough, before the "create-index" script was done, he was back online and sent her an instant message:

> **Mike:** I see that the create-indexes is still running.
> **Christine:** it just finished. i'm running the primarykey.ddl

Christine encountered a problem with Mike's "primary key" script, which she found and fixed. She discussed and verified the fix with Mike. When the primary key script was done, Christine sent Mike an instant message to make sure she was seeing the expected output:

> **Christine:** is that the normal message you were talking about? sql0598w
> **Mike:** that error message is a good message.

Christine jotted down the times and moved on to the next step to drop views, which went quickly. She was close to the end. She had two more scripts to run for renaming tables, which were also done rather quickly.

In the meantime, she had asked Sasha to access the tables that were just moved and to verify her changes. Sasha was online waiting for his verification step and responded quickly:

> **Christine:** how does it look?
> **Sasha:** everything looks fine for VBAP and VBEP.
> **Christine:** ok did you do a sto4, too.
> **Sasha:** not yet just a min.
> **Christine:** it has that on our proc, ok.

Christine, well aware of the procedure, was also keeping an eye on what Sasha needed to do and made sure he did everything as documented. After a few minutes, Sasha responded back that everything looked fine:

> **Sasha:** the accesses to zsapbta4d and zsapbta4i looks fine.
> **Christine:** good. I'll do the runstats now.

Christine passed along Sasha's verification to Mike and continued on to the next step: generating statistics on the database tables for performance tuning. The final step was to have Sasha check the consistency of the tables.

She was just about done, and she seemed to us very relieved. She had found and fixed errors in several scripts, and verified the timings for the tasks. Furthermore, the task times were reasonable for the given change window, especially given that the production machine was going to be faster than the test machine.

Here, we see careful collaboration, communication, and coordination of work. The close mentorship between Mike and Christine, whether sitting side-by-side or communicating over the phone and instant messaging, was very helpful in bringing Christine up to speed on the table-move operation. Christine's timely communication with the monitoring and support teams was also important, ensuring that they were aware of what was going on, and that everything was proceeding as expected.

Multiple Checks for Risky Operations

Christine and Mike frequently found themselves multitasking when long-running tasks and immediate demands intersected. We saw them listening to conference calls in the background while doing other things and only reacting when they heard their names being called. Sometimes we saw them fitting in short tasks while waiting for long scripts (such as table creations) to finish, but these context switches could lead to trouble.

While Christine was rehearsing the table-move, waiting for the create-indexes step to finish, she received an instant message from a colleague on a conference call with a customer: "Christine. We encountered another DB problem. Can you call back in?" She was not happy about the interruption, saying aloud, "Oh God!" but it was her responsibility because she was on call. She investigated the problem reported on the phone, occasionally checking the progress of the create-indexes script and working with Mike on the script to run after that. She also discussed with another DBA instructions for an operating-system upgrade, which required an *offline backup* of the DBMS on a certain machine—an offline backup stops the database completely to create a backup of all its contents from a single point in time. While all this was going on, Christine needed to schedule two backups of the production DBMS as part of the table-move: She needed to do an *online backup* that afternoon, which permitted the DBMS to continue operating, but she also needed to schedule an *offline backup* for the next morning, because the DBMS would not be running during the change window. Mike told Christine that they needed to schedule the backup commands.

One part of backup scheduling was to ensure that blank tapes would be available in the tape drive (where the backed up data would be stored), and that morning Christine had spoken with Larry, the admin responsible for making sure the right number of tapes were in the machine. She still had hand-written notes on her desk,

> 1 set of six tapes on Friday online
> 1 set of seven tapes on sat offline with tarfs

It was time to set up the backup commands.

> **Christine**: Did you talk to Larry about the tape load?
> **Mike**: Yes.
> **Christine**: Cause he's got to go in and load the tapes for tomorrow's offline.
> **Mike**: Yes, I am going to remind him, in case he forgets.

At this point Christine had quite a few balls in the air. She was monitoring the create-indexes script, thinking about the subsequent script, talking about offline backups for a system upgrade, working out the details of tapes for both online and offline backups for the table-move operation, and all the while the conference call about a customer's database problem was droning on in the background. It was not surprising when Christine came very close to dropping one of the balls.

Christine's group scheduled and executed their backups using a UNIX utility called *crontab*, which was based on a configuration file that specified commands to be executed and when to execute them (Figure 4.3). Crontab is commonly used for any regular task (backups, audits, monitoring, maintenance), and the crontab file on Christine's machine already had a variety of such tasks listed in it. Each line in the crontab file began with a set of numbers indicating when to execute a command (e.g., every day at noon, every Saturday at 1 AM, the fourth Wednesday of every month, or even a single date and time such as November 8, 2002, at 4 PM), followed by the command to execute. Lines beginning with a '#' character—the comment character—were ignored. As seen in Figure 4.3, some commands were active, and others had been commented out. Commented out commands were left there as examples.

110 Taming Information Technology

(a)
```
#================================================================================
#=======Normal Backup Schedule- should match web page====================
#================================================================================
##Lotus requested an online backup for 09/21
00 16 * * 0-4 /dba/lib/db.control onltape.cntl > /dba/logs/db.out 2>&1
#20 19 04 11 * /dba/lib/db.control onltape.cntl > /dba/logs/db.out 2>&1
#55 23 02 11 * /db1/lib/db.control onladsm.cntl > /dba/logs/db.out 2>&1
#00 06 * * 6/dba/lib/db.control ofltape.cntl > /dba/logs/db.out 2>&1
00 16 0 11 * /dba/lib/db.control ofltape.cntl > /dba/logs/db.out
#Lotus usually wants online last and first weekend of the month . . .
#00 06 * * 6 /dba/lib/db.control onltape.pluster.cntl > /dba/logsdb.out 2>&1
#================================================================================
```

(b)

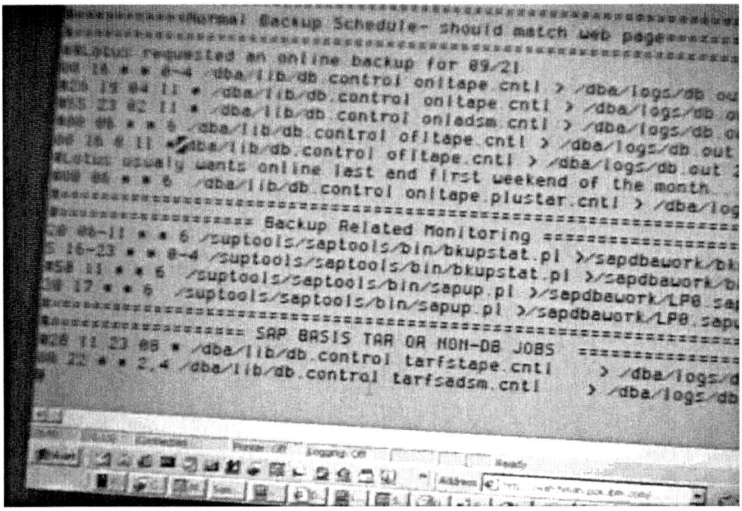

FIGURE 4.3   Part of the crontab file Christine edited for creating a backup, with text of the file shown in (a), and screenshot of Christine working on the file shown in (b). Note that her cursor was on the wrong line of the crontab file in (b), the line for starting an offline backup rather than an online backup, which was just two lines further up.

To schedule the online backup for the afternoon, Christine edited the crontab file. The file was fairly long, so she searched for an existing backup command. By mistake—perhaps because she had been discussing both online and offline backups recently—she searched in the file for the text "ofl." This brought her to a line with "ofltape," which was an example of an offline tape backup (and which was just below the example for an online backup). She copied and pasted the line, changing the scheduled time. She then ran a command to get the current time, which was 15:58:53. Christine specified

```
00 16 8 11 * /dba/lib/db.control ofltape.cntl > /dba/
logs/db.out 2>&1
```

which would cause the command to run at 00 minutes past 16 hours on the 8th day of the 11th month, about 60 seconds in the future. She double-checked the time. It was now 15:59:27—in 33 seconds. Then she typed !wq (to save the file) and waited several seconds to hit "enter," looking at the file and making sure things were correct before saving it. She then hit enter, which saved the file and scheduled tasks for execution. About three seconds later, however, she exclaimed in a panicked voice:

Christine: Oh, shoot!! [21 seconds to go]
Mike: What??
Christine: I think I got the wrong one.
Mike: No!! [his voice panicked as well now, Christine had already re-launched the editor on the crontab file, with 19 seconds to go]
Christine: Oh, no.
Mike: No!! It was offline???
Christine: I think, I did! [Christine searched for the line in the file, 16 seconds to go]
Mike: No!!
Christine: Yes, I think it went off . . . [Christine disabled the line in the crontab file with a '#', 12 seconds to go]
Mike: No!
Christine: Yes!

Christine rushed to save the crontab file to prevent the offline backup from being launched. In a panic, she made several typos before getting it right and successfully saving the file with just 6 seconds to go.

As observers with videotape, we could tell in retrospect how close Christine came to the edge. At the time, however, there was no countdown timer and she did not know how close it was or whether she had in fact brought down the customer's DBMS in the middle of the business day. So she needed to verify whether the offline backup was running.

Christine: What can I do?
Mike: Is it running?
Christine: I think it might be.
Mike: It's okay ... [in a reassuring voice]

She executed a command to see if there were any running processes containing the text "ofl":

```
ps -ef | grep -i ofl
```

She saw none, but ran the command again to double-check (in case it had just started). Seeing that there was none, she was relieved:

Christine: I always give myself time.
Mike: Just page, do page, backup, dba/logs/backup ... .log, just to make sure ...

Following Mike's advice, she checked the log file directory to see if the backup process created a log file, indicating that the backup had started. She noted that the last modified date of the backup log file was the day before:

```
Nov 07 20:21 backup.log
```

Now, really relieved, she said:

Christine: My God! Just in time ...

Christine was lucky. The offline backup process had not started. She later told us that she usually configured the crontab file to give herself more than one minute to allow time to catch these sorts of errors. Although crontab gave her time to catch errors, this use of it certainly allowed for these types of mistakes. The commands for offline and online backup were right next to each other in the crontab file, and the two commands differed only by one character (onltape versus ofltape). In addition, there was no mechanism to ask for explicit confirmation for more serious commands. Another problem was that Christine had been discussing two different offline backups just before, possibly leading to confusion. And in any event, this was a rather interesting use of crontab. When asked why her group used crontab, she responded:

> **Christine**: We always do it through crontab. We always use these backup files [selecting the respective line in the crontab file] so it is just easier to do it through cron. You don't have to worry about directing the output. It is all taken care of. You could manually do that from the command line, but it is just a little time saver, I think.

Here, we saw the practice of using crontab beyond its typical use case. The crontab utility was already used for recurring, regularly scheduled tasks, so if an additional backup needed to be run just once, it was straightforward to copy and paste the recurring command instance and modify it to run once at a particular time. In this way, the crontab file over time accumulated commands for all the important tasks, with the syntax and parameters set appropriately, making the crontab file a kind of menu-based task execution user interface. They did not have to remember the syntax of the commands each time because the last working example was always in the crontab file. There were other advantages to crontab: The tasks would continue running even if the admin's connection to the remote machine was lost, unlike commands launched from the command line. Crontab also gave the administrators an opportunity to stop commands they submitted before they were executed, if they happened to have second thoughts on the command syntax or semantics. As Christine said, she often gave herself more time. In this case, however, she had only about 30 seconds to reconsider the task submitted, but even that was enough to stop the incorrect command.

Crontab was not designed to be a user interface for launching one-time tasks, and although it was flexible and reliable, it certainly had limitations. There was no ability to ask the user for confirmation with particularly serious commands, as in, "are you sure you want to stop that DBMS?" The amount of lead time was not standardized; it was just whatever the admin happened to type in. Documentation was limited and commands cryptic, making it relatively easy to confuse similar commands.

On the whole, however, repurposing crontab for ad hoc tasks did work for these administrators. It reduced risk by protecting long-running processes from lost connections, and also by ensuring that commands submitted had the right syntax. Most importantly, it gave the administrator time to reconsider tasks even after they were submitted. Although Christine had only barely enough time to correct her mistake, there are few GUI tools that give the user any time to cancel an action after it has been launched.

This episode also demonstrated many instances of verification as a practice for avoiding errors, grounding her understanding of the state of the system (Brennan, 1998, Velasquez & Durcikova, 2008). Before saving the crontab file, Christine ran a command to check the current date and time twice, and then she waited a few more seconds to look over the command to make sure her changes were correct. Though there was still an error, she did her job appropriately by taking time to go over commands again and again. When things did go wrong, she examined the state of the backup process in multiple ways. First, she corrected the crontab immediately. Afterwards, she searched for backup processes twice to see if the command from the crontab had started executing. Though she did not find the process, she went even further, based on Mike's suggestion, to see if any logs had been produced. Only then was she confident that the backup command had not started. This practice of verifying system state from multiple perspectives was important for tasks that were complex, risky, and long running.

Managing Risk

In the story of Christine and Mike, we saw database administrators working on critical customer systems in which unscheduled outages and data loss were simply unacceptable. We observed a number of methods and practices aimed at mitigating the risk inherent in making *any* changes to such operational production systems, including:

- Rehearsing complex, long-running tasks on test systems to get them right before performing them on production systems.

- Collecting task instructions, scripts, and logs in a structured repository for use whenever a task is performed, creating a kind of organizational memory that ensured admins did not need to recreate process, syntax, and best practices each time.
- Automating long tasks as a series of small scripts, with human verification of system state after each one.
- Using a second pair of eyes to verify risky commands before they were submitted to the system.
- Ensuring that all interested stakeholders remained aware of the ongoing processes of critical tasks.
- Copying and pasting (rather than typing) cryptic file, database, and server names into scripts and commands.
- Delaying command execution to allow time for verification.
- Avoiding simultaneous use of both production and test systems so as not to perform an operation on the wrong system.

Overall, it seems that the most critical practice for managing risk was the pattern of interactions among participants. Like George (in chapter 2), Christine acted as a hub, responsible for getting the job done, managing the activities of others, and establishing common ground on the task with others. Unlike George, Christine had Mike, who functioned as a kind of "co-hub"—he did not perform work directly, but monitored the process, helping Christine avoid mistakes and correcting gaps in her knowledge and understanding.

Christine and Mike's various risk management practices differed in scope and maturity. Some required extensive support from the organization, such as performing rehearsals for long risky tasks, which required technical infrastructures, processes, documentation, and supporting roles. Some were merely an individual practice, such as Christine's almost religious use of copy and paste. All these practices had been established by the sysadmins and their organization without support from the database software vendor.

One aspect of Christine and Mike's story is how local innovation—changes to work practices, including procedures and technologies—is disseminated effectively in the broader organization. We saw sparks of innovation come through human interactions. We saw innovation disseminated by word of mouth and also through documentation in shared

> **Box 4.2 Observations for Design—Christine and Mike**
>
> The story of Christine and Mike lies at the intersection of risk and innovation. Database adminsitrators take the risks of data loss and unscheduled outages very seriously. To manage risk, sysadmins adopt a wide variety of methods and practices, including rehearsal of complex tasks, human verification, and extensive documentation, refinement, and sharing of best practices.
>
> The database administration tools we saw, however, did not support any of these risk-mitigation techniques, so the sysadmins implemented them on their own: (a) There was no explicit tool support for rehearsal—for moving scripts from machine to machine—which led to problems, such as the missing semicolon that resulted from manual script editing; (b) timing and documenting each step of the process was entirely manual, with Christine scribbling notes on her instruction sheets; (c) the DBAs adopted crontab for running critical jobs because the lines in the crontab file described the precise, site-specific options for each command, serving as a template to ensure that the commands ran consistently; and (d) the database system did a poor job of indicating success or failure of executed commands, as was the case when Christine and Mike tried to delete a database table that had not actually been created.

repositories. We saw extensive use of documents in defining, adapting, and improving tasks. Documents conveyed innovation and provided flexibility. Christine could embody her experience in plain English in the instructions or in more structured commands and template scripts. As Mike said, inheriting scripts allowed others to inherit new practices. These seem clear cases of evolution at work—incremental improvement of tools and practices through adaption and use over time. When local innovations are taken up in new situations, they both change the situations and are changed by them. Here, documentation and scripts passed along from one sysadmin to another shaped the context of work and were constantly updated in new contexts.

Of course, in the context of complex social and technical systems, innovation—any change, really—can be risky. But when dissemination of innovation is managed properly, for example, by incorporating appropriate reviews and tests under different use cases, the potential benefit could be large. In such cases, whole organizations may evolve *standard* practices. We now turn to a story about standards.

The Story of Patrick, Capacity Planner

Information technology service providers must support customer needs while making money. The key to this is *capacity planning*, the intersection of business and IT management (Menascé, Almeida & Dowdy, 1994). Its purpose is to ensure that sufficient server and network capacity is allocated to match customer demands in a manner that is cost effective for the service provider. Consequently, a capacity planner works with key stakeholders to ensure that business demands are translated into appropriate IT infrastructure configurations that yield service levels within the formally defined SLAs—while remaining profitable for the provider.

We interviewed Patrick, a capacity planner in a large service delivery organization that hosted an enormous server infrastructure shared by many customers. His tasks included understanding capacity requirements of each customer application and making server assignments after careful examination of potential impact on the overall infrastructure. He had to decide what kind of system to use for any new application depending on whether the application required more processing, storage, or memory. The decision had to satisfy the customer in terms of performance, and it had to satisfy his organization in terms of cost.

In Patrick's story, we examine trade-offs between standards and experience. As an employee of a large organization, Patrick's work was circumscribed by several standards and guidelines (Brunsson & Jacobsson, 2000; Leidner, 1993; Schmidt & Werle, 1998). They defined how he was supposed to conduct his work, with whom he was to coordinate, and which tools and metrics he was to use. These standards and guidelines had been developed by a committee of technical leaders in his organization over a long period. They were extensive and detailed. Each had a list of people associated with it, and a well-defined formal revision process for changing the standard. Perhaps because of the heavy weight of the revision process, we heard that the standards and guidelines did not change very often. Patrick used standards and guidelines as his starting point. Without necessarily breaking the rules, he also relied on his own experience by collecting additional contextual information, and developing and using his own tools to support him in his tasks. In what follows, we examine how Patrick described his work, the standards and guidelines he used, and the practices he developed to make the right decisions when planning server capacity in a large, shared environment.

Allocation by the Book

Capacity allocation requests came to Patrick as part of a formal change-management process. He received details of the request by e-mail in the form of a spreadsheet file. During our interview, we discussed one such request. He explained that the application in this request had been already preassigned an initial capacity estimate by the global application delivery (GAD) group using a standard points-based system:

> **Patrick**: What they [GAD] do is, they take an application, they size it, they determine how big the application is going to be, [...] based on the information given to them by the customer, that is, how many Web hits per hour, or something like that, that they are expecting. And they look at the application code, run through a series of tests, couple of algorithms, and they assign a capacity point to it. It could be anywhere from 5 up to 600.

The capacity points, as Patrick explained, were really a general measurement of the overall demands of an application. It was a standard measure for all applications, whether the application was more CPU-intensive or more I/O-intensive. The problem was that the standard measure focused mainly on CPU requirements, creating possible problems accounting for I/O intensive applications when planning capacity.

Looking at the capacity request (see Figure 4.4), Patrick said that this application required staging and production Domino servers in global Web architecture (GWA) and a Domino server in global notes architecture (GNA), where GWA and GNA were architecture and practice standards used by his organization. Given his experience, Patrick judged this to be a pretty small application, one that he would usually put on a shared server with several other applications. Patrick explained that, in addition to the current standard measure of capacity points, the request also used an older measure, total silver node (SN) CPU, which described capacity needs in terms of a percentage of a standard server:

> **Patrick**: [...] prior to capacity point measurements, they did total silver node CPU percentage. And the sizing was based off a four-way silver node, which of course, silver node is a 4 332 megahertz (MHz) 604 processor, 3 Gig (GB) of memory. There, you see percentages instead of capacity points. They are getting away from that now. Since our machine architectures has changed and it is kind of spread out from B50 to P690. They decided percentage is obviously not a good measurement.

Computer performance and architectures changed quickly, and a standard measure based on a particular machine became obsolete quickly. The move to a point-based system that accounted for an application's general CPU and storage requirements was a step in the right direction. This was a good example of how the standards changed over time, following the changing environment.

PLAN Sizing Assessment Summary		
Domino Server (GWA)	Domino Server (GNA)	Staging Server (GWA)
SN partition %: 4%		
Total SN CPU %: 4%	Total SN CPU %: 2%	Total SN CPU %: 1%
Capacity Points: 13	Capacity Points: 7	Capacity Points: 3
Risk = H M [L]	Risk = H M [L]	Risk = H M [L]

FIGURE 4.4 An application capacity request received by Patrick, showing capacity points for each server along with risks.

Patrick's organization had developed standards and guidelines, including the GWA and GNA standards. These were adopted by the whole service delivery organization and defined all aspects of Web application architectures, including mandatory rules for design, development, and maintenance. Capacity planning was a subset of the tasks covered in a 500-page GWA standards document. The overall GWA standard—and the individual subtasks within it, such as capacity planning—had been developed over time with contributions from a number of organizations using a formal process that governed the definition, review, and publication of content. It involved many people, such as authors, contributors, content coordinator, business, and executive owners.

Development of standards was quite involved. Before work on any standard began, the responsible business owner worked with a content coordinator to identify the standard's scope. Coordinators were responsible for ensuring that the new standard would be compatible with existing standards in the area. Once verified, the business owner designated an author for the document and provided the content coordinator with the formal review plan. Authors prepared the first draft of the document using the common standards template, which included information about business and technical scope and value of the proposed standard, dependencies, criteria for compliance, implementation and migration, geographical considerations, tools, and support. Use of this template was required, and it enabled stakeholders to easily find information that was critical to the effective implementation of the standard. Authors were supposed to ensure that all fields in the template were addressed appropriately, especially the value to the business. Authors needed to clearly and succinctly state compliance criteria, including what must be done, how to comply, when compliance was required, and dependencies.

Each standard was subject to a multi-tiered review cycle. One team did an initial review to ensure that the standard was compatible with other standards in the same field. The business owner was responsible for resolution of any business and technical interlocks, and associated issues were addressed prior to publication based on cross-organization review and approval. The review team included key decision makers, representatives with area expertise, and unit and corporate team representatives. Once the standard was approved and published, it was assigned another review in 6 months, even if there were no updates since publication. Notifications of new standards were sent automatically to appropriate people within the organization, such as the system administrators and business representatives. It was also published on the organization's Web site.

Standards were important in Patrick's organization, as can be seen from the formal development and review processes. In shared environments in particular, it was important to measure each application's requirements using the same criteria to achieve fair and balanced allocations. However, standards need to change in response to changing business and technical requirements. It was in the interest of Patrick's organization to review and update standards from time to time and to have a bottom-up process in which feedback from the front lines was taken into account.

Allocation by Experience

For Patrick, the standards provided a good starting point and general guidelines for his capacity planning work, but they failed to capture the real-world details, which changed as architectures and workloads changed.

Patrick often revised the capacity measurements of an application because the initial capacity points were *expected values* based on customer input, not actual values based on use. Initial capacity points could be significant overestimates. This was where Patrick's expertise came into play. To make capacity allocations in a cost effective way, he collected more information once the applications were deployed and were in use for a while. He then examined what server performance actually looked like using the service resource management (SRM) tool.

Validating customer requests was critical, because the customer view of application needs and the standard GAD measures might not match reality. Patrick used several tools to help him determine actual requirements, such as SRM, which measured system performance when the application was running. Service resource management took basic system performance information about processes, memory, I/O, and CPU activity and put them into graphs and tables displayed on a Web page.

Through SRM, Patrick might discover that even though a server was supposed to be working at full capacity, in reality it was only working at 10 percent capacity.

Because of the shared IT infrastructure, Patrick found overall server-level performance data were often insufficient. He needed data at the application level, which was not easy to get:

> **Patrick**: I would like to see, on a shared WebSphere cluster, what the heap size is for each application. That has actually bit me a couple of times. I run into problems where we have a box where the CPU isn't doing anything but you have 4 apps on it with 256 meg heap sizes with 1 Gig of memory, and so you know you are out of memory on the box.

Once Patrick arrived at a reasonable capacity-point estimate for an application, he needed to find a suitable server in the IT infrastructure to host it. He explained that he maintained a spreadsheet of all servers. Each entry in the spreadsheet contained hardware specs, installed software, a list of applications along with capacity points. He also maintained a column for his own comments about server health based on his experience. These comments played a significant role in his allocations:

> **Patrick**: I also try to incorporate in there how the box is doing. You know I have comments in there which says: "O.K. January 23rd, this box is running at 90 percent for the entire day" and stuff like that. It is all manual entry.

In summary, though Patrick had firm guidelines at hand to allocate capacity, often he relied on his tools, practices, and experience:

> **Patrick**: I don't consider it written in stone. This is what I base it off of. I don't really follow standards and guidelines. It is more . . . experience.

By the Book versus by Experience

Overall, standards play a critical role in making the modern world function correctly, efficiently, and safely. They ensure that nuts and bolts fit together, that weights and measures are uniform, and that drug dosages are the same from bottle to bottle. Information technology is full of technical standards—ensuring that telephones and computers can connect to networks, that software can run on standard computing hardware, that computers can use disk drives from different manufacturers, and so forth (Cargill, 1999). In IT management and delivery, there are also best practices or conventions, which are sometimes adopted by organizations to become standard operating procedures (Office of Government Commerce, 2000; 2001; 2002a; 2002b; 2005a; 2005b; Meum, Monteiro, & Ellingsen, 2011).

Standardization offers many benefits in the IT environment. Standards ensure that workers share a certain body of knowledge, and they help workers establish a common understanding of the systems. Standard procedures may lead to improved efficiency, reduced risk, and improved quality. Standardization often happens slowly because of the need for alignment and ownership among many stakeholders. Because standards must be stable, yielding repeatable benefits, they do not change very often. Unfortunately, this static nature can prove to be problematic in dynamic domains, such as IT, in which technologies and requirements can change quickly (Rada, 2000; March & Olsen, 1989).

Patrick had developed his own tools and practices that went above and beyond the standards and guidelines he was provided. He examined server performance data, application architectures, and application-specific performance data. He revisited assumptions made in different parts of his organization. Patrick developed the practice of doing his own bookkeeping with a spreadsheet in which he kept server capacity and application information. Furthermore, he recorded in the spreadsheet his own comments on the systems. This was purely subjective, yet clearly helpful in understanding the details of the servers. Patrick was responsible for the whole IT infrastructure, and he needed to keep it all in perspective—he considered not only the specific application performance but also impact on the overall architecture. Patrick evolved these techniques over time, adapting them incrementally to new circumstances until he had developed the fairly reliable practices we observed. This sort of evolution—arising from the interaction of environment, technology, and people—is never smooth. In this case, technical circumstances and standards changed at different rates, affecting what Patrick could do to keep up. Nevertheless, it seems to us that Patrick struck a good balance,

> **Box 4.3 Observations for Design—Patrick**
>
> The story of Patrick examines broad practices more than specific episodes, showing the interplay of organizational standards and individual experience. In this case, standards guide consistent operation of large-scale IT service delivery, often involving detailed procedures to develop and update their content. In fact, standards from different periods can co-exist, with older standards falling from use gradually. Despite their level of detail (and perhaps because of their heavyweight change procedures), standards may not successfully handle all aspects of real-world operation, meaning that sysadmins must often gather additional information and apply their own knowledge and experience. With respect to tool use, Patrick's process of reconciling standards with the actual system behavior was entirely manual: He decided what information to collect, and he put it in a spreadsheet by hand.

incorporating both standards and his own experience into the work. Standards were the starting point, but he relied on experience to make final capacity allocations.

Managing Innovation Reduces Risk

Information technology systems change constantly under pressures from business, regulations, and globalization (Kamsin, 2004; Kauffman & Walden, 2001; Kumar, 2004; Spohrer & Riecken, 2006). System workloads and configurations change at an even faster rate in response to day-to-day demand fluctuations. Projects and customers change. Over the long term, roles and responsibilities of the system administrators, as well as organizational structures, change, too.

Change drives innovation, and, at the same time, standards help maintain consistency of the work. In most organizations, the way work is actually conducted differs from the way it is described in the standard procedures and manuals (Brown & Duguid, 1991). Organizations aim to improve work practices by prescribing formal work practices, but on the front lines, the practitioners learn, innovate, and adapt when confronted with real-world constraints.

This chapter gave examples of innovation in practices in several forms and at several scales. We saw examples of individual innovations. We saw how strictly Christine practiced copy and paste, using it for almost all the server, database, table, and file names she entered. We saw her avoid executing even a single command on a production server while working on the consolidation server to avoid errors by typing the wrong command into the wrong window. We saw her writing a script even for a single-line command and reusing it rather than having to work through the syntax each time. All these practices served one purpose: to eliminate human error as much as possible, whether a typo of a server name or an incorrect option for a command. These practices were developed in direct response to the complexity and risk in her work environment.

We also saw some individual innovations that grew to be shared in the larger community. Documentation of procedures was one such example. We saw Christine using and improving instructions and scripts from a shared repository for the table-move operation. Sample scripts codified the practices, such as using quotes consistently with schema names to avoid potential problems. It was a practice she inherited, one that was built into the scripts she used. We also saw her contributing back to the community by updating the shared documentation; she added the "-s" option for DB2 commands to address the problem she encountered when her script kept executing despite hitting an error.

For Christine, free-form documents and scripts were the right way to describe the methods used by her organization. Documents included the collective experiences of others who went through the same procedures in the past. They often included sample script code, but they were less like blueprints and more like templates with written instructions on how to produce new scripts for specific needs. The form of these documents was a good fit, allowing practices to be improved based on personal experiences captured and improved over many generations. The document was flexible, providing exactly the right level of detail, in specific computer executable code or in simple natural language, relying on the recipient to interpret and understand missing and domain-specific information when it was actually put into practice (Halverson & Ackerman, 2008; Carlile, 2002; Star, 1989; Star, 1995). Such documents in shared community repositories helped both to support individual practice and to become institutionalized and adopted by the community at large (Carlile, 2002; Meum, Monteiro & Ellingsen, 2011; Orr, 1986; White & Lutters, 2007; Yates, 1989).

For Patrick, formal documentation was central to standardization. The GWA standards he used for capacity planning were contained in a 500-page document with detailed descriptions of policies, scope, exceptions, and mandatory and recommended practices. The document's content was managed through a formal process, with clearly defined procedures for authoring, revising, and approving changes. Business benefit was a clearly stated objective for inclusion in the standards documents. The process for updating documents was much more involved in Patrick's organization than in Christine's. Whereas Christine updated documents immediately to reflect her experiences, Patrick did not contribute his experiences back into the organization, perhaps because updating the standards documentation was a complicated process.

An innovation might introduce risk if it is untested—yet when managed appropriately, an innovation might lead to substantial productivity gains when deployed in the overall organization. Sometimes the larger organization can benefit from local innovations that enable the organization to expand its view of work overall (Schein, 1990). One way to manage innovation effectively is to have processes for reviewing new methods and approaches. In Patrick's case, however, these processes seemed too demanding for him to contribute back to the larger organization.

We saw validation emerge as a common feature in many practices that dealt with environmental factors, such as change and risk (Velasquez & Durcikova, 2008). On a small scale, we saw Christine hold off hitting "enter" to submit a command to the system, verifying command syntax and semantics multiple times, or submitting commands only after Mike's confirmation. Likewise, Christine's use of crontab to submit commands with built-in delays gave her one more chance to abort potentially erroneous commands. Other examples include using separate scripts for each step of a procedure to verify system state after each step, which makes sense not only because error handling is difficult, but also because human judgment may be needed between steps to verify and analyze system state.

We saw other examples of validation in planning and rehearsing, which pushed their changes up the testing, consolidation, and production servers, verifying operations and solidifying scripts. Everyone in the organization practiced this discipline, given organizational mandates and infrastructure support built for it. We also saw validation built into other formal and informal organizational practices, such as the strict approval process for changes, which were examined and sanctioned by several people in various forms, whether informally through e-mail or instant message, or formally within the change ticket system.

Standardization can be a powerful tool to manage work. It can manage cost and risks in a business, streamline processes, and improve coordination and communication. Standardization promotes interoperability of tools, systems, and people with clearly defined lines of responsibilities within an organization. Standardization of technology, tools, and practices can help narrow the IT solution space, making configuration, deployment, and troubleshooting simpler. Yet there are limitations to standardization (Egyedi & Dahanayake, 2003; Schmidt & Werle, 1998). In Patrick's case, standard capacity measurements were insufficiently nuanced to reflect real behavior, and Patrick had to rely on his own experience and measurements to find optimal resource allocation. Standardization can also be risky when it prohibits adaptation to changing conditions (Deetz & Kersten, 1983). Effective standardization, however, must be rooted in actual practice, and it takes time to develop. It is best suited for maturing practices that have clear definitions of work. To be effective, standards need to be supported by tooling, architectures, and organizations.

Innovation in methods and practices is critical for the viability of any organization, because change in the work environment is inevitable. The key to success is to manage innovation at the organizational level while encouraging innovation at the individual level (Brown and Duguid, 1991). In the stories here, we saw many organizational mechanisms and procedures for effective evolution of innovation. Such mechanisms and procedures include proper reviews, organizational standards, and validation of innovation by incremental introduction to broader use.

5

Tools and Automation

> *"It's a living tool."*
> —Shawn, operating system administrator

Shawn and his colleagues had developed a very handy tool, a database and a Web front-end to keep track of hundreds of systems and their patch levels. It supported their work precisely. And it was a living tool. They improved it whenever they could find time in their busy schedules, automating more and more of their work. Not only was the tool central to what Shawn's team did everyday, it also helped maintain relationships with their customers by enabling them to set appropriate expectations for upcoming work.

In this chapter, we focus on *creation* of tools by sysadmins for sysadmins, and on the forces that spur this activity. Given the complex environments in which administrators work, it was not too surprising to find that they needed tools to help to coordinate, configure, monitor, and troubleshoot both technical and social parts of their environments. Often available tools do not adequately support their complex, lengthy multistep tasks. We saw many situations in which tools provided by system vendors were imperfectly aligned with the particular needs and work practices of sysadmins (Barrett et. al., 2004). Vendor tools often appeared to be designed to permit a single admin to manage a single system component (e.g., a DBMS), and such tools did not provide a high-level view of the multiple components that form the system as a whole, nor did they help communication and coordination between all the parties involved in IT management. Consequently, administrators built their own tools to fill the gaps. Tools range from one-line scripts that reliably execute a single command, to full-fledged Web applications for continually monitoring and analyzing the status of hundreds of systems, to spreadsheets and databases that keep track of system or server information. Some of these tools are created in an ad hoc fashion to solve a problem at hand and collected in a personal toolbox. Some of those prove to be generally useful; over time they are shared with others to become a community resource. Some are even used to automate tasks.

We illustrate sysadmin tool-development practices through several stories from our studies. First, we describe tools created by Shawn and his colleagues to coordinate their work monitoring, installing, and maintaining software patches on a large number of Unix servers for one particular customer. In Shawn's story, we examine tools they created to reduce labor and increase consistency. In creating these tools, Shawn and his colleagues thought through not only the technical aspects of the work but also the social and business aspects. Much of their work required careful coordination and negotiation with the customer, and the tools they developed facilitated this. Customers demanded special exceptions to the formally established patch schedules, and so formal tools, procedures, and processes needed to be complemented with informal negotiations.

Second, we describe storage administration at a government lab, where Diana and Mark depended heavily on scripting to perform tasks such as monitoring system performance, moving large data sets between storage systems, and automating responses to well-understood system failures. One unique aspect of Diana and Mark's work was that, as a part of government research lab, they were required to push the limits of technology as far as it could go—their environment was very large and depended on a complex heterogeneous collection of tape and disk storage systems.

Finally, we describe the sophisticated script-generation framework developed by Jimmy and his fellow database administrators over many years working at a retail customer site. In Jimmy's story, we see how the longitudinal focus facilitated by long-term employment with one company, a multi-year service deal, and a single customer-dedicated service organization enabled investment in customization and automation.

Overall, we found that sysadmins created tools to fill their own particular social, organizational, and technical needs. Some tools aimed to improve information flow and, therefore, grounding among sysadmins and the systems they manage. Sysadmins improved their tools incrementally in response to changing needs and changing circumstances. Sysadmins shared the most useful tools with others, creating community resources that then got taken up by others and adapted for use in different settings.

The Story of Shawn, Operating System Administrator

Shawn worked at a service delivery center for a large IT services company. His group was dedicated to a single long-time customer, a large telecommunications firm. Shawn and his team supported three customer sites at different locations across the United States. About seven years before our visit, the telecommunications firm had outsourced their IT services to Shawn's company. Shawn had supported this customer account from the beginning, and then, about 5 years later, he moved to a sister account, which had spun off from the original customer. Shawn had been a sysadmin for his entire 11-year career, primarily responsible for Unix-type operating systems.

Shawn introduced himself as the "patch focal," a coordinator responsible for management of the overall patch process for hundreds of Unix servers that the customer used, ensuring all machines were up-to-date with the latest operating system fixes. *Patches* are software updates and patch management has become an increasingly important aspect of systems management. Its main purpose is to help maintain systems so they are secure against known problems in operating system and application software. Patches are often grouped into *bundles* that vendors release on a regular basis. Some patches may have undesirable side effects, so patch management is a balancing act through which the problems that a patch fixes must be weighed against downtime to install it and against any possible side effects.

Balancing Customization and Automation

Shawn was responsible for the entire patch process. We watched him work on everything from improving the patch distribution infrastructure to maintaining a database of every machine and its installed patches. One of Shawn's major tasks was customization of the patch bundles. He would start with the whole set provided by the vendor and remove any patches that he identified as problematic.

> **Shawn**: There is a lot of customized work here, 'cause you could just take the bundles and throw them out there. That is it. Then you run the risk of backing it out, spending the time to back it out, trying to figure out which patch it was that messed up…Now the machine would not boot up, then you are in, you know. We take a lot of…We have got quite a procedure.

To do the actual patch installation work, Shawn and his team had developed an architecture of local patch *depot servers* at the three client locations, aiming to mitigate potential network performance problems that might crop up at inopportune times. Synchronization among the servers was done manually by Shawn. He downloaded the bundles and copied them to each of the depot servers. Shawn's team also wrote a set of scripts to copy the patches from the depot servers to each client and then perform the installation. These scripts allowed them to automate most of the patch installation process.

We watched Shawn install a patch on a domain name system (DNS) server. This type of task was outside his normal duties. Normally, the actual work was done by the other sysadmins. However, Shawn told us, "I am still just a regular SA [sysadmin]." He was helping a colleague who was working on another problem. Shawn installed a Solaris 6 patch bundle on a DNS server, following a very detailed and lengthy set of instructions (Figure 5.1). He explained that patch installation was typically automated, but, because this was a DNS server residing outside the corporate firewall, they needed to follow special procedures.

> **Shawn**: Normally, we would have this automated. But this is a DNS server. So, it is a firewall server. Normally…all this would get exported, all the patches, so we just remotely NFS-mount [Network File System] the file system that has all the patches from a depot server. And all this would be automated. But since this server doesn't allow you to come into it, and doesn't allow the kind of access to it, we have to copy all the data. […] We have to go through couple of hoops to get to it, and then we get in. So, I have

```
11. Solaris 9 servers
  # op /etc/inrt inetd.conf etc/inet/inet.conf.
12. Change directories
  # cd /usr/local/bin
13. Run the install script
  # inst_clust
  #########################################
  # IF YOU DO NOT USE THE inst_clust SCRIPT#
  # BE SURE TOENTERTHE BUNDLE NAME IN
  # /var/sadm/install_data/CLUST
  # i.e. Jul_2003
  ####################################################
14. Answer questions
  y: if you wish to proceed
  n: if you wish to quit
  y: if you have console access [proceed to step 15
     **BE SURE TO VERIFY THAT YOU HAVE CONSOLE
  n: if you do not have console access [proceed to
15. Script will install maintenance patchs. When complete
  ** VERIFY THAT YOU AN TELNET INTO THE SERVER BEFORE
  sync, sync, sync
  shutdown -ls
  cd /var/patch
  patchadd ketnel patch [this will install the kernel
  Once kernel patches are installed
  Compare differneces (if any) between new and old /etc/
  # diff /etc/name_to_sysnum /etc/name_to_sysnum.MMDDYY
  #diff /etc/inet/inetd.conf /etc/inet/inetd.conf if
  add any missing entries to the new file.
16. Copy safe copies back
  # cp /etc/mail/sendmail: MMDDYY etc/mail/sendmail
  # cp /etc/name to
  # cp et/c/motd: etc/motd
   FOR SOLARIS 6 SERVERS
  # cp /etc/inted.conf if /etc/inetd.conf
  FOR SOLARIS 7 SERVERS
  # cp /etc/inet/services if /etc/inet/services
  FOR SOLARIS 8 SERVERS
  #cp /etc/inet/services if /etc/inet/services
  #cp /etc/intet/inetd.conf if /etc/inet/inetd.conf
  FOR SOLARIS 9 SERVERS
  #cp /etc/inet/services if /etc/inet/services
  #cp /etc/intet/inetd.conf if /etc/inet/inetd.conf
  #sync, sync, sync
  # halt
```

FIGURE 5.1 Part of instructions to patch a DNS server. Each step is detailed with commands to type, including alternatives for different kinds of systems (e.g., Solaris 6, Solaris 7,...)

to do all these commands by hand. Normally, we have a script that does all this.

He paid close attention to the instructions not only because of the unusual manual process but also because of past problems in which this particular patch bundle had incorrectly overwritten certain system configuration files. Before applying the patch, he saved the old configuration files, as indicated by the instructions—even though the old and new ones were the same. He explained that, normally, verification of configuration file updates was also handled automatically in the script, which would compare the configuration files before and after patch application, and then notify them if any files were overwritten.

Having completed the patch installation, Shawn rebooted the system. He explained that they were currently revising some of their patch procedures, and he was rewriting the automated script so that it would handle patches in two phases. In the first phase, it would automatically identify the patch server based on its proximity to the client machine, download all kernel patches in the appropriate system mode, and begin installing kernel patches. Once this was completed, it would reboot the system and download and install the maintenance patches, which did not necessarily require a reboot. Kernel patches, which change operating system software, usually required a reboot and installation in a special mode. Maintenance patches often did not require a reboot, so it made sense to organize patches into two categories and use a two-phase patch installation process to avoid unnecessarily rebooting the system multiple times. Central to the new procedure was the need to isolate kernel patches from more common maintenance patches. This was important when things went wrong and patches needed to be taken back out. The new procedure helped them to identify problematic patches quickly:

> **Shawn**: If the operating system is going to come out, so then you only got a small amount of patches you have to try and back out, and you know which ones they are. Whereas, if you had a whole list to go through, you are like, Oh, man!…Well, you probably end up backing out the whole bundle because it takes so long to go through. We had that problem in the past. That is

why we are trying to minimize that kind of problems now, as much as we can.

They wanted to avoid problems—when errors occurred installing a large set of patches, it took too much time to determine which patch was at fault. Because they had limited time, they would simply restore the system back to its original state, and do a post-mortem after the machine was back up. After they understood what went wrong, they could notify the customer and schedule another time to redo the patch on that server.

Once he completed his work, Shawn communicated his findings via a Web site he had created, where he would post warnings for the sysadmins about potential problems with some of the patches. In fact, it was the sysadmins' responsibility to check the Web site for relevant warnings before beginning any patch installation. Shawn showed us one such warning in which a particular patch in a patch bundle had created problems by overwriting configuration files. They put out a warning and also pulled that particular patch out of the bundle they used:

> **Shawn**: We had a problem with this patch. This HP patch 29284, with any servers running MQSeries [pointing to a warning] and it wrote over a config file. It was an on-demand patch to actually fix a certain problem, not a security problem. We got the bundle down from HP and then we put that patch into the bundle on the depot. And then we found the problem that night, people were pulling everything out to find out what it was. So, now we got here [a warning]. We have gone ahead and pulled it out of the bundle.

Shawn explained that after downloading patches from the vendor sites, he and his team would read the README files, which were published by the vendor and contained important information about the fixes in the patch. Because README files were typically long, Shawn wrote a script to quickly scan the files for certain basic information. The script extracted parts of the README files that helped them identify patches that updated the kernel, required a reboot, or had dependencies on any of the customer's software. With the script, he would make a quick first pass on the README files and identify potentially problematic patches. He would then read through these patches' README files in greater detail:

> **Shawn**: We can then go through and say these are the ones we need to read through. You kind of watch for anything that has an application name in it, you just kind of go down the list, looking for anything that would say, fixing something for like MQseries, or Oracle, cause that is going to raise a flag, like, well, we better read into that. So, we go through the README files, and check them all out. We do pull certain patches out that we say, "Oh, this isn't going to work. This is going to cause us a problem." So, we pull those patches out.

Shawn had to carefully analyze the patch information while keeping in mind the customer's applications to ensure that the patch would not break any installed software. Some cases were even more restrictive: for certain machines, the customer required that one of their staff must always first read through the README to see if it would cause problems. For such cases, Shawn had put warnings in the Web site to alert the sysadmins to install patches only after getting approval from that particular user:

> **Shawn**:…here [pointing to a warning] we have a user who, he wants to go, he likes to go through the entire patch. We give him the patch bundle to look. He goes through all the README files, and he tells us specifically which patches he wants put on these servers. So, that is why this warning here…

Clearly, manual work was still required, despite many years of effort in automating patch management. It seemed that there will always be special cases requiring human intervention. Though some special cases could be added to the scripts, human supervision would still be required, given the complexity and dynamic nature of systems, to monitor automatic patch management, identify problems, and fix them manually.

Homemade Tools

The patch process was repeated at least once per quarter for every machine on the customer account. In fact, the service agreement contained an explicit customer policy stating all servers must be patched every 120 days. To help in this, Shawn's colleague Chuck had developed (completely in-house) a database with Web access containing information about servers, available patches, and which patches had been applied to which servers. There was no automated data collection; Shawn had to enter and update the data manually.

The database and Web site were used by both Shawn's team and the customer to track patches. There were three types of patches: (a) patch bundles, patches grouped together by the vendor for general software updates; (b) security patches, updates to resolve security-related issues; and (c) on-demand patches, special updates requested by customers to resolve specific software issues. The database allowed Shawn to add and modify information, such as server information, warnings, and patch information. He could query the database by patch name, type, date, server names, and operating system version, and he could examine server patch status individually for each server and create summary status reports by operating system type and patch level. The customer could use the Web front-end to see warnings and to create reports, including an overall patch report (Figure 5.2) and a list of servers that had not been

```
OVERALL PATCH REPORT
Category                    Number      Percent of Total
Current                     87          49.15%
Not Current w/ Exceptions   74          41.81%
Not Current NO Exceptions   0           00.00%
Not Applicable              16          9.04%
Total                       177         100.00%

OVERALL PATCH REPORT BY OS
OS Type  No Current  % Current  No Not Curr. w/Ex
$ Not Curre. w/Ex  No Not Curr. No Ex.  % Not Curr.
No Ex. No Not Applicable.
Hp-UX 11.00
Solaris 2.8
Solaris 2.7
HP -UX 11i
Solaris 2.6
Solaris 9
Solaris 2.5.1
AIX 4.3.3
. . . .
```

FIGURE 5.2 Shawn's overall patch report, showing a total count of servers that are current with their patches, servers that are not current with exceptions, and so forth. Also shown is the patch report by OS type.

patched in the last 120 days (Figure 5.3). However, the customer did not have the ability to add or modify data in the database.

The patch database and Web site played a central role in their practice, and Shawn considered it an evolving, living tool:

> **Shawn**: This is an ever-growing tool. As things come to us, we make changes to improve it, as best as we can, if we can come up with a new idea that can help us out with something. So, it is a living tool, it does get changed, we do make updates to it. […] I know one thing we would like to be able to do is to get the connection between the HP service desk, the change control tool, to update my patching database. So that I wouldn't have to have the report on Monday and go through it manually and update my database. […] I mean that is one of our goals, but when you got everything else going on, you know sometimes, priority. When we got time we work on stuff like that as time permits.

Despite the difficulty in finding time to work on the development of the database, it was an extremely useful tool. Not only did it aid

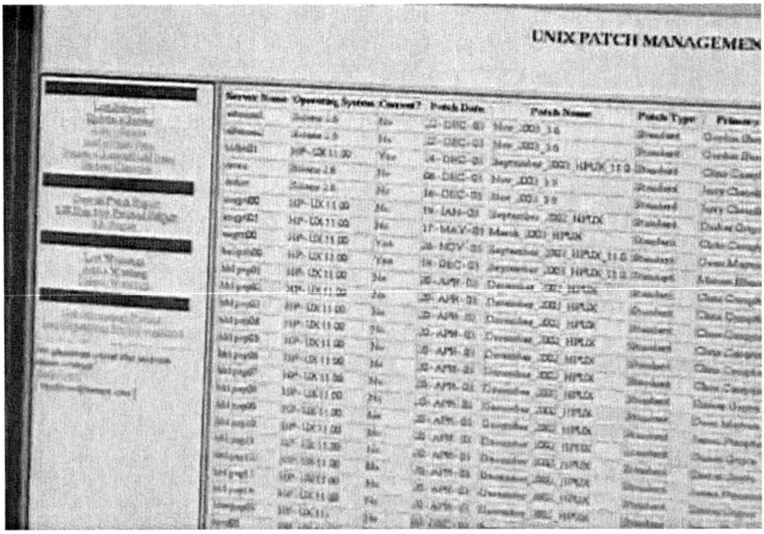

FIGURE 5.3 Patch database showing all the servers with an exception to the policy—servers that had not been patched in the last 120 days.

Shawn, it also built support for the patch process from the customer side, helping set appropriate expectations. Customers could see what was being planned and what was happening at any moment:

> **Shawn**: At first a lot of people weren't used to it, on the user side. At the end of the first patch process, they are like, "Hey, okay we are done!" They also hear the [new] changes come again, "What are you doing? I thought we are done." "That was last quarter. This is this quarter!" Then, everybody kind of got on board with it. I think by now, it is like two years, so everybody is pretty much on board with it, by posting the schedule, and putting it out there, DBAs, application owners. We also put the README files out on the Web site, so all this information is out there, so they can actually go ahead look down the line and see what is going on. We get a lot of positive feedback, from the customer.

The overall patch report showed the percentage of servers that were current with the latest patches, servers that were not current with or without exceptions, and servers that were not to be patched. As can be seen in Figure 5.2, about 40 percent of the servers were not current with the latest patches; each had some sort of exceptions to the customer policy. Shawn showed us the list of servers that had not been patched in the last 120 days (Figure 5.3). The list displayed server name, primary sysadmin, and operating-system information, along with explanations of why servers were not patched. Shawn explained that there were several possible reasons:

> **Shawn**: Now, some of these...HP is now at a point, where they are no longer putting any new bundles after March 11 for 11.0. So, the last December bundle only had for 11i. So, what happens is these servers, like this one here, it is an 11.0, well, it has passed it's...It was last patched on November 26th with the September patch bundle, which was the last one for it. It shows that it is over 120 days, but it says it is current over here. Server is current with the latest release. [...] Here, the customer doesn't want us to patch these guys. And for here, it has been pushed out for one reason or the other. Someone has asked that it gets scheduled later down the line. Either they are doing testing, maybe on the box, or there

is something else going on. They just don't want to get interrupted. So, it gets pushed out. We keep all that here.

Quite a lot of the servers were not patched because of customer-driven exceptions to the policy. Those exceptions required extra effort on the part of Shawn and others to keep an eye on them and to treat them accordingly. There were many reasons why a machine might be an exception. For some, it was simply that there were no new patch releases in the 120 days—so there was nothing to update. For others, it was a matter of coordination and negotiation with the customer to find a suitable schedule to do the install or to work with them to select and apply patches. Exceptions were common. They were a legitimate part of the process. This was just the nature of it. Shawn and his team developed not only a patch installation tool, but more broadly, a patch management tool that incorporated features to coordinate scheduling and monitoring of patch management with the customer.

The database and the Web front-end were clearly very useful, both to Shawn and to the customer. It was developed to satisfy a particular need. Yet there were similar tools in the marketplace. Some customer systems came with a patch management tool that was developed by the system vendor. When asked about that tool, Shawn told us that they could not use it:

Shawn:...Because it doesn't meet what our customer requires of us. Sun is kind of changing its ways right now. Now, they have maintenance updates which they put out every quarter, and the maintenance updates are patches that have been tested by them on a bunch of machines. They group together and they put out once a quarter. They also have what they call recommended clusters. Recommended clusters can come out every other day. These are patches that they put in there and they haven't necessarily really tested very much. And what our customer wants us to have on this account is a benchmark when we can show every 120 days are all the same. And if you use just that recommended cluster, well, every day I run the Solaris patch tool if I patched one server today, and let's say next week I did another one, it could be a different recommended bundle, and they wouldn't necessarily be, the servers, wouldn't be at the same level.

The vendor's tool simply did not support the patch schedule they needed. The issue was that their customer wanted to have all the servers with the same level of patches. The automated tool would load all current "recommended patches" and install them, but because those recommended patches could change every day, systems patched on different days might wind up with different patch levels. In addition, the recommended patches were insufficiently tested. Thus, Shawn's team built tools themselves.

Coordinating with the Customer

Shawn did as much as possible to make sure that patches were okay before installation began, but he did not actually have a test environment. He explained that this was just not practical because the customer had so many different kinds of systems from several different vendors. Consequently, Shawn used the customer systems to progressively test patches. He had developed a patch rollout schedule that initially tested patches on a variety of noncritical systems before moving on to more critical machines, such as production servers. The idea was to hit as many different kinds of system as early on as possible so that potential problems could be fixed before hitting more critical systems:

> **Shawn**: We do the test boxes first, and then the production boxes and we usually save the really high-end production, cluster boxes to the very end, the ones that are most critical. Make sure that we encounter any kind of possible problems we could have...

To help him determine a rollout schedule, Shawn had created a spreadsheet that contained information about servers sorted by primary functions, such as Web server, production database, cluster server, production application server, or research and development server. In addition, he kept a column for each server with special instructions for comments regarding specific system versions and general availability times for patching. This spreadsheet was also published on the customer Web site so they, too, could view and update the information as necessary:

> **Shawn**: This is all their servers here. Their production servers are called gold servers. So, you see the gold ones are at the very end.

So, you see these are production database servers. At the bottom are cluster servers. Previously, it is more production application, and then before all that is the development boxes. And in the first week, as you can kind of see, I try to get in as many HP 11, HP 11i, Solaris 6, 7,…So, the first week or two we hit all the different operating systems…

As logical as it seemed, this scheme of staged installation on increasingly critical systems did not always work. For example, Shawn told us about the time a patch installed successfully on development systems, but failed on a production server—the difference was that the development system's files were not as large as those on the production system:

Shawn: 'Cause what happened was we had patched the development box, but the development box was different enough from the production box, that when they tested it on the development box, "Oh, it is okay," so then we went, put it on the production box, and then there was a problem. It was something about anything over a certain size of file was a problem. […] 'Cause the development box never had any files that big, so it never rendered a problem.

Usually, however, things proceeded as planned, and they caught problems early by patching the less critical development systems first. On the whole, vendor patch bundles were reliable because they were tested extensively by the vendor, and had been out long enough for any problems to have been detected by the community at large.

Shawn: 'Cause some patch bundles have 400 some patches, and there is only so much time. So, you kind of have to trust the vendor to a point, that is why we really like HP and the Sun maintenance updates, cause these have been tested in their environment. So, by using the ones that have been tested, and usually by then they have been out a while, you know we get the patch bundle like, right now I am doing the December patch bundle for HP 11i, so it is…by the time they get it out to us they have tested them pretty well. Well, it is time-tested that way.

Shawn published his patch schedule spreadsheet on the customer's Web site, and also created change tickets for each server in the order of the patch schedule. The tickets provided the formal mechanism for getting approvals for the patches directly from the customer. He typically did this about two-weeks in advance so customers knew what was coming down the line and had plenty of time to approve or reject them. But actually getting customers to act was not always so easy:

> **Shawn**:...because what happens is certain people need a little reminding, cause I might put the ticket out three months or two months in advance, and they forget. [...] Usually Mondays and Tuesdays I spend an hour or two each day, sending e-mails, saying, "Okay, come on! What is the holdup here? This has been out there so long. Could you please either reject it, or approve it? And if you are going to reject it, let me know why. You know, so I can reschedule it." So, usually that kind of stirs them up a little bit. And if they do reject it they will come back and say "Oh, that is not a good weekend for us, we have got testing we are doing on that box all weekend. So, we just can't afford to have it down for four hours while we are doing that." So, they will give me a date, they will say, "after such and such date, now, it is good. You can do whatever you want after that date." So, then I re-change, I go back in, and change the dates on the change request and resubmit it out there. That is a constant process of tracking, keeping up with those.

Shawn's tools, the spreadsheet, the Web site, and the ticketing system kept the entire process on track. The tools were not enough: it was the people that made it all work. Customers needed to check the information on the Web site, and then approve or reject changes. System administrators needed to check the service desk and the Web site to see if there were any warnings for the systems they were going to work on. Though there was a formal process for changes, there was almost always an informal follow-up negotiation by e-mail and phone. For example, Dan, Shawn's backup, would e-mail reminders to the relevant sysadmins about upcoming patches:

> **Shawn**: It is every SAs [sysadmins] responsibility to check service desk on a daily basis to look for any patches that are assigned to

you. But Dan, as part of his job as patch focal, he is a nice enough guy that he actually puts out an e-mail. Like today he will put out an e-mail for all the patches tomorrow, and so that goes out to the team. I mean the service desk shows all the patches for our group. He sends that out just as a friendly reminder to everybody.

Sometimes Shawn too would check on the sysadmins via instant messaging a few minutes prior to patch installation time, just to make sure they are aware of any warnings and had no issues:

Shawn: There has been times I've been kind of a mother hen. And it will be like changes somebody is supposed to do in five minutes. And I will [instant message] him, "Is that change going to be okay?"

In return, the sysadmins would e-mail Shawn to let him know that the work was done. To complete the cycle, Shawn would also execute a script weekly to pull information directly from systems about configuration changes. He would use that information to confirm the changes and update his database. In many ways, these activities helped Dan and Shawn improve their situational awareness (Sarter & Woods, 1991) of past, present, and future activities of the team, helping them establish a common ground among all those involved. Situational awareness is especially important in fields such as IT management, where activity is coordinated among many participants, flow of information is complex and dynamic, and human error can lead to serious consequences (Endsley, 1995).

Customization, Automation, Coordination

Overall, patch management is a critical and complex task (Cavusoglu, Cavusoglu, & Zhang, 2008). By definition, patches fix known problems, yet the process of applying patches can make a machine unavailable, with extended outages when patches have unintended side effects and need to be removed. Patches often could not be applied because of technology limitations and customer constraints. To understand the scope of exceptions, it was necessary to coordinate and communicate with all the stakeholders to manage each exception in the proper way. Shawn's team started without any specific tools or practices. Over time, the demands of the work inspired them to create databases, spreadsheets, and scripts for the group as a whole, and to establish practices around existing tools such as e-mail, instant messaging, and the ticketing system. The team's tools and practices evolved over time to meet changing technical, social, and business demands. The tools and practices were instrumental in both managing the technical complexity of the patch process, and also for managing the social complexity of coordinating patch management activities within the team and with the customer.

The patch database played a central role in Shawn and his team's practice. Patch focals used the patch database to keep track of server patch status, server configuration information, and warnings and comments about patches and bundles. Administrators would check the database for warnings that might apply before conducting any work, and the customer used the database to get reports on overall status and to check compliance with the service level agreements. This is why Shawn's team had built a Web-based front-end that enabled others to easily access information in the database and establish common ground about current and future activities. It was a useful tool, but it had limitations. Shawn had to enter all data manually and had to validate data regularly. He had plans to automate this step, but tool building was not an official part of his job. He could only work on it in the margins, when time permitted.

As with many sysadmins, Shawn created scripts. There was the script for automating the patch process, which Shawn was enhancing to separate kernel and maintenance patches into two phases. He also mentioned the script for analyzing the README files distributed with patches, looking for key terms that would indicate a potentially problematic patch. He had a script to gather information for the database, pulling configuration and patch information directly from the servers. Each of these was developed in response to the particular needs of Shawn's job, and they were being updated as circumstances dictated.

Shawn created tools because vendor-provided tools did not meet the requirements of his environment and customers. Automated patching programs were available, but they did not ensure different servers would receive the same patches, they did not install kernel patches first to allow for easier rollback, and they did not provide the option of selecting only those patches that had been tested over time. And no vendor tool even attempted to perform the information-sharing and

> **Box 5.1 Observations for Design—Shawn**
>
> The story of Shawn shows the importance of innovation and automation in complex IT environments. We saw teams of sysadmins coordinating work across a large number of heterogeneous machines by creating and using tools, such as databases and Web sites, to manage and share information. We also saw sysadmins create tools to better manage the volume, complexity, and risk of their work, such as automatically scanning README files in huge patch bundles to better spot problematic patches and automatically installing patches in two phases to simplify recovery when patches failed. Overall, it seemed automation was the goal, but special cases were inevitable and had to be handled through human intervention. Moreover, considerable informal communication with customers was required to achieve consensus on the details of changes and schedules, despite well-defined service-level agreements.
>
> Shawn's team added considerably to the tools at their disposal. For instance, there were vendor-provided patch management tools, but these did not meet Shawn's needs with respect to installing patches in multiple phases, detailed validation of the patch bundles, and achieving buy-in from the customer before patches were applied.

operation-scheduling needed to coordinate the patch process with multiple customers, operating systems, and administrators.

Through the various tools Shawn and others on his team created, they could encapsulate critical aspects of their work, reducing labor while increasing consistency. They did so by thinking through all aspects of the work, and they tried to incorporate informal as well as formal processes, given the unavoidability of special cases.

The Story of Diana and Mark, Storage Administrators

Diana and Mark were storage administrators at a major government facility that received, stored, managed, and analyzed data from spacecraft.

The facility housed many petabytes (1 PB is 1,024 TB, and 1 TB is 1,024 GB) of data, which, by congressional mandate, had to be maintained for at least 100 years. The only way to manage data on that scale was to use Hierarchical Storage Managers (HSMs), huge systems that store data in vast robotic silos housing thousands of magnetic tapes. Because data on tape is slow to access and cannot be manipulated directly, HSMs also include disk systems large enough to hold a few percent of the data. When data is accessed, the HSM automatically moves it from tape to disk, eventually copying it back to tape when it is no longer needed. Diana and Mark worked on a four-person team that managed one of the two different HSMs at their site.

The HSMs were mostly automated, but sometimes required sysadmin supervision. When analyzing data, users could pretend all their data were present on disk, and the HSM loaded the data from tape to disk transparently. If the data were changed, the HSM moved the data back to tape when finished. Yet the process was not completely transparent: If users required certain files to remain on disk, they needed to ask a sysadmin to ensure that these would not be moved back to tape automatically. This required care, however, as Mark recounted from a recent incident in which a user inadvertently filled up all the HSM's hard drives:

> **Mark**: I set a directory so that it would not archive any of the data and release that data out of the directory, so the user could pump in and fix some files, then pull them right back off. Well, they exploded so much data into the directory. They didn't realize that they had filled it up.

In this case, the user was given temporary space on disk where files would not be moved back to tape automatically. However, the user put far too many files there, eventually filling up the entire shared disk system, preventing anybody else from using it.

Mechanical problems were also common. The tape robot would fail several times per month because tapes got stuck or because the machine-readable tape labels fell off or became dirty.

> **Mark**: They are highly mechanical devices that are used all the time, and we know that the weakest point of any failure is going to be mechanical. The robot arm swings around and picks up tapes and moves them from location to location, in and out, sometimes

the gripper doesn't want to let go of a tape, it doesn't quite line up to go get a tape...

Automate as Much as Possible

Mark and Diana's job was to monitor the state of their HSM for short-term problems, while performing longer-term performance and capacity analysis to determine how the system could be improved. For short-term monitoring, Mark used the open-source Nagios package, which he had configured to keep track of the HSM's components, sending him e-mail or paging him when disks got close to full or when failures occurred. He had also created a script for automatically collecting and recording daily HSM activity, e-mailing it out to the team for use in troubleshooting any problems that arose. The facility also had a ticketing system in place for users to report errors or unexpected behavior. Diana and Mark often spent the first part of each day dealing with new tickets.

Scripting was the cornerstone of their work, from collecting data for analysis and planning, to automated monitoring scripts, and to responding to system problems automatically. Script-based monitoring was common. They had implemented a platform for automatically running any script at scheduled intervals, handling the script output in a standardized manner, and notifying administrators when necessary. This platform made it straightforward to establish monitoring and notification for any aspect of system state.

Mark: We live and breathe...we live on scripts...
Diana: Most of us write a script a day to accomplish something...

Indeed. One morning we observed Diana write three different scripts. She wrote one script to move 800 tapes of data from one HSM system to another. Because the tapes could not be physically moved, the data needed to be carefully loaded from one tape system to disk, and then written to new tapes in the second tape system. Care was required to keep the process going with minimal supervision, and to avoid "thrashing" (using up all available tape, network, or disk capacity), resulting in bad performance for all users. Diana also wrote two other scripts to help troubleshoot two possibly related failures: a robotic tape silo and a server application. One script aimed to reproduce the failure by stressing the system, that is, reading or writing files of increasing sizes until the performance limit of the system was reached. As part of this effort, Diana needed yet another script to generate identical file directories on the systems whose performance was being compared. Diana and Mark thought that a similar script might have already been written, but because they did not have a common script repository, Diana could not find it and ended up writing the script from scratch.

To automate some operator tasks, over time they had developed scripts to respond automatically to well-understood system failures.

> **Mark**: We do have a mindset here that as much as can be automated needs to be automated, so we don't have to do as much human work...One is predictable behaviors that I can predict on the system. I can go to the test system, introduce failures of certain types and then understand what those predictive failures are, or predicted behaviors. So that, to me, it's key to understand, this is how I know when the system is operating correctly, under different loads, under different configurations, under different parameter changes.

Although certain situations can be predicted and automatically responded to, Mark noted the limitations of automation in that, "other types of unpredicted failures usually take a human to execute [fix] when notified by a monitoring program."

Beyond day-to-day work, Mark and Diana also created scripts for analysis of existing system resources and uses, aiming to help establish requirements for next generation systems by building and testing performance models:

> **Mark**: We're always trying to be forward thinking, into reorganizing the system, improving performance here. We spend a lot of time, Diana and I, doing analysis of our file systems: how much data do we get in a day, how much do our users retrieve a day, what's the average file size that people retrieve, what's the average age of the file...so we can properly understand how do we need to architect our next system. We have a test system that

sits side-by-side with the same architecture, and I spend a lot of time on the test system simulating different scenarios to see how it would react.

Clearly, Mark and Diana were not only system administrators but also system designers: they monitored and collected use-data and prepared requirements to design architectures for the future systems based on current and future use scenarios.

Building One-of-a-Kind Tools

Diana and Mark's environment was unusual, large, and complex, with heterogeneous tape and disk storage systems, computer servers, and desktop machines. It was unlikely that any of the vendors could have imagined their particular use case, how the components in the HSM would interact with each other, what potential failure modes would emerge, and how monitoring, testing, troubleshooting, and maintenance of such scale would be performed on a day-to-day basis. Some tasks were complicated and would be tedious to perform manually without a script. Others needed to be run on a regular basis or over long periods. No outside party could have anticipated all the tasks involved in all possible configurations, so it was most effective for the local administrators to create and customize the tools they needed. Diana and Mark's environment was a one of kind, yet many sysadmins also must deal with their own unique circumstances. Thus, the practice of customizing and developing one's own set of tools was not at all unique—we saw tool building at most sites we visited, though with varying levels of complexity and collaboration.

The Story of Jimmy, Database Administrator

Jimmy was a database administrator at a large IT services company, working on the account of a large regional retail chain store. Until two years earlier, he had been an employee of the retail firm itself. When the store had outsourced its IT management, the IT employees were hired by the service provider as part of the deal, with more or less the same responsibilities.

> **Box 5.2 Observations for Design—Diana and Mark**
>
> The story of Diana and Mark provides further examples of the potential roles of automation in system administration practice. For instance, automation can be critical for long-running tasks, such as migrating hundreds of tapes worth of data, for continuous tasks, such as system monitoring and automatically handling some error conditions, and for tasks requiring precision (and that may be tedious), such as creating multiple identical file systems for testing, and for highly repetitive and time-sensitive tasks, such as stressing a file system by continually reading and writing files.
>
> It seems off-the-shelf tools are lacking because of the idiosyncrasy of systems and tasks. Diana and Mark's environment was very unusual, perhaps unique, and so scripting was their stock and trade.

The retail chain was rapidly expanding through acquisitions, and one of their primary challenges was IT integration and scalability. The IT assets and processes from each acquired store needed to be integrated into the overall corporate IT (Giacomazzi, Panella, Pernici & Sansoni, 1997; Stylianou, Jeffries, & Robbins, 1996). Furthermore, rapid growth meant that the retail store needed scalable IT solutions to support business growth. Technology was not their core business; retail was, and the outsourcing agreement enabled them to focus on what they knew well.

In our interviews with the technical staff of the IT services company, we heard about many challenges related specifically to the retail industry. One of the managers told a story from the early days of the takeover. He told of how new IT administrators, unaware of the retail-market environment, took servers down for operating system upgrades the day before Mothers' Day—one of the most important sales days of the year for retail stores. A normally routine operation had serious complications—unforeseen downtime—causing significant loss of revenue for the customer and headaches for the provider in fixing the relationship. Clearly, the IT services company needed to know more than just technology. They needed to understand the business environment of their clients and adapt their practices accordingly. They needed to have close relationship with the customer. In fact, the agreement allowed the old and new staff of the IT services company to remain at the old location—on the bottom floor of a store. Because the group was dedicated to a single customer, co-location helped them build a close relationship with the customer.

Jimmy was part of a team of four database administrators who worked very closely together in four corner cubicles, at a central location in a large cubicle space with lots of other IT staff. During our visit, it was not uncommon to hear them talk with each other across cubicle walls. They were all very aware of what everyone else was doing and offered help frequently, without even getting up from their seats.

Because of a recent acquisition, Jimmy had recently taken on the task of integrating PeopleSoft databases into their routine practices. This meant that they would be responsible for maintenance of these databases. Jimmy (and others before him) had developed a mechanism for automatically writing scripts to perform all routine database maintenance tasks. The development of these tools began about eight years earlier, even before Jimmy and any of his current colleagues were onboard. For the most part, these were mature tools that required only occasional modification.

> **Jimmy**: The good thing about here, we try to make everything pretty much portable…And you don't really have to make that many changes. Like on the mainframe, we have maybe seven or eight different subsystems and in order to get [our scripts] to work with those, you just have to point it to the correct subsystem.

What they developed was not simply a collection of scripts they could run. They invested time to develop a model-driven scripting methodology using REXX, an interpreted macro language for IBM mainframes. The basic idea was that they created a database of model scripts and a database of input parameters for various system settings. They had about 10 to 12 such programs for regular tasks, such as backup, reorg, and copy. They would run a program to generate new scripts in the mainframe's scripting language, JCL, and another program to submit these jobs and get them scheduled on the mainframe. Their elaborate scripting scheme facilitated the batch processing needs at their site fairly well:

> **Jimmy**: We have a database called DBA1000, and it has tables in there that controls parameters and different things we use as input to these programs. This right here...is the main program that we use. It runs and generates our copies utilities, reorg utilities, whatever we are going to run for that day...So this program would pull in any parameters from our outside database. And once we put in those parameters, it actually goes through and it generates JCL, and it would put it over here. For each database, we have a library where we store the generated JCL for that.

Jimmy explained that most of the time, it was just a matter of pulling the right parameters from the database and replacing them in the model scripts to generate new scripts. The model script contained variables (e.g., DB, TS, $DSNUM$) that were replaced with the actual values at the time of creating new scripts. The execution of the JCL scripts was controlled by a table in the database, which had an entry for every script that needed to be run during a given evening:

> **Jimmy**: Once we have all this generated, later on that night, I think we kick out stuff around 8, 9 o'clock...We will have a job out here...and it goes in and it starts all the jobs we generated and this is controlled through some tables that we have on our database too....it writes a log to a table that we called DBA107....it is looking for rows in 107 to submit, it will start submitting those jobs that are in 107 for whatever utility we are running until it is complete....And if it fails, we either get a call on that or sometimes we get a call on it but most of our JCL we have some things coded that will cleanup the failure scores.

They also developed another program that tracked script execution and removed the corresponding entry from the database:

> **Jimmy**: We have a program [that] watches; it goes through and looks to see what is out here in 107 table and if your job is completed successfully it will remove these rows for you.

Jimmy and others put a lot of time into customization and automation of tools to deliver a solution best suited for the customer. The fact that they were able to step back and use sophisticated model-driven scripting suggests that they were focused on long-term gains. They could afford the initial investment because of their long-term employment with the company, the multi-year service deal, and their work in a single service organization focused on a single customer.

Creating System Administration Tools

Tool development was pervasive throughout the system administration work we observed. System administrators developed tools, automated common tasks, created Web pages, wrote command-line scripts, created databases, and repurposed existing tools in support of systems management tasks. Sometimes these tools were created for personal use; other times they were explicitly created for the use of a group. Groups might also adopt and adapt tools from outside, optimizing them for their particular needs. In addition to performing technical tasks, tools were also developed to support coordination and negotiation among staff and customers and to support inventory management, thus covering social and business aspects of work as well. These informal sysadmin-created tools complemented formal tools and processes, filling gaps in functionality, and providing additional channels for communication and negotiation (Botta et al., 2007).

Scripts spanned a broad range in terms of complexity, from a few lines thrown together in the moment to elaborate scripts that included error handling, and to complete automation solutions with automatic monitoring and response. The simplest scripts were usually *shell scripts* written for one of the command line interpreters (also known as "shells") available on the operating system. It is worth noting that all the scripting we saw involved command-line interfaces (CLI). System administrators are known for preferring CLIs over GUIs—one survey showed that a majority of administrators find CLIs to have greater trustworthiness, speed, and reliability (Takayama & Kandogan, 2006)—though scriptability is probably also an important reason for this preference.

Despite the value of scripting, system administrators often complained of the difficulty of finding time to work on scripts, as they often had to account for how time was spent on customer work. The problem was much less severe for administrators on dedicated customer accounts, particularly if these were on long-term service contracts, as in Shawn and Jimmy's cases. For example, Jimmy's team had the time to develop an elaborate framework of REXX programs generating JCL scripts based on system information stored in the database. The value of automation was much more apparent in such cases, justifying the cost of tool development.

Many administrators we observed kept "cheat sheets," a collection of useful scripts, text instructions, and sample commands for performing various tasks (Halverson & Ackerman, 2008). When system administrators could not remember how to execute a certain command, they could look up in their cheat sheets and then copy and paste samples from these files. Given the diversity of the systems that administrators touched daily, there were many tools they used infrequently, and it was helpful to have a list of useful commands handy. We observed this at virtually every site we visited. For example, Dot's Web administration group (chapter 3) had a shared repository of Unix shell scripts that were available to the whole team. Many instructions in these cheat sheets were specified at a high level, but they covered all important aspects of a complex task. They came from many sources—some were jotted down or copied from a command line after a tricky debugging session, others were copied from Internet discussion groups. To provide quality control of the repository scripts, they had instituted a formal approval process that some described as cumbersome and saw as a barrier to making contributions or updates, clearly limiting evolution. Nevertheless, the use of tool collections was an important response to the complexity administrators faced everyday. They had too many tools, too many systems, too many tasks, and too many commands to keep entirely in their heads. They did not need to know every detail; they just needed to know how to find the details when necessary (Hrebec & Stiber, 2001). When they found the details, they had the background and expertise to interpret instructions and carry them out as needed.

Why do sysadmins create and collect their own tools? Well, at the very least, administrators created their own tools whenever the tools they were given were not up to the job they needed to do. Sysadmins must perform long, complex tasks involving multiple systems and people. Consider Shawn's case. He and others in his organization, as well as the customer, were trying to coordinate patch management. They developed a database that contained information on all customer servers and whether they were compliant. The database helped everyone to be on the same page, including the customers, and it set the expectations about what needed to be completed. This database was central to their work but it did not capture all aspects of it. Patch change schedules were not part of the database; Shawn kept a separate spreadsheet to determine schedules. He also mentioned that they would like to automate more to close the loop in change management. Shawn updated his tools based on his needs, time permitting.

In Shawn's story, we also saw a vendor-supplied patch automation tool that failed to provide a viable solution. It did not comply with the customer's policy that all systems be on the same level. It was not flexible in allowing enough customization. Of course, automation can be very helpful if developed right. We saw this in Jimmy's story, in which a sophisticated model-driven approach to automation helped them be very productive because it provided sufficient customization.

Custom tool development was also necessary when system administrators needed to maintain situational awareness of complex systems involving numerous different components (Bailey, Etgen & Freeman, 2003; Hrebec & Stiber, 2001; Sonnenwald, Maglaughlin & Whitton, 2004). Many vendor tools only provide management software specific to a single system component, lacking the necessary high-level view of the system as a whole. Recall the crit-sit story (chapter 3) in which several administrators worked to solve a transient problem that involved several interacting systems. They did not have a single tool to extract the state of the system as a whole, which would have helped them understand what was going on more easily.

In some cases, there might not be a sufficient user base to develop and market a vendor tool. A task might be too idiosyncratic or a configuration might be too unusual. Consider the script that Diana developed to migrate files between two different HSMs. Diana could well have been working at the only site in the world that had the two different types of HSMs in question. In other cases, there might be a market for vendor tools, but no "official money" to purchase them. In one case, we observed a Web administrator using a monitoring tool he had purchased with $50 of his own money to improve situational awareness after a customer Web site became bogged down without anyone noticing.

Regardless of the reason, we saw many instances in which existing tools did not effectively support sysadmins' work practices. Diana and Mark were doing performance tests, building performance models, and developing solutions to be run on test servers first. On the test servers, they were simulating how the system would behave under different workloads before actually deploying their solutions to production systems. There were no tools for modeling system behavior, so Diana and Mark developed a set of scripts to simulate and measure system performance on their own. When existing tools fail to adequately support administration tasks, sysadmins fill the gap with tools of their own.

At several sites, we found sysadmin script-development practices to be informal and collaborative. Maintenance of scripts was ad hoc at best. This was not surprising, given that sysadmins often lacked software development training and experience (Kolstad, 2001–2006). Yet they still developed their own tools using various scripting languages that they had learned on the job through self-study and with the help of more experienced colleagues.

System administrators frequently create tools informally, in the moment or in between other tasks. They might not have the time to invest upfront to build more robust systems. In IT service delivery, there is no clear release cycle for system configuration and maintenance. A large part of the work is reactive, done in response to emerging issues such as external workload demands or internal system errors. Design time is clearly limited. A precise understanding of system model and behavior would put a significant burden on sysadmins, because systems are significantly complex and, in many cases, no single person has a full understanding of the complete system. Moreover, the required behavior is often hard to capture and communicate, so it was not surprising to see high-level, English-language descriptions of system behavior being used heavily in practice. Such descriptions are vague compared to precise computer code, and they rely on experts to understand and to fill in necessary implementation details (Sandusky, 1997; Halverson & Ackerman, 2008).

Given the complex, risky, collaborative, dynamic, and reactive nature of sysadmins' work, a systematic approach to software development may not be ideal or even possible. Nevertheless, there is potential to develop solutions that carefully consider the sysadmins' relationship to the systems they manage—in environments in which design, implementation, testing, and maintenance of software artifacts are tightly integrated— and offer incremental and collaborative software development methods (Kandogan, Haber, Bailey & Maglio, 2009).

6

Organizations and Information

> *"Nobody has everything. You sort of merge, you try to learn from one another."*
> —Henry, storage administrator

As team leader, Henry needed to manage his people on the fly, allocating sysadmins to tasks by taking into account technical expertise, personal holidays, work schedules across projects, task priority, and more. He had to know his people and their situations—Henry distributed the work based on where people had expertise or on where they could gain expertise by working together. In addition to his team-lead role, Henry also acted as an organizational bridge, an interface with other groups in his organization and with customers, translating designs into technical specifications and coordinating work across the organization.

In this chapter, we examine organizations, how people with different specializations, roles, and responsibilities work together to deliver IT services. An organization is a formally defined group that plans and coordinates work through shared tools, processes, and practices to achieve collective goals (Gibson, Ivancevich & Donnelly, 2002; March & Simon, 1958). IT systems are complex in composition and in lifecycle—from purchase to design to deployment to eventual decommissioning. IT service providers create a variety of organizations specializing in different aspects of IT to concentrate expertise, organizational knowledge, and best practices. These organizations must work together smoothly to ensure the correct operation of the system as a whole.

In this chapter, we consider how the structure of organizations and the interaction between organizations can be arranged to help create and manage complex systems. When expertise and responsibility are distributed across many different people and groups, it is important that they work well together to achieve the overall goal of satisfying the customer. Our focus is not so much on the structure of organizations in terms of who reports to whom, but more on the flow of information within and across organizations to coordinate work and establish common ground among stakeholders. We will examine formal as well as informal roles that support an effective flow of information as it is distributed, filtered, and transformed within organizations, and we will examine the evolution of tools and practices to support these activities effectively.

We present two stories illustrating how organizational structures and practices figure into IT service delivery. The first is based on interviews and observations of Henry and Ryan, team leaders for two organizations in Managed Storage Services (MSS) that worked together in providing computer storage services. Henry was a team leader in the Storage Operations Center (SOC), handling the day-to-day operations side of the MSS group of a large IT service provider. Ryan worked on the design team for MSS, interfacing with customers and turning their storage requests into designs that Henry's team could implement. Both Henry and Ryan worked at the boundaries of their organizations, bridging between groups within MSS. Both were aware of the interaction among groups, and personally adopted practices and developed tools to improve the overall effectiveness of the organization. To keep the organizational interactions running smoothly, they relied on standardization, such as using standard forms for communicating requests and standard configuration practices.

The second story is based on interviews and observations of Amy, a transition manager at a large IT service delivery center. In this story, we examine a services organization in terms of the lifecycle of IT service, from sales to transition to steady state. Once a customer agreed to purchase IT services from the sales team, the transition team's job was to ensure that the appropriate hardware and software were purchased, installed, configured, and running before being handed over to the steady-state operations team. Amy used a wide variety of tools to track and coordinate large IT provisioning projects, dealing with other organizations to ensure that all the necessary work was done correctly and on time. Sometimes Amy also had to stretch her role beyond transition to assist the organization in charge of steady state because of the knowledge and expertise she had developed in the earlier phases. Overall, her role was that of a coordinator, translating and filtering information in build sheets, tickets, and finance codes between different organizations to ensure that new IT systems would be created properly.

Overall, we see that the technical complexity of IT service delivery requires interaction of people, groups, and organizations at various levels. Organizations exist to coordinate work and information, establishing common ground between people within and across organizations. To make it all work, people coordinate activities, transform information, and develop and evolve tools and practices to ensure that everyone has what they need to work together smoothly.

The Story of Henry and Ryan, Storage Administrators

Henry and Ryan worked on different teams within MSS, Henry on the operations team, and Ryan on the design team. Managed Storage Services was in the business of offering enterprise-level storage solutions with allocation-based pricing, meaning that customers paid for the amount of storage available to them at any given time. This enabled companies, particularly those too small to afford their own dedicated systems, to buy high-end storage solutions at convenient prices. With an attractive offering that delivered high performance, high availability centralized storage services—including on-demand storage capacity allocation, 24/7 monitoring, and management services—MSS's customer base had grown rapidly within just a few years. At the time of our study, MSS had been operating for 2 years and had grown to 27 customers. They had more than 50 subsystems (referred to as SHARKs—huge systems of hundreds or thousands of disks with intelligent, optimized controllers and high-speed network ports) distributed across 10 different sites around the world. The customer computer systems at each site were connected to the SHARKs via storage area network (SAN) *fabrics,* collections of high-speed fiber channel switches, and interface cards (for more about storage area networks, see Box 6.1). This provided high-performance, reliable storage that could be shared across computers and expanded as needed. This also meant that a large number of devices needed to be carefully connected together.

Work at the operations center was highly technical. It also frequently crossed organizational boundaries, requiring extensive communication and coordination. For example, provisioning new storage involved transforming customer requirements into storage designs, and then implementing those designs, requiring input and often verification from the customer, design team, and operations team to keep the requirements, design, and actual allocation in sync.

Optimizing within an Organization

Henry worked as a storage administrator at MSS in the Storage Operations Center (SOC). Though the storage systems Henry managed were distributed around the world, the whole operations team was located at a single site, which was also home to Ryan's design team and numerous other IT services, such as Web hosting and help-desk services. Henry identified himself as the operations team *focal,* a role that included communication and coordination between the SOC and other groups in MSS and between the SOC and customers. He had been with the group from the beginning, when they had only two customers and two SHARK storage subsystems.

Henry's group was active 24/7 with hands-on technical work of storage operations, including routine activities, such as *provisioning* storage (creating storage volumes out of subdivisions in a SHARK system and making those volumes available to specific computers), *boarding* (bringing onboard) new servers by connecting them to the SAN via host bus adapters (HBAs), and *updating* firmware for the SAN switches, HBAs, and SHARK systems. Firmware updates also involved significant customer interaction, because the updates often required SHARKs, SANs, or customer computers to be restarted, which meant extensive negotiation and coordination with customer schedules (see also the story of Shawn in chapter 5).

Managed Storage Services aimed to give customers the same quality of service they would have if the infrastructure were dedicated to each customer alone, even though the centralized storage service supported many customers together on a shared infrastructure. This required considerable human judgment in prioritizing customer requests dynamically based on knowledge of customer context, employees, and work

Organizations and Information 163

> **Box 6.1 Storage Area Networks**
>
> Most of us are familiar with computer storage in the form of hard disk drives inside or attached to our personal computers. In enterprise computing, however, individually owned and operated disk drives are not sufficient to satisfy business needs for performance, capacity, and reliability. High-end enterprise solutions make use of large storage systems containing hundreds or thousands of disks made available to many computers via specialized high-speed storage area networks (SANs), along with specialized management software to provide high levels of flexibility, recoverability, availability, and reliability (see Figure 6.1; also see Wilkes, Hoover, Keer, Mehra, & Veitch, 2008).
>
> Connecting computers to the storage area network and allocating storage requires considerable human effort, with storage designers developing a specific design for each customer request. This requires a deep understanding of the system architecture and the customer's needs. For instance, connecting computers to storage systems involves creating one or more *paths*—connections from a computer's host bus adapter (HBA) port through the switches of the storage area network to a port on the storage system. For reliability and performance, multiple paths are the rule. This way, access to storage could be maintained even in the case of multiple component failures. Paths are defined through the process of *zoning*, which specifies how the SAN permits communication (unlike general purpose networks, SANs are often configured to allow communication only between certain end-points for better data security). Defining paths carefully helps ensure reliability and performance, because each HBA provides only so much network bandwidth.

itself—all these factors came into play when determining who should do what and when:

> **Henry**: If we get an expedited change or if there is an outage, let's say, file system has reached 99.99 percent, and it is about to crap out and cause the server to break down, we may have to push

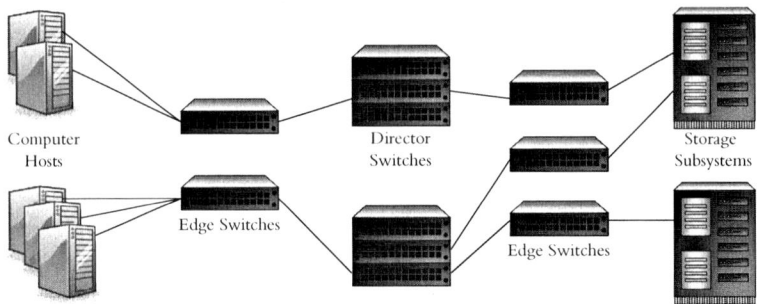

FIGURE 6.1. Enterprise storage architecture: a detailed schematic of one specific connection through the storage network.

doing that allocation before that one. That's where the human intervention lies, since we may have to page out the architect and say, "this guy needs new storage and there's no room on this SHARK."

Because Henry's group worked with so many customers, and issues came up unpredictably, resource allocation had to be reactive rather than proactive for certain kinds of work—the big question every day was how to allocate people to the issues that came up:

> **Henry**: We never know on a given day what we are doing. On any given shift you could work for any customer. Like right now, I have five people on shift, including myself. Based on the need, the shift lead would say, okay, we got an issue here, we got an issue there, you do this, you do that.

As team leader, Henry needed to allocate staff to tasks based on expertise, holidays, schedules, severity of the issues, and more. To do this, he needed to have good situational awareness of current and upcoming work, as well as knowledge of his people's availability. Team members had different backgrounds and different tenures at the SOC. Some had extensive experience with Unix, some more specifically on storage systems, and still others had more hands-on experience with test equipment. The team leader's responsibility was to understand these diverse backgrounds and leverage them in the best possible way to solve problems—and at the same time, have team members learn from each other, both to develop technical skills and to help establish and maintain common ground across the team.

> **Henry:** There are some people who have been on the SOC several years. There are some people [who have] been here only a few months. You can't expect the same. Nobody has everything. You sort of merge, you try to learn from one another.

Resource allocation was complicated further because MSS had a policy of completing customer requests within 48 hours. For some requests, this required exceptional effort, which Henry tried to provide through ad hoc resource reallocation. He would simply "pull someone out"—based on skills and experience—to devote all time to some urgent task. In such cases, he had no option but to ask people to work solely on one issue and nothing else.

The shift schedule was an important aspect of the organization's work practice. It had changed over time as the team sought the most effective and flexible arrangement. In the past, they experimented with 12-hour shifts, in which people worked 3 or 4 shifts on alternating weeks. They settled on five 8-hour shifts per week with people occasionally on call. Henry's group felt that this provided a lot more flexibility, because they could move their shifts back and forth depending on staff availability and business needs.

Henry's team also used organizational structure to better address their unpredictable work load and varied experience base. The SOC was organized into two teams: Investigation "I-phase" and Research "R-phase." I-phase people were "face people," as Henry liked to call them. They talked to the customers directly and did the initial investigation of customer issues. Tough problems were escalated to R-phase for detailed research and analysis when necessary.

> **Henry:** Their [I-phase staff] job is your first point of contact that you speak to. If they can't fix the problem, say within the 15-minute period, they then escalate to me or the shift lead, and the shift lead would delegate that to whomever appropriate, what we call R-phase or research phase, which would be somebody

who is a little more, technically inclined, used to troubleshooting problems.

Henry's team developed software tools to support their work. The SOC used an online repository to share information internally, such as procedural and departmental documents, references, project plans, reports, shift information, hardware inventory, user accounts, and staff data, including educational background and skills, vacation schedules, telephone numbers, and so on. They also used more ad hoc tools, such as a publicly visible whiteboard listing all the current tasks and problems to facilitate situational awareness. This helped staff, especially I-phase, to be grounded in current issues as they interacted with the customers:

> **Henry**: If I am doing a change, to add storage or rezone a server, and the customer calls, saying they can't see, my server just went down. I would expect my I-phase person [to] be able to say, "I know about that because we just did a change to rezone that server and that is why you can't see it."

Henry's team appeared to do a good job managing the pressures of a customer-driven, diverse, and dynamic work environment. They adapted to this environment through organizational structures and practices: ad hoc and adaptive resource allocation, flexible shift schedules, I- and R-phase groups, and locally created tools for grounding the team in the current work state.

Reducing Friction Between Organizations

The SOC did not operate in isolation—storage-services work involved interactions among a number of groups. Within MSS, storage provisioning involved both design and operations. Once an initial request came in, a change record was created and a design architect was assigned. Architects would then design the storage, determining which disks on which storage subsystems would be used, but the actual allocation was performed by the operations group, the SOC. The policy was that provisioning requests had to be completed within 48 hours, requiring tight coordination between design and operations. Though this period was usually sufficient, occasionally problems with the storage designs were discovered at implementation time, requiring direct interaction between design architects and the operations team. These interactions might be difficult if the problem was spotted during the evenings, as the operations team worked 24/7, but the design team worked normal business hours. For this reason, the SOC followed a practice that required all provisioning requests to be reviewed and verified by the operations team in advance, before implementation.

> **Henry**: Our motto is not just to take what they have architected to be the gospel. [Otherwise] you can get 90 percent of the change and find out that the other 10 percent is messed up. Now you lost time because now you gotta engage the designer, who doesn't work 24/7, who is now not on site.

In another case, Henry told us that they had to resort to technical solutions to reduce friction between groups. In this case, the problem was that, whereas MSS did the storage operations work, computer servers were managed by a group of sysadmins outside of MSS, and these sysadmins might cause problems for the SOC by attaching their systems to the wrong SAN port. Henry told us how they used two technical solutions to address this issue: port blocking, which disabled unused ports, and port binding, which enabled access only on a given port to a single HBA from a single computer. This prevented incorrect connections from computers to the SAN.

> **Henry**: We had SAs [system administrators] walking to the raised floor and saying, "It is not working on the port so I am going to use this port." That doesn't work! So, what we had to do is come up with a way to fix that. […] What we do is, once we receive a phone call from a server admin, they would say, "Okay, I am getting ready to plug my firewall into port 13." We would then check to see to make sure that port logs into the fabric. Once we do that, we would go back and port bind that port, so this way nothing other than that unique 16 digit can log in to that.

Henry's team could work much more effectively when they had visibility onto future work. The key to getting such visibility was to situate people in the right positions within the flow of information in the organization. Henry appointed a team member to represent the operations team at meetings of the transition team. This representative would note potential upcoming work items and convey them to the operations team so they could plan for them:

> **Henry**: James is our transition representative from the SOC. Anything that comes through, like, say, we had a new customer, say, <customer> wanted to board tomorrow. And they wanted to board 50 servers. James would attend the meetings and he would turn that over to the shift lead, and say, "we got 50 servers coming from <customer>."

Even though IT delivery was structured into many separate groups and roles—operation, design, system administration, transition, focals, local liaisons, and others—from the customer's perspective, it was still a single organization. So it was important for the different groups to work together smoothly because the customer did not care who was at fault if a failure occurred. For example, the interactions between the design and operations team for provisioning was fairly involved, but Henry seemed to think that it worked well in keeping the IT workers and customers happy and aware of each others' work:

> **Henry**: It's the old adage: "Don't step on anyone's toes." If I were to go over there and tell, okay, well I just decided that I am going to do it this way; he would feel like, "you're doing my job for me." They may not want to do it that way. From the customer's standpoint the MSS is viewed as one entity. It is not viewed as designers and storage operation center. If there is an outage, we all share the blame. Even though from our standpoint we know it is two separate groups that it has to pass through.

From the customer perspective, there was no difference which group within MSS was responsible for a problem. Managed Storage Services was one entity; good and bad were shared. Yet coordinating work required careful scheduling, attending the other group's meetings to maintain awareness of upcoming work, and even implementing technical fixes such as port binding to prevent different groups from stepping on each other's toes.

Grounding Past and Future

One challenge of working with a large customer base was diversity of customer hardware. Whatever type of server a customer had, MSS worked to support it. The bottom line was simply that customers were paying for the service, so MSS did what it had to do.

> **Henry**: The main thing is that the customer dictates what type of server they have. [If] they want to board an HP server, we don't tell them no. They want to use VMware, we say fine. It is compatible with the SHARK. I guess the bottom line is…if you are paying, we are playing.

But this came with a caveat: Henry's group needed practices that brought some order to what could otherwise be complete chaos. For one thing, they had to maintain detailed information about customer systems to ensure they remained compatible with the storage area networks. To help in this, Henry had created a checklist for tracking necessary details for every customer server (Table 6.1). This checklist standardized his interaction with the customer, and enabled him to ask the right questions and monitor operational prerequisites, such as operating system versions, firmware levels, adapter types, level of fiber channel, and so on.

Upgrades to the SANs required careful planning, especially in an environment like Henry's, in which different customers used the same storage infrastructure, and operations could affect many customers at once. Because storage was vital to customers, MSS aimed for no outages and no downtime. They achieved this by taking advantage of the inherent redundancy in storage area networks, taking down only part of a SAN while redundant portions remained in operation, continuing to serve customers. Yet upgrading the SAN sometimes required customers to upgrade their own systems, so Henry had to establish a year-long update schedule so that all customers would know the deadlines to make their own computers compatible with upcoming upgrades. It took considerable planning and interaction with the customers to come up with a schedule that worked for everyone.

Henry told us that he had chaired a working group that formulated a process for conducting these SAN firmware updates. The goal

Table 6.1. Checklist used to guide interactions with the customers when performing a software upgrade.

	D03DBR05H/ GN1C0/GN11C1	D03NM124/ GN11D0/GN11D1 ...
Server Information		
1. A Operating System and version	AIX 5.1	AIX 5.1
1. B SDD version installed or "none"	SDD 1.5	SDD 1.5
1. C Server HBA adapter (Make/Model)	IBM 6228	IBM 6228
1. D Cite any problems this server is currently experiencing with SAN Storage	None	None
2. Does this server meet minimum requirements?	Yes	Yes
3. If minimum requirements are not met,		
3. A Will server be upgraded to minimum requirements before (insert data one week in advance of microcode install date)?		
3. B If the server will not be upgraded can it be quiesced from SAN storage during the change?		
3. C What is the change number for the server upgrade?		
4. Minimum requirements for [Insert OS]		
4. A Minimum multipath software	SDD1.3.3.11	SDD1.3.3.11
4. B Insert patches from "Minimum Patches/PTFs required, found in the ES code installationinstructions		

was to standardize the interactions between customers and the SOC to maintain common ground about the state of the work. The result was a standardized four-week process that was documented as a flowchart (see Figure 6.2) outlining all interactions and all work to be completed. Weeks 1 and 2 were primarily for establishing requirements, schedules, and so forth. Handshaking happened during these weeks, both from a technical perspective and a social perspective, including getting customers to agree to specific upgrades to their own systems if necessary. This established common ground between the customer and the SOC, setting the right expectations, requirements, and responsibilities regarding who needed to do what in the upcoming change.

Whereas the first two weeks were primarily for establishing common ground, the remaining two weeks were mostly for technical work. In Week 3, the customer made any necessary upgrades agreed to in the first two weeks, so that customer systems were ready for the SAN upgrade. Here, customer sysadmins performed any necessary changes and reported status to the SOC once the work was completed. Week 4 was the final check with the customer, giving them a last chance to withdraw from the plan. If all parties agreed, it would be recorded as such, along with all other relevant information including change schedules, parties involved, contact information, and so forth. Finally, operators in the SOC would do their part:

> **Henry**: Week 3 [...] gives you a week in order to fix your stuff. All we expect back from them [customer] is an answer saying, "We upgraded this weekend." We add it to the change record saying, "Okay now the server is compliant, fine." Week 4 is where we finally say [to] this customer, "That is the last chance to back out." We publish the last timeline, so the customer knows everything that is going to happen. What time the servers have to be down, what servers are quiescing, who needs to be contacted there in the change, all that stuff. The night of the change we execute the change. At that point we send out the necessary notifications to the customer, saying, "Well X change is successfully completed tonight at so-and-so time, whatever."

In this case, we see a fairly detailed process, embodied as a flowchart, which set up the necessary information flows among parties involved to ensure all necessary actions were performed in the right order. It was more a social process than a technical process—initially grounding all participants with the details of the process, and handshaking at different points along the way. Only the last week included actual technical work and details of that were not even explicitly described in the flowchart. This complex process was necessary to ensure that a large shared IT infrastructure could be upgraded while being available to customers.

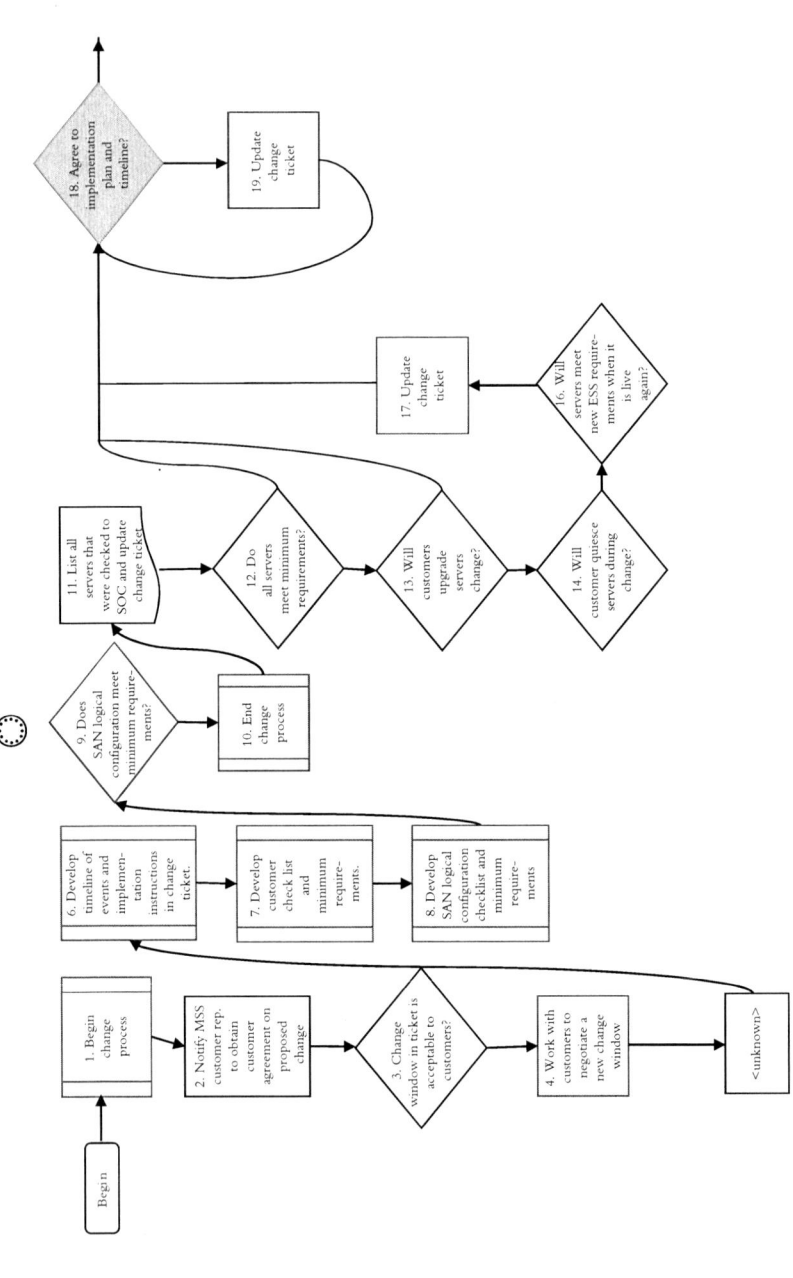

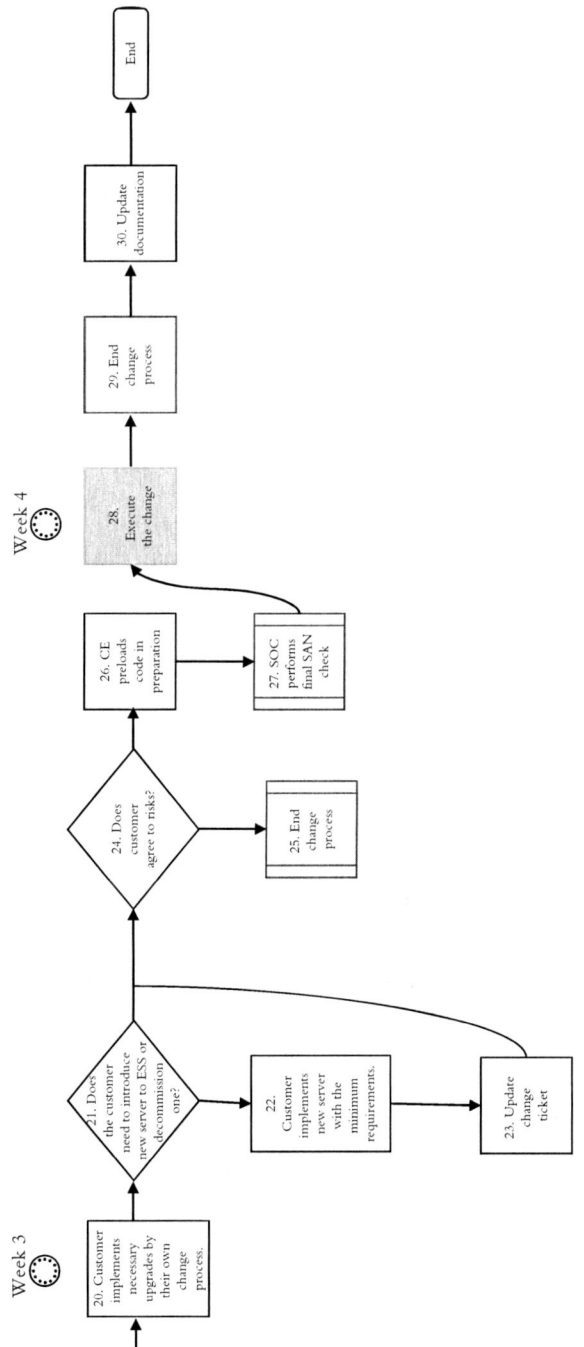

FIGURE 6.2. Flowchart developed to manage a specific sort of customer upgrade process.

Developing and maintaining organizational memory was also important for meeting customer needs in this diverse environment. Operators served multiple customers, and there were often extended delays between the time when storage was made available and when the customer started using it. Thus, problems during implementation might not surface until much later; sometimes the operator who implemented the change might no longer remember it.

> **Henry**: You may go ahead and execute that change today. The SA may not board the server [until] three weeks from today. You have already zoned, you have carved the storage, but the customer is not ready to use it. So, you are thinking everything is fine. But until a server…SA actually goes out, "Oh yeah, I can't see my LUNs." Now, you go, "Well, I closed the change three weeks ago!"…One of the problems we have is that how do you track that, because I did something four weeks ago. Do you really remember what you did four weeks ago? Because if I am working on customer A today, three weeks from now, customer C says, well you worked on my stuff a month ago. Customer A is on my mind right now. I am not thinking about customer C.

To help themselves maintain a memory of past work in the face of current problems, they had implemented a change-tracking database that they referred to when they needed to ground themselves in the details of past work.

Central to supporting customers in such a dynamic environment was the establishment of common ground among all involved, across past, present, and future. The change-tracking database supported memory for past work while addressing current issues. The status whiteboard enabled everyone to be on the same page with respect to ongoing work across the group. Future work was informed by liaisons positioned in bordering organizations. Finally, the SAN upgrade process showed the full complexity of establishing common ground on complex upcoming operations.

Synchronizing Work Across the Organization

Ryan was a storage architect at MSS, and like Henry, he had been with MSS from the beginning. As a storage architect, his responsibility was to design the allocation of storage space—or "carve storage," as he said—in enterprise storage systems. The particulars of storage allocation could significantly affect performance, so he needed to know a lot about the architecture, current allocations, utilizations, and typical workloads to meet customer needs effectively. Even though MSS was a shared environment serving many customers, design architects like Ryan were each dedicated to only a few customers.

Ryan's main collaborators worked at the SOC, where the actual allocation was done. He kept in close contact with them throughout the design process to ensure that his design stayed in sync with the actual allocation of storage. Because design and allocation were done by different teams, discussions went back and forth as teams worked to ensure that constraints on both sides were met. As we heard from Henry, they reviewed designs before implementation to help this.

During a day of observation, we watched Ryan and Ronald work together to fulfill two storage requests, one of 1.5 TB and another of 5 TB in size. Ronald had joined the team just a week before, so Ryan was mentoring him. In fact, Ronald's computer accounts had not yet been set up, so he had to submit his change requests through Ryan as part of a learning process: his designs were first reviewed by Ryan, and then sent to the SOC for actual allocation. This mentorship was important, as it helped Ronald understand not only the complexity technical work but also local practices.

Two storage design changes a day were typical. But Ryan told us that the account they were working on that day was a big customer and three or four changes were more the norm. The number of customer requests could also change over time, with more changes during periods when many new machines were added and connected to the fabrics. Once the fabrics were stable, storage allocation requests would still come in, but they could be fulfilled using existing paths through the fabrics.

Design requests typically came from the customer representative in a standardized form: a spreadsheet that specified the total amount of storage requested, intended use (e.g., database server), kinds of services requested (e.g., backup, flashcopy), along with technical information such as host name, host world-wide port number (WWPN, a globally unique network address), and preferred LUN sizes (a LUN was the basic unit of storage allocation). For this particular allocation, the customer requested a total of 1.5 TB of storage in LUN sizes of 32 GB, shared between two specific servers. Ryan explained that the customer representative who sent the request was always very specific about where he wanted his storage allocated because he had such a large environment.

The practices used for allocation had evolved over a number of years. One example of such refinement was in the basic units of storage allocation, the LUN size. In the past, they allocated storage in whatever sizes the customer had asked for. Ryan explained that once an LUN of a given size was allocated, it could not be unallocated, so odd-sized LUNs could be difficult to reuse. As a result, their organization had settled on standard sizes. Now storage was allocated using a standard LUN size—a terabyte of storage comprised many LUNs of smaller sizes (e.g., 32 GB) located on different disks or clusters. This was critical for shared environments, as customers requested and released storage frequently. Having standard sizes allowed storage to be reused efficiently. It was also good for performance:

> **Ryan**: So, you come in and you say, okay, I don't need this storage anymore I take it back. So, when you come in and you say I want four 8s [8 GB LUNs], I might have some 8s out there. There are certain parts of this we didn't understand. So, when somebody said, "Well, I want a 420 gig mail file," sure, I go out there and 420 gigabyte LUN. "Here is your 420 gig mail." It was okay for a while but we found out that the standard sizes needed to be there. We also found that it was not a good match for performance. Of course, we didn't find that out until after the fact.

Earlier, Ryan had assigned Ronald the task of transforming the customer storage request into a design that could be implemented by the SOC. This design was in the form of a standard spreadsheet that Ryan himself had developed. Originally, the form contained highly detailed information, including details for each and every LUN on every server. This level of detail could result in very large designs, for example, the single 5 TB allocation that day would involve 160 LUNs of 32 GB, each accessible from two servers. At some point, Ryan adopted a more abbreviated format.

> **Ryan**: You can probably guess, this is a very large spreadsheet, and it just got to be too cumbersome, and it was very confusing. You

see on here [showing an old spreadsheet]. This goes on forever. So, what we have done is, I backed away from adding all the LUNS on all the servers we used to use for the carving. So, that is why I turned around and made that spreadsheet that I showed you, it is just an abbreviated spreadsheet.

They had standardized even the name of the spreadsheet; encoding in the file name the site where the hardware was located, the change number, and date, all to help reduce potential misunderstandings between designers and operations staff. This type of standardization helped improve grounding between designers and operations.

After Ryan received the design sheet sent by Ronald, he carefully examined it to ensure its correctness before sending it along to the SOC. He commented that it was easy to make cut-and-paste errors because information was entered manually:

Ryan: Basically what I am doing is, I am going through a verification process to make sure that we have all our ducks in a row before we send it down there. So, we don't send them storage to the wrong server and have them undo it.

The design sheet contained columns of very similar strings of letters and digits, the host names and WWPNs for servers, storage subsystem port numbers, and so forth. In verifying the spreadsheet, Ryan needed to check every detail of Ronald's design, including verifying entries using the "capture database," a tool that automatically pulled information from their storage infrastructure each day and provided an ad hoc query mechanism to support their design work. This database was also known as "Ted's database" because a sysadmin named Ted had developed it over the years to improve the process of designing storage:

Ryan: I started with MSS in the beginning, and everything was 100 percent manual for the most part. That environment ended up very very large as it is now. Trying to keep track of all that on a spreadsheet and having eight changes a day and that type of thing was an absolute nightmare..... Once he [Ted] saw, how cumbersome it was to work, he decided and said I think we can do x y z. So, that is how we ended up with this.

Ryan explained that this database was essential to his work. Here again, we see that sysadmins created their own tools in response to pressures in their work environment. A manual and cumbersome task initially forced them to design a database that automatically gathered the data they needed. The database evolved over a number of years, as they added capabilities such as various ways of querying the data.

We watched as Ryan verified Ronald's design. He copied one of the server names from the spreadsheet, GB02QDS05102PX7, and entered it in the hostname column to search the database, but this did not return any results. After a while, he realized that this might be because this server had recently been added and perhaps had not yet logged in to the fabric, which would explain why it did not show up in the database. He then searched for the server by the WWPN number in the request, and this time found an entry in the database:

```
complex   hostname          fc_xwwpn_x      portal
     WARWICKGB02QAS05102PX7  fcs0 100000C93BF8D6  WWK380
```

Seeing this, he said,

> **Ryan**: All right, there, he is there. "QAS051"…Is that what he has got up here? [Comparing server names on the request and the design sheet] No, he has got QDS. What is wrong with that picture? Here is where you starting running into a rhubarb. These server names are so alike!

Looking around a little more, he finally decided to go with the server name specified in the customer's original request, arguing that the database was probably not up-to-date. They later confirmed that the servers for this storage request were, in fact, brand new, and had not yet been connected to the fabric.

Later, Ronald walked in to see what Ryan thought of the design. Ryan was a bit confused about the way information was organized in the design sheet:

> **Ryan**: All right, let's do this…Red, green, red, green [referring to fabrics each path is routed through]. I guess we are okay…That is

of many different groups. Amy worked in On Demand Data Center Services (ODCS), and had been there since the group's inception two years earlier.

Before ODCS, the traditional IT outsourcing model, often referred to as "your mess for less" or "lift and shift," involved a service provider simply taking over existing IT equipment, processes, and often employees of their clients (as seen in the story of Jimmy, in chapter 5; see also Dossani & Kenney, 2003). In this traditional model, the service provider had to deal with all the idiosyncrasies of the customer's existing set-up. In contrast, ODCS sold specific business applications, supporting them with standardized hardware and software configurations and processes. Outsourcing of IT functions was a growing trend, driven primarily by the high cost of managing and maintaining IT infrastructure internally (Crow & Muthuswamy, 2003; Lackow, 2001).

ODCS had defined phases of service, each managed by a different group, starting with sales, then transition, and finally steady state. In the *sales* phase, the service provider's sales team worked with a potential client to specify a technical solution that addressed their business requirements, and then the sales team negotiated a price, terms, and conditions, ideally culminating in the signing of a contract. In the *transition* phase, technical teams began building and deploying the IT solution as defined in the solution architecture document that had been developed jointly with the client during the sales phase. In the *steady-state* phase, the service provider managed the ongoing daily operation of the IT system.

Although ODCS had been in operation for two years when we visited, the processes, tooling, and people needed to support its service model were still evolving. As often happens in such cases, people adapt, using their tools and talents to meet demand while more efficient and scalable processes are being designed and deployed. As can be seen in the following episodes, Amy ensured—sometimes by sheer force of will—that people across organizations worked together to meet their commitments.

Amy worked in the transition phase of ODCS as a transition manager. Her office was along a short connecting hallway, situated among offices belonging to fellow transition managers and to other professionals, such as accounting, procurement, and legal, all of whom also worked in the transition phase. Amy's office was decorated with nicely framed family photographs, designer vases, and a landscape painting. "I figure I'm here 80 percent of my life, I want to be surrounded by happy things," Amy laughed. However, the majority of her office walls and desk space were dedicated to the equipment and information that she needed to perform her job. There were the obvious things, such as telephone, laptop, and printer, but also a PDA and a bulletin board covered in cards and notes with names, numbers, and instructions for handling special requests. On a wall to the right of her chair, there was a large whiteboard covered with hand-written reminders and a few printed pages taped along the right edge. These were Amy's *cheat sheets,* which she used to help her remember how to perform infrequent tasks. She also used the white board to track the status of change tickets and things that she needed to do, such as:

```
578456—Install Phase I LPARS.
Need to plan for Phase II servers
```

She told us, "The brain gets kind of full."

There were more printed pages taped to the wall to the right and below the whiteboard. The wall to the left was also covered in printed pages taped together to show the process flow, steps, and individuals involved in the overall ODCS process. Because transition touched almost all the ODCS processes, Amy had to be able to navigate them if called upon. Indeed, she had become an information resource and was often called upon by many in her organization.

The demands on memory were very high, and there was no way she could get by without notes and reminders: "At one point I was managing four different projects, so it [white board covered with notes] helped me figure out what I needed to do." Because Amy tended to be working on many activities at once, her focus shifted minute by minute to what needed to be handled at any time. As with other information technology workers, multitasking was common for Amy (Mark, Gonzáles & Harris, 2005), and surrounding herself with notes helped her switch context more easily.

In what follows, we present several episodes from Amy's day. They do not follow a sequence of events and they do not tell a single story; rather, they reflect the patchwork of details and happenings in transition, just as Amy experienced them.

Information Hub

Although Amy was officially part of the transition team, she spent much time communicating and coordinating with groups beyond the transition team. A large part of her job involved responding to requests for information. She had become a de-facto hub of the information flow in her organization. Her communication tools included instant messaging, telephone (for individual and conference calls), and e-mail. She also had a Blackberry sitting conspicuously in its cradle beside her laptop, though we did not see her use it.

As we watched, she reviewed the hundreds of unread e-mail messages in her inbox. "My e-mail is such a mess," she said. There were messages from project managers for Unix and Intel server builds, disaster recovery, and strategic outsourcing. There were messages from her peers in the client IT shop, and messages from transition leaders in operations. There were messages from finance, purchasing, and inventory. It was easy to see how Amy could feel overwhelmed at times. "I get more e-mail than I know what to do with." In the messages, people asked Amy any number of questions, for instance, about the architecture standards and how they were supposed to work, about the CPU utilization procedures, about the procedures for increasing capacity, and more. Many of these messages required Amy's response before operations could proceed, so she needed to get back to them promptly. Others were just informational, keeping Amy abreast of the many activities in which she was involved. Amy had created filters so that messages for which she was only on the "cc" list were automatically put into a separate folder. These were of secondary priority and she would check them when she had time.

Amy played a central role coordinating the information for the build process. She often received the initial specifications for new servers in the form of a large, multitabbed spreadsheet, which she referred to as the "build sheet." There were tabs for VMware, Windows, AIX pSeries, Server IP addresses, and change history. The server tabs could have hundreds of servers, listed in the rows, with dozens of server properties listed in the columns. Her current project involved building 200 servers. The project had 10 phases, distributed over 2 delivery sites. There were separate build sheets for each site, and each was versioned any time a change was made. To reduce the frequency of new versions, Amy would wait for sets of related changes to come in, and then make all the changes in one session, save the build sheet as a new version, and then upload it into the repository, marked as the latest version.

Because other people could not easily parse the build sheet, Amy had to copy certain information from the build sheets into fields in change tickets for different parts of the build process. To do this, she followed a tedious process of copying the information from the spreadsheet to a text editor, which helped her get the formatting right, and then she copied and pasted from the editor into the change ticket. The build sheet information that she brought together included server name, serial number, vendor, model, CPU, RAM, IP address, and applications. Because build sheet data were in different tabs, she had to move from tab to tab to get all the required information into one place in the change ticket. If a build sheet changed after the ticket was opened (and it usually did), Amy had to go back into the ticket and check the numbers again.

There were many components and issues that Amy had to be aware of. For example, if there was hardware to order, she had to anticipate and plan for the lag between placing the order and receiving the hardware. Amy was very familiar with the capacity requirements: each box (which might be shared by multiple clients via partitioning) had to have a 60/40 utilization/overhead ratio, and each client also had to have a 25 percent built-in capacity overhead. This policy allowed them to increase capacity up to 25 percent instantly, without requiring a request for service, which was the formal process that a client had to use to request additions or changes. Amy also had to understand how servers were deployed in the data center. She explained to us that a frame (or rack) held 32 CPUs, and that the CPUs were then allocated to various logical servers. Although, as she explained, there were some special-purpose servers, such as an HACMP (which was made for high-availability architectures) that needed to be isolated—not shared—to ensure they would work successfully in fail-over situations.

Amy worked with the solution architects on the account to fill in all details in all the build sheets prior to starting the actual work of building the servers. This process could take several days, but it was important to make sure the information was as complete as possible. The sysadmins on the build teams did not like frequent changes once they began the build, although they expected some. There was a build-sheet approval process, and once the build sheet was approved, Amy could take the next steps to get the build work started.

During the transition process, Amy quickly became the authority on what was being built for an account. She knew more than almost anyone else about the servers, configurations, and policies. Because of her detailed knowledge, it was sometimes difficult for her to shed old accounts as she took on new ones. People would continue to contact her for support, even though an account had officially been moved to the steady-state phase. In one case, Amy continued to support an account for two years after transition was completed. The client kept submitting project change requests (PCRs), and the account manager kept sending them to Amy. As we watched, Amy got another question about one of the accounts that she had supported in the past: "How many pSeries boxes on this account are in Southbury?"

To keep up with all this, Amy relied heavily on tools such as spreadsheets and databases to keep track of technical and financial details for each account she supported. Some of these tools were used across the organization, whereas others had been created by Amy to meet her specific requirements. Amy often created customized documents to help disseminate information because the build sheet, which defined every detail about the IT system under construction, was so complicated. Amy ended up transcribing custom versions of it for what she estimated to be 12 different audiences, including operations and networking services. For example, one of her custom spreadsheets captured server system information and client contact information for the operations team, which then used the spreadsheet to update one of the databases they used when a problem ticket for a particular client came in.

When system administrators were assigned to build new servers, they needed *claim codes* that they could use to bill their time. It was important that everyone charged their time to the right account in the right amount—this is how they made money after all. The financial analyst (FA) on the account determined claim codes. One of Amy's tasks was to give all the administrators their claim codes. Usually, there were standard claim-code categories based on equipment or activities, such as all work associated with Intel servers. Amy worked closely with the FA because claim codes could change and new ones could be added. She kept a list of claim codes in a spreadsheet on her computer. Additionally,

Amy needed to keep track of what was billable to the client. For example, the particular software applications running on the client's servers could affect licensing and whether the application was billable: "And that's always kind of fun to, to figure out what is billable and what is not billable."

Amy also worked closely with the asset manager, who maintained a financial database to track assets. The asset manager used two sources of information to populate the financial database, (a) the charge-back worksheet, and (b) the change tickets that Amy opened to track the work of provisioning servers for an account. The change ticket had more technical information than the charge-back sheet did, almost as much as the build sheet, such as the server name, serial number, function (e.g., Web server, application server), CPU, RAM, SAN storage (external disk space), and applications.

Overall, Amy was the hub of the information flow in her organization. She often had five or more IM sessions going at any moment, while also answering e-mail and talking on the phone. She had to make sure that every one had the information they needed to accomplish their work as efficiently as possible.

Activity Hub

In addition to being in the middle of the information flow, Amy was also in the middle of the action. Amy was responsible for managing the entire server build process: installing the base operating system, installing and configuring management tools, setting up back-up and recovery services, registering the server, running a health check, and mounting file systems. It was her job to make sure that the people responsible for each step did the right thing at the right time. Once all this was completed, the server was ready to hand off to the team that installed and configured the applications requested by the customer.

Amy started managing the build process once the system build sheet was approved. She opened a change ticket. She attached a copy of the final build sheet to the ticket and set the due date for 35 days in the future to give adequate time to build all the servers, knowing, however, that they might finish sooner. The ticket was under the name of the account manager for the project, and Amy assigned the ticket to herself as owner. They used the change tickets to manage work across functions (e.g., operations, availability, server build, capacity planning, and networking), to know who was doing what and when. Because everybody could access the ticketing system, task assignments were visible to all. This prevented multiple people from working at cross purposes on the same system. The change tickets also served as an audit trail.

Once the change ticket was opened, work could officially start. Amy would schedule a team kick-off meeting to review the account, set expectations, hand out claim codes, talk about dues dates, and answer questions. Typically, these meetings included everyone involved in the build process, as well as representatives from operations, such as an operations transition lead, to help them prepare for taking over the servers when they were ready to "go live." These meetings served to establish a common ground on the specifics of the work to be conducted.

In addition to the well-defined activities of the build process, sometimes Amy had to scramble to get something done quickly. At one point we saw Amy receive an instant message reporting that several recently deployed servers lacked hardware management consoles (HMCs). Hardware management consoles were physically co-located with the servers on the data-center floor and allowed sysadmins to access a server when their normal remote methods failed. They were critical for maintaining server operation in certain situations. It usually took two weeks from the time an order was placed to when a console was installed and functioning. There were many people who had to be engaged and coordinated to install an HMC, including hardware planners, rack and stack physical designers, networking specialists, and client engineers. In this case, because of a contractual deadline for completing a transition, Amy had to try to make it all happen in two days. Failure to order an HMC was not unheard of, but such oversights were relatively rare. When they did happen, resourceful people like Amy stepped in to help recover.

At times, Amy seemed to be juggling multiple time-critical activities. For example, at one point during our observations, Amy was on the phone, checking on the status of server disk partitions being created at two sites. She learned that network services were backlogged, so it would take at least two days to run the cables, preventing the servers from being configured. She developed a strategy to appease the client, trying to "buy a day or two" by giving them alternate servers while they waited for their own, dedicated servers to come on line. During this call, Amy had six instant messaging sessions going. She used instant messaging as a back channel to check on particular tasks with some of the other participants on the call. Even though she had bought them some extra time with the alternate servers, she was still nervous about the cables being installed in time to meet the deadline. Because a holiday was coming up, everyone might be scrambling to get last-minute requests submitted and completed on a tight schedule. As she was mulling over this problem, she got a phone call asking about the status of a Virtual Machine (VM) host request—"not together yet"—but she could open the change ticket that day if they would send her the source and destination port numbers and IP addresses. At the same time, the delivery executive on the project submitted an exception to raise the priority of the cabling work, allowing Amy to get overtime approved so the cables could be installed immediately.

Amy had a project manager to work with her on some of the many activities for which she was ultimately responsible. One of these activities involved installing and configuring specialized software for monitoring server performance. Monitoring was critical in the steady-state phase, when the operations team needed indicators of server performance (e.g., RAM and CPU utilization) to ensure they were meeting all service-level agreements specified in the contract. As part of transition, monitoring software and configuration settings needed to be set up and verified before the server was turned over to steady state. Relying on a project manager to help with this task was one way Amy could meet transition schedules.

Amy's organization divided responsibilities to ensure that all phases of work would receive appropriate attention. This could be an issue resulting from tension between fixing and building. In IT services, when a production server—one that is actively handling business transactions—was down, contractual agreements stipulate the maximum amount of time within which it had to be operational again. Inoperable servers could potentially result in lost business and revenue for the client, and if they were not made operable within the allotted time, the provider would have to pay large penalty fees. For this reason, a sysadmin responsible for both building new servers and fixing broken servers would always prioritize *fixing over building*. This ended up delaying the server build schedule, which was not acceptable to new clients. Management addressed this problem by assigning administrators to either building servers or supporting servers, not to both. This gave Amy much greater control over the build schedule, including an improved ability to meet deadlines: "We needed delineation of roles and responsibilities...so that we could insure that we get the servers built in a timely manner."

Orchestrating Organizations

Amy faced significant complexity in putting all the IT pieces together, and engaged in extensive collaboration and coordination to make sure that all the people in all the different groups did the right thing at the right time. She planned and coordinated different parts of the deployment process, extracted and transformed information for different groups, and stayed aware of everything that was going on. Clearly, Amy was at the center of much of the activity in her organization, orchestrating the information and work flow between groups (Yates, 1989). She was the person to go to when people had questions or needed a piece of information, and she even covered other phases of the IT service lifecycle, such as steady state. Amy was available to others above and beyond her defined role to ensure that customers received the best possible service.

Orchestrating the Flow of Information and Work

Providing IT services depends on expertise and responsibility distributed across people, groups, and even companies. It is the work of more than just individuals, more than just groups, but of many organizations that must carefully communicate and coordinate their activities, develop and evolve tools and practices, and continually modify and structure the flow of information within and across the organization to reflect new demands. As always, it is the people who make this work, the team leaders who establish practices and tools, and the information hubs who make sure that the right information moves to where it is needed at just the right time and in the right form.

In this chapter, we examined two organizations that provided IT services to many customers from a centralized location. Managed Storage

Services provided storage services for customers' existing computers, and ODCS provided end-to-end support for specific applications. Both required the coordination of many different groups to provide customer service. Managed Storage Services was structured into a storage-design group and a storage-operations group (which was, in turn, divided into I-phase and R-phase workers). They worked closely with sysadmins responsible for the computer servers, liaisons at remote sites, and the transition team that kept them informed of upcoming changes. ODCS was also organized around a division of labor: Amy worked closely with sales, accounting, procurement, and legal, all in addition to her work with traditional sysadmins, who were assigned exclusively to either operate and maintain systems (operations) or to provision new systems (transition).

Orchestration of information flow was critical, both within and between groups, for effective collaboration and coordination of work. Customers usually do not care which group was responsible for a problem; they simply want their IT systems to work. At the SOC, Henry developed a number of tools to capture and disseminate information within his team, and also with other groups and with customers. These tools helped establish common ground related to current, past, and future work. The tools included the publicly visible whiteboard of current operations, the change-tracking database that recorded who did what for every customer, the spreadsheets for tracking customer interactions and scheduling upgrades. Though each MSS customer used a different ticketing system for making requests, Ryan and Henry standardized the spreadsheets for communicating customer requests and the resulting storage designs within MSS.

In addition to tools, practices were also an important part of orchestration of information flow within the organization. Consider the elaborate practice for orchestrating upcoming firmware upgrades (described by the very detailed flow chart in Figure 6.2). This was especially impressive, with the four-week process demonstrating a large amount of coordination required to make changes across multiple connected computers and storage subsystems. They carefully designed an information flow, defining who has the information, what transformations to apply, and how and when handshakes occur when information is passed from one person to another. Managed Storage Services also used technical practices to limit access and reduce friction between groups. Henry's use of port blocking and port binding ensured that the sysadmins working on the computer systems could not accidentally plug in to the wrong part of the SAN fabric. In designing the connections between fabrics and storage subsystems and the paths used by computer systems in making connections, Ryan followed the practice of odd-even port numbers and symmetry between parallel fabrics to make connection and zoning simpler for the storage operations team. These standard practices helped in maintaining common ground, and in ensuring that the distributed cognitive system of MSS worked effectively.

In addition, Ryan and Henry developed and evolved work practices in response to pressures in their environment, such as the 48-hour deadline for handling customer requests. The differences in responsibility and job schedule between operations (which was 24/7) and design (regular business hours only) demanded that Ryan's group carefully validate the parameters on receiving a request to ensure that errors might be communicated with the customer immediately, and carefully validate the design when it was complete. Henry's group, in turn, reviewed storage designs against current system parameters as soon as they received them, giving themselves ample time to address any problems while the designers were available and before actual implementation started. One practice that helped speed the SOC's responses to customer requests was I-Phase and R-Phase teams, ensuring that there was always a group of people who could address customer problems in 15 minutes, if possible, while also keeping available greater expertise for more difficult problems. Finally, Ryan's practice of mentoring new people was invaluable in helping bring Ronald up to speed on the complexities, tools, and practices of the design group.

At ODCS, Amy was the glue that held processes together, coordinating people in multiple organizations, roles, and responsibilities to resolve issues. She knew the technology, the people, the teams, their workload, and their capabilities so she could coordinate work dynamically, hold status calls, and rearrange work to satisfy customers. She stretched herself over different phases and reached out to different teams, even though she was responsible only for transition. To remove potential impediments to establishing common ground, she translated and filtered information in build sheets, tickets, financial charge codes, and so forth, so that other groups would receive information in a form appropriate to their context and work. To help her in managing all these different aspects of her work, she surrounded herself with handwritten notes; printed documents; and notes on the whiteboard with information about her work, such as contact information, process flows, financial information about accounts, and more. In a way, these were her external memory, allowing her to switch between concurrent tasks with less effort (Landsdale, 1988; Malone, 1983; Bernstein, van Kleek, Karger & Scraefel, 2008; Campbell & Maglio, 2003). In addition, she had automated e-mail, sorting to separate informational e-mail from that requiring immediate action.

Although Amy was not personally responsible for the technical work in provisioning systems or diagnosing and fixing problems, she was a key player in the IT service delivery system. Skilled in communication, coordination, and organization, she ensured that the right tasks were done at the right time and that everyone knew what they needed to know to do their job. In a sense, she was regularly and iteratively engaged in establishing common ground among all of those involved in provisioning. Her activities ensured that the distributed cognitive system of ODCS operated smoothly.

Both Amy and Ryan filled the role of organizational bridge, translating information from one domain to another (Velasquez & Weisband, 2009). Ryan took the storage requirements from customer requests and transformed them into highly specific technical designs that could be implemented by the operations team. Amy played a similar role, translating the customer requirements in build sheets to the wide variety of documents needed to build large IT systems. Within IT service organizations, the various interacting groups had different responsibilities, worked with different tools, and were judged by different metrics—it was necessary to have people located at the boundaries to help bridge these gaps.

In both organizations, work was constantly evolving, so tools and practices had to evolve in turn. Ryan and Henry had been with their groups for the entire two-year lifetime of the organization, and over this time they observed and addressed problems through development and refinement of tools and practices. With their extensive exposure to the particulars of their organization's work and interrelationships, they were in the best position to improve things. To help cope with large storage requests, Ryan eliminated the LUN information from his design sheets. To help cope with diversity in customer hardware, they evolved practices to standardize system levels, to schedule upgrades, and so forth. Though developing tools and practices required a significant investment of effort, with a longer term view, these investments clearly paid off.

In conclusion, the technical complexity of modern IT systems, when combined with the business of IT service provisioning, resulted in sets of interrelated people, groups, and organizations interacting on various levels, with expertise, responsibilities, goals, and tools varying throughout. Careful orchestration of the flow of information and work was required at all levels, as was translation and transformation among domains to help establish common ground. The successful organizations we observed also relied on a significant body of tools and practices that had been developed locally, by those with the closest view of the problems and challenges of the work—the sysadmins themselves. These tools and practices were updated by sysadmins, evolving over time as the context of work changed. Most importantly, these tools and practices established by individuals and organizations enabled them to orchestrate the movement of information and work among organizations, ensuring that everybody had what they needed—at the right time, in the right form, and with the right content—to create and operate IT systems as efficiently as possible.

7

Communities and Trust

"These guys are getting better and better. We've got to stop this."
—Joe, security administrator

Joe, a security administrator at a university, was on the phone with a security administrator from another university. He sounded worried. They had been desperately trying to stop an ongoing series of malicious attacks that were persistently targeting systems at university and government sites. The hackers were getting better and better, sharing tools and techniques within their underground community. Joe and his colleagues tried to keep up, collaborating across institutions and forming their own ad hoc security community specifically to respond to these attacks in an organized way. They shared computer system logs, information about compromised accounts, and exploit tools. They discussed their findings on weekly phone meetings, and tried to adapt to the ever-changing tactics of the hackers. It was hard work. And the attackers kept coming back, making Joe and his colleagues ask, "What else could we possibly do?"

In this chapter, we examine communities of sysadmins. More precisely, we are talking about *communities of practice*, groups of people who share an interest, craft, or profession, and who engage in collective learning in a specific domain (Lave & Wenger, 1991). Practices develop through activities, such as shared problem solving, requests for information or experience, building and sharing tools, coordinating work, and documenting common problems (Wenger, 2006). Sysadmins are members of a number of communities. They are members of teams and organizations that coordinate work at a local level. Within a single company or a single geographic area, they may often get together to share knowledge, tools, and practices. There are also broader, online communities as well—those facing similar problems and challenges specific to their expertise, regardless of employer or geography. Administrators working with the same type of system can help and learn from each other, even if located halfway around the world. Web search, online discussion boards, local-interest-group meetings, larger conferences, and open source software projects are venues for sharing information and tools. This can be as simple as pasting an error message into a Web search engine to find how others handled the problem, a practice followed by virtually every sysadmin we observed.

We examine communities at all levels through episodes from our study of Joe, Aaron, and their colleagues, security administrators at a large university data center, as they worked together monitoring systems for vulnerabilities or signs of attack. Their work involved communication and collaboration within their local team to analyze and resolve security alerts related to their own systems. Among the broader security community at the university, knowledge and strategies were exchanged about more general threats and trends. At the global level, we saw Aaron working with and customizing open-source intrusion-detection systems, as well as using security mailing lists and Web sites to learn about new threats. We also saw Joe's close collaboration with security administrators at other institutions to develop a concerted response to a long-running worldwide security incident—working together in an ad hoc security community to handle a common threat. (For more about computer security, see Box 7.1).

Communities are critical to system-administration work, yet there are challenges to collaboration when knowledge is exchanged beyond local organizations. Lack of context and trust may impede grounding when collaboration moves from the comfort zone of one's own organization or trusted social group out to public forums such as newsgroups and Web sites. Particularly in the domain of security administration, trust is critical; it can be disastrous if the wrong information falls into the wrong hands.

The Story of Joe and Aaron, Security Administrators

Joe and Aaron worked at a large public university supercomputing center. Joe, a senior security engineer, managed Aaron and two other security administrators at the center. Previously, he had worked as a system administrator at the same center, and he had also been a software developer at several local companies. The computing center provided services for about 300 employees as well as for many external collaborators throughout the United States. Joe and his group were responsible for setting up, configuring, and monitoring intrusion-detection systems, and for responding to alerts to resolve security incidents. They also worked proactively to eliminate vulnerabilities and performed forensic analysis on compromised systems. As a manager, Joe was responsible for defining center-wide security policies, and as such he interacted with other concerned groups within the university. Joe spent quite a bit of time on the phone and in meetings; he still did day-to-day technical work but tried to delegate a lot of it to his staff.

We met Joe in his office, which had a bookcase full of various puzzles and games (see Figure 7.1). He told us that this hobby was "a nice metaphor for my day job," suggesting that security administration was a lot like solving puzzles. Joe typically started his day at nine in the morning. First, he read e-mail and launched the MOO (Evard, 1993; Fox, 2004), a text-based multi-room chat system used for communication between all IT staff at the university. Joe typically left work around five, but quickly logged in again from home to stay in touch with his colleagues and to continue monitoring the systems. At around 9 PM, one of the automated systems would send out a daily report, which Joe read before going to bed, hoping that he could sleep with some peace of mind. Joe had been officially on call 24/7 for 8 years, though he told us he had received only a few off-hour calls in that time.

Aaron was a junior security engineer who reported to Joe. He had graduated with a masters degree in computer science the year before, and had been working in this position ever since. He shared an office with Tom, another security administrator. Aaron's schedule was similar to Joe's, but offset by an hour or two. The security group members staggered their hours to ensure better coverage at both ends of the workday. In fact, one of their team members worked remotely two time zones away, further increasing around-the-clock coverage.

Aaron's day was centered on e-mail. Automated monitoring tools generated e-mail security alerts, which needed to be evaluated and acted upon immediately. He checked his e-mail frequently for these alerts, at least every five minutes. Based on his experience, Aaron could quickly

Box 7.1 Computer Security

Computer security administration is critical because hundreds of millions of users rely on secure access to computing and information services for their business, educational, and personal activities. The Internet, which permits global communications and commerce, also allows for global attacks that compromise machines, steal data, and reduce productivity (Grow, Epstein & Tschang, 2008). Computer attacks vary depending on the type of computer. Personal computers often fall prey to *malware* such as viruses and worms, which can copy themselves from computer to computer, often over a network. Attackers can also gain access to and control of larger enterprise and university computers, which are shared among many users and often accessed over wide-area networks, using compromised user passwords or software vulnerabilities. In either case, the malware or attacker might steal or destroy data, log computer activity to steal user passwords, or use the computer to surreptitiously send out spam or attack other computers.

New computer vulnerabilities are discovered every day, and security administrators try to patch system vulnerabilities as quickly as they become aware of them. There are numerous online resources, such as Web sites and e-mail lists, to help administrators stay on top of the latest threats. Security administrators must also continually monitor systems for any signs of attack, including unusual activity by a user or program, or increased network utilization as the malware or attacker scans nearby computers for vulnerabilities to find a way to spread. Security administrators often rely on automated intrusion detection tools, which analyze computer and network traffic logs for suspicious activity. Once an attack is discovered, administrators must react quickly by investigating the traces left behind, to piece together clues to identify the vulnerabilities that were exploited (to cut off the means of attack), and track down the perpetrators. Most importantly, they must work together as a community because security threats are a worldwide problem.

FIGURE 7.1. Puzzles in Joe's office.

determine which alerts could be ignored and which could indicate an ongoing attack. When an alert looked serious, he immediately began an investigation, preempting any other work he might have been doing at the time. He would scan through system logs, check network ports, search for exploit information on the Web, and consult with his co-workers. Though detection of anomalous activity was largely automated, discriminating between real attacks and false alarms required human judgment. On normal days, most alerts were false alarms or simply harmless, but it was up to Aaron and other administrators to make that call. This required intimate knowledge of the environment—of system workloads, network traffic, application use, hardware and software architectures, and so on, built over years of experience.

Aaron also had e-mail subscriptions to security-related e-mail lists (e.g., Call Center Industry Advisory Council (CIAC), Forum for Incident Response and Security Teams (FIRST), and university lists), which kept him up-to-date on new vulnerabilities, and to lists related to various publicly available security tools (e.g., Honeynet, Bro, Tripwire, and Nessus) that they used at the center. On hearing about new vulnerabilities through these mailing lists, he would usually search the Web to learn more, and sometimes he would download sample code and logs of attacks to better understand how they worked. Once he understood a specific vulnerability, he tried to find machines at his institution that might be susceptible.

Human Judgment Required

We watched Aaron for several days follow his routine of checking e-mail frequently for alerts from the automated intrusion detection systems. In almost every case, he examined the alert summary and quickly disregarded it—an obvious false alarm. In one case, however, an alert needed further investigation. There was new network activity between a computer at the university and a remote host that was known to have been compromised previously in an ongoing attack (Figure 7.2).

> **Aaron**: Right now we got an alert, which is totally related to the incidents going on right now. So, this takes, like, most priority. So, I will leave everything and start looking into this.

The ongoing attack was a very serious threat in which a small group of people overseas was using a wide variety of vulnerabilities to gain access to military, industrial, and university systems. The e-mail alert said that there had been recent network activity between a local machine (IP address x.x.63.22) and a remote, formerly compromised machine (host name nyx.xx.xx.edu, and IP address x.x.31.10). Past experience suggested that formerly compromised machines were often targets for new attacks, so they received extra attention. The activity was an HTTP transfer of a 711kb file recorded in the log with ID 77125. The report also said that on June 8, Victor, a fellow security administrator, had identified the formerly compromised machine.

```
Watchdog found the following alerts in tcpread. These seem
to be coming from the known compromised hosts. Please take
time to investigate.
Non-XX IP (Once Compromised IP's)
x.x.31.10 #nyx.engine.xx.edu (6/8 from victor, used as
login to XX)
X IP's Connections
On1
> Jul 27 15:10:14 x.x.31.10 0.1kb > x.x.63.22/http 711kb
0.0b %77125
```

FIGURE 7.2. An alert about activity on a compromised host.

All the contextual information surrounding the alert came from customization of the open-source Bro intrusion-detection system (Paxson, 1999), which allowed Aaron's team to register certain hosts as compromised and add further miscellaneous information, such as who reported it and when and how it was compromised. In fact, Bro could be customized in many ways, allowing the sysadmins to define signatures of suspicious activity and alerting them or terminating a network connection whenever it detected these events. But customization was not a simple task. Attack patterns can be difficult to define. Yet customization proved to be critical for them, because it permitted the administrators to adapt their tools to new attacks and new vulnerabilities, and to manage growing numbers of alerts.

Noting that the alert referred to an HTTP transfer with id 77125, Aaron looked at the Web server log for this particular id:

```
$ grep %77125 http.log
10900959014.04476 %77125 start x.x.31.100 > x.x.65.22
    %77125 GET/download/perftools-0.5.1b5.tar.gz
```

The log revealed the name of the file (`perftools-0.5.1b5.tar.gz`) that was downloaded:

Aaron: It looks like performance...for parallel computing...so, most probably it should be legit.

Aaron judged that the filename indicated a legitimate file; specifically, it looked to Aaron like some performance monitoring software had been transferred. The filename was not suspicious.

Tom had also noticed the e-mail alert and was investigating it in parallel. In fact, he had already replied to the e-mail telling others that it looked okay. However, Aaron went further, determined the host name of the machine, sutter.xx.xx.edu, and then tried to find its owner by querying an online database, but with no luck. He asked Tom for help:

Aaron: Can you look at this machine, 65.22?
Tom: Look at it how?
Aaron: Like it is not on DNS. The entry is not there. sutter.xx. This is the machine which downloaded perftools. Which machine

is that and who is the admin? [...] Like, if it is some guys in parallel programming, then it should be okay.

After a little while, Tom replied with the login id of the administrator. Aaron immediately did a Web search and found the person's home page. Based on the Web page, Aaron concluded that the user worked on high performance computing. He sent the URL to Tom on the MOO by whispering (sending a private message) to him:

```
You whisper to tom, http://<site>/~user/perftools
```

Aaron was convinced this was a legitimate file, and not related to the ongoing incident:

> **Tom**: Did you Google?
> **Aaron**: This guy, I think, basically wrote this thing... So that was a false positive.

Both were relieved, as the alert might have been important:

> **Tom**: It is totally related to a machine that has been compromised in this incident.
> **Aaron**: The machines which have been compromised, they use it again and again. But the problem is this machine is compromised because that user is somewhere related to the [center]. So it is compromised and because of that we got compromised, now that user is still related to [center], so he still interacts with [center] but because of that, these attackers enter in the same way. We know that they are coming from this machine but it is highly likely a legit user is also coming from the same machine and we cannot block that machine because it is being used. So we cannot block them, so we have to monitor them.

This was a fairly easy case. They recognized the file that had been downloaded and they were able to identify the users and their purpose after only a little investigation. However, there were times when things were not so easy:

> **Aaron**: I mean it was fairly straightforward. We knew what application has been downloaded, we knew... which guy downloaded it, and we can associate it. But then there are times

when somebody would download any tar file, which is like source code or something else, then we have to...It gets a really tricky thing, like, is it an exploit, or what is going on there?

Aaron and his colleagues adapted to new security threats by customizing network-monitoring tools to the highest degree possible. In this case, they had customized the Bro alert based on information shared by another site, where a machine had been compromised in the current incident. They leveraged knowledge of the community at large by incorporating that knowledge into their monitoring and detection tools to customize the reports. Seeing the relevant context of the alert allowed them to assess the importance of the alert quickly and guided them in their investigation, facilitating establishment of common ground on system state among sysadmins and their systems. In this case, because the alert was related to the ongoing incident, it became top priority for Aaron and Tom. In this case, Aaron first collected as much information as possible from the logs, such as the name of the file transferred and the host machine, worked with Tom to better identify the local machine, and then he did more. He looked up the owner of the local machine and examined his Web page, finally convincing himself that the alert had, in fact, been generated by a legitimate action. He integrated a variety of information from a number of sources, including Web search, to support his and Tom's original judgment.

Working with the Local Community

When not occupied by alerts, Aaron and his colleagues spent time researching new tools, vulnerabilities, and security threats. Based on information found on mailing lists and discussion forums, he often searched for vulnerabilities at his site and worked proactively to remedy them. During our visit, we saw him undertake several such investigations. Here, we report one case related to the MyDoom worm (Kanellos, 2004), in which he made use of both the broad community through Web-based research and also the local community of other university administrators through the MOO.

Through his research, Aaron learned of the emergence of a new variant of the MyDoom worm, which spread extremely quickly from network to network and caused infected machines to send out spam e-mail. This was a bad thing. He had scanned the systems on his subnet earlier in the week, and he discovered at least one computer that exhibited suspicious network traffic involving port 1034, which, according to his research, was MyDoom's network communication port. He notified the system's owner of the situation and immediately took the system off the network.

Having taken preliminary action to limit the damage, Aaron now needed to assess the situation more closely, trying to verify whether, in fact, MyDoom actually had affected this system. If it had, he had to clean the system before bringing it back online. He also assessed the scale of the problem by looking for other affected machines on their subnet. For this, he examined Argus network flows (Qosient, 2011), which contained logs of all network traffic at their site (typically several gigabytes of data per day). Because of their size and detail, these flow logs were impossible to read and understand directly. Aaron used small programs to filter the logs for port 1034, homing in on the specific sort of network traffic he was looking for:

Aaron: Right now, I was interested only in this port, which is the source port. Because I found out this is basically the port which is being used [by the MyDoom worm]...and how do I get this information? Through mailing lists, or going to different Websites like USCert...

He used Argus command utilities to examine a network flow on a particular port:

```
$./bin/ra -zcanr argus.out—port 1034 | more
27 Jul 04 13:16:44 qd tcp x.x.90.162.1034 ->
x.x.232.51.80 6 6 968
27 Jul 04 13:19:25 qd tcp x.x.109.163.1034 ->
x.x.50.116.3017 4 5 46
27 Jul 04 13:19:46 q udp x.x.2.2.53 <->
x.x.164.117.1034 2 2 4957
27 Jul 04 13:30:50 qd tcp x.x.90.162.1034 ->
x.x.80.23.80 6 3 695
```

The output was still several pages long, even though it was filtered to show flows only to and from port 1034. He picked a few of the IP addresses involved and executed the host command to get the host names of the machines, such as ach-wireless-127.x.x.edu, and urat-wireless-130.x.x.edu, and so forth. He then extracted the complete list of all the IP addresses involved, copied them into a file, and ran a small script to get the host names into a nicely formatted list.

The resulting list suggested to Aaron that the worm might have infected four other systems. He read up on MyDoom on the Web to understand how it worked. He verified from security Websites, such as uscert.gov and dsshield.org, that this particular version of the worm caused problems on some search engines, as it queried them for valid e-mail addresses within a particular domain, keeping them extremely busy. He shared his findings with Tom over the MOO, telling him that the worm was very easy to spot because its search activity left a clear signature in the search engine logs (Figure 7.3). They discussed how the computers might have gotten the worm. Tom pointed out that the infected machines were mostly laptops connected wirelessly to the university network, making it likely that they picked up the worm outside

```
dube (to tom): regardless, if it came through with a
standard attachment, it shouldn't have had it past the
filter (unless we aren't currently blocking zips again)
tom (to dube and linda): one machine was infected
yesterday, but its also a laptop, so might of gotten it
else where
linda (to tom): here's is the list of MyDoom variants that
we scan for ....
linda (to dube): and yes, we still block .ZIP files
tom (to linda): i'm thinking all of them got it somewhere
else. Two of the other machines are wireless connections,
so they are also laptops.
melliott says, "silly promiscious users"
You whisper to tom "dalat.xxxx.xxxx.edu probably a win
machine"
dube (to kender): did you fund out more about that titanium
2 machine?
dube says "Can someone with Fedora Core I and without the
OpenSS binaris do an "ssh -V" for me?
tom (to dube) give me a sec to fire up my vmware
```

FIGURE 7.3. Conversation between sysadmins on the MOO about the recent virus issue and more.

the university. The MOO conversation grew to involve a number of other system administrators at the university, all of whom contributed information or speculation on the matter. The MOO maintained a series of interwoven—and not always related—conversations.

Based on their findings thus far, Tom and Aaron also discussed this issue verbally in the office:

> **Tom**: What is weird is that all the other ports, it is going through sequentially. So, it might be just (unclear).
> **Aaron**:...but then there are so many 1034 connections. Do you see 1034, 1035, 1036?
> **Tom**: I don't know. All I know that it was going incrementally up.
> **Aaron**: We should just run the flows and look at it.
> **Tom**: I grep'ed on that file from yesterday. There were like four 1034s in there.
> **Aaron**: What if we run it today and see how many connections we see.
> **Tom**: Yeah, I started too. [...] Yep, that is what it is. 1034, 1035, 1036.
> **Aaron**: Ohh.
> **Tom**: Again and again.

At this point, both Tom and Aaron began to doubt whether MyDoom indeed had affected the laptops in question. They suspected that because the pattern was sequential, it could have been some sort of port scanner or another application that had searched for an available port over and over. In any event, they had done their job and asked the system owners to run virus-scanning software to clean it up if anything was indeed affected.

Here we saw the MOO used to share information among IT staff at the university. The MOO was essentially a persistent messaging system comprised of a set of chat rooms representing dedicated spaces for administrators to communicate on preagreed topics. Joe told us that he liked the MOO system because it provided a way to catch up on things quickly in the morning using the history to show past messages. We also saw Aaron and Tom use it to exchange private messages, such as URLs, even though they were in the same office. The MOO was also used for obtaining a quick advice from administrators, such as, "Is there a quick way to get a list of configured hosts?" or domain-specific issues, such as mail filter options. One of the interesting features of the MOO was that one could whisper to another person so that only parties involved would see the messages exchanged. Aaron described why this was used:

> **Aaron**:...but there are certain things which we don't know if they should know it or not, generally not, unless need to know basis thing...so if we are to exchange IP addresses here, we whisper.

In other cases, even though a discussion was held among a few people, others could view and join the conversation if they had something to add. Most of the people on the MOO congregated in different rooms based on the function of the room, such as the "cluster room" (for IT staff working on the supercomputer cluster) or the "networking room."

Aaron's community involved many layers. Closest was his officemate and immediate team, with whom he worked moment-to-moment. At the next layer were the other administrators at the university, following similar policies and facing similar problems, and exchanging information mostly via the MOO. The MOO was essential for many of the administrators to ground themselves with emerging technical issues. Joe relied on the MOO to catch up every morning on what had happened since he left work the night before. Despite the fact that everyone on the MOO was a system administrator at the center, Aaron and others were very cautious when sharing sensitive information by "whispering" so only selected people could see certain things. The outermost layer was the security community as a whole, which used Web sites, discussion groups, and e-mail lists to disseminate information about threats and vulnerabilities. Regardless of the layer, collaboration was central to Aaron's work. Given the rapidly changing landscape of security administration, with new software, vulnerabilities, and attacks occurring daily, it was simply unimaginable how he could conduct his work otherwise.

A Global Response to a Global Attack

Though minor security incidents occurred every week or two, during our visit, Joe's team was in the middle of a long-lasting worldwide incident that affected military, educational, and government sites across the United States and Europe. This incident was first noted when a researcher at a university received an e-mail message from someone bragging about breaking into military sites. Unlike many other security incidents, which were often contained in a matter of days by patching the vulnerable software on compromised computers, in this case the attackers were extremely persistent, taking advantage of a wide variety of vulnerabilities and continually changing their tactics. Once a computer was compromised, the hackers would capture the passwords of legitimate users and try those passwords to gain control of other computers on which the users had accounts. With these techniques, the attackers had an ever-expanding set of compromised machines at institutions across seven countries, a situation that demanded broad collaboration among security professionals. In the end, it took more than a year to bring the attacks to an end, with prosecution of individuals in several countries.

When we were there, the center had not been attacked for about four weeks, but Joe still coordinated work on the incident across the affected sites. It became something of a personal issue for him. So Joe looked sad when he dropped in to Aaron and Tom's office to break some bad news:

> **Joe**: Well, [a different university] pulled the machine. Friday afternoon. They weren't able to get all the TCP dumps and they just figured that they didn't want to leave it up, so they pulled it. Now, we don't know where they will be coming in from.
> **Aaron**: So, they have no dumps at all?
> **Joe**: No, no dumps. They have flows, and when I asked him to give me all those flows, he said he is going to talk to higher-ups and find out if he can do that or not. So, we will see…
> **Aaron**: This is not good, actually. So the thing is, basically, that machine would give us a lot of other information about what exactly is going on, like where are these guys attacking now. So back to square one, Tom.

To track the attacks, security administrators allowed some computers to remain compromised but under close surveillance. This enabled them to monitor which other machines were under attack and find out when the attackers were active. In this case, another institution had shut down one of the compromised machines without getting critical data, the network traces. Without this machine, the attackers would come in via other unknown computers, making it harder to keep an eye on their activities.

> **Joe:** We have been able to track within the last eight weeks or so where they are coming in, you know, they basically take a path in. Once they get a path in, they will use it for a couple of weeks. [...] Usually they come in from Europe to a machine in the US, and from the US they make either one or two more hops before they start launching any attacks. If we can find the point of origin in here, and monitor that, we can get a lot of information: where they are going in the US and stuff like this. So we knew that machine, we knew the second machine they are hopping to, and there is a third machine that was here in town that they are using as well. This machine, I need to call them today, the place in town here, and talk to them, and I need to track down some of these other sites, the admins there.

And in this case the attackers were relentless:

> **Joe:** ...but these guys, unless they are caught, the problem is not over. Because they tend to come back and back and back, and they try all kinds of different things to get into...They have a set of things. That is why, we know these are the 10 or 15 attacks they are doing. So we scan the network, did all kinds of testing, we stopped those services which were vulnerable on most of the machines. So they are not able to get into the network, but we don't know what they are going to do tomorrow. Then CVS [Concurrent Versions System] exploit came in before it got published, we got attacked with that exploit. [It was] most probably by the same guys because of the various other signatures which were left on the machine.

Having received a new scan from another site, Joe asked for Aaron's help to discover the exploits the hackers used.

> **Joe:** I moved all the files, that we were connecting to the [machine name] machine, and moved all those files over into the scans directory. Remember the scans/remote directory? You look in there under files [...]. It is kind of interesting, I haven't figured it out exactly what they are doing yet.

Aaron looked in the directory <attack name>/remote-info/scans and opened the latest scan file. Joe and others at the center had developed a standardized directory structure to collaborate on incidents. They had directories for each incident, which contained scans, exploits by year, and names of the compromised machines. Joe pointed Aaron to a recent scan he received and asked him to examine two exploits in the logs and to report his findings:

> **Joe**: This is the directory, the rootkit directory. If you look at the tools that are in there. They have two new things in there that I didn't notice. I told [another university] about identity key there [pointing to ingresd.x.x.edu.identity] and I am not sure what it is from. They are trying to figure out what it is from as well. I don't have a copy of it because it is binary data. So I wasn't able to get it, but that mod_rootme, we need to find out what that is…The other thing they are using is that ussl thing. Take a look at that as well, and see exactly what that is because this one is new and this one is new [pointing to mod_rootme and ussl].

Aaron made several online searches to find out more about these things. Several security sites revealed that mod_rootme was in fact a high-threat vulnerability that set up a backdoor inside the Apache Web Server, whereby a simple HTTP request would allow a remote party to gain privileged access in secret. While researching this, he downloaded a copy of the code for the exploit and examined several files. In one, he noticed several individuals identified by user name or e-mail address:

```
printf("[*] named 8.2.x (< 8.2.3-REL) remote root
exploit by lucysoft, Ixix");
printf("[*] fixed by ian@cypherpunks.ca and jwilkins@
bitland.ne\n\e");
```

As Joe and Aaron told us, many people created exploit tools for fame and glory in their community, so it was not unusual to find nicknames or e-mail addresses in the code. Aaron did a Web search on each of these—lucysoft, ian@cypherpunks.ca, and jwilkins@bitland.ne—and the last one led him to yet another vulnerability, the BIND exploit. Once he completed his research, he wrote an e-mail message to the team describing his findings, including the URLs and documents he found.

Aaron explained to us that trying to understand source code was very hard, whereas references to identities often led him to further clues easily:

> **Aaron**:…and that is what I generally look for. Like most of them have assembly code or something else. Rather than spending time on what exactly the exploit is doing most of the time, first I try to.…What I was doing right now is, I got the source code, I started looking at the comments to see explanations, and the signature of the authors. Because generally all the hackers…tend to write their own signature handle or something.

His research led him to an OpenSSL exploit, which had been well studied by the security community. In fact, he found a comprehensive report on it written by a security professional elsewhere. After reading the e-mail, Joe spoke with Aaron:

> **Joe**: I am printing off that PDF file, see what that is. Did you find the tool out there?
> **Aaron**: Oh, yeah. I found two of them, this mod_root one,…
> **Joe**: Yeah, I saw that.
> **Aaron**: So, that was one and then a.c
> **Joe**: See, what you say about rootme…It is a backdoor for Apache but I was wondering how it gives you root access on the machine.
> **Aaron**: Well, I think, they are making connections on port 80.
> **Joe**: Right. So, everything is over port 80. So, it is going to make it look like it is normal traffic…but I can see it giving you the, you know, a shell, as the user that is running the Web server. […] So, if there is a local exploit you can do that. It is just basically masking the traffic, normal, it is coming across port 80.
> **Aaron**: and then the OpenSSL exploit, that was an interesting.
> **Joe**: Yeah, did you find the tool for that?
> **Aaron**: Ah, no. I was looking for it but, I mean there were two or three different Web sites but they did not have this tool.

Had they found the tool, Joe said they would try the exploits in quarantined environments, such as virtual machines with limited connectivity, to learn how they worked:

> **Joe**: What we try to do is put them into like a quarantine environment, setup VMware. We have a number of hosts in VMware we can just bring up VMWare host, throw some tool on it, run it, see what it does, or maybe setup a couple of hosts inside VMWare, where we can actually use the client servers and stuff. And once we play around, we can just delete that whole thing and just have a copy of the VMware stuff.

Collaboration was essential to tackling large-scale incidents such as this one. Once the scope of the incident was understood, security staff at affected institutions held weekly calls and exchanged information through e-mail, phone, and more. In fact, Joe played an important role coordinating some of the effort, passing on information he found, and asking others to help him out. Beyond the regular weekly calls, Joe also had several individual calls with security staff at several institutions on a daily basis to discuss their findings. In one such call, he reported the latest exploit details to a security administrator at another university:

> **Joe**: …also there is another one, a tool that we have finally, and Aaron found a copy of that out there in the Internet. It is basically, it is a BIND, a DNS vulnerability, so these three things we have never seen them use before.

This incident clearly required an unusual amount of effort to contain; most of the time an incident could be resolved with a patch that fixed a vulnerability so attackers could not come in the same way again:

> **Joe**: …the last time we did this it was a 16-year-old up in New Jersey. A slap on the hand and it is like, you know, that kind of thing. So we haven't pursued anything for quite a few years. Cause most of the time, like I said, you discover something and you clean it up, they are gone, you don't really see them back.

Joe and others were very close to catching the attackers, and that made it all the more important for him to work with others to bring the attacks to an end:

> **Joe:** We are, you know, fighting our time to catch these guys back there. But, we are also tracking who they are affecting, and trying to notify all these sites and being proactive and saying, "hey you have compromised machines" and so forth. Because these guys are very prolific in what they have been doing, and there is a large number of affected sites, so we are just trying to help them out; it is just a point that we don't have to do this, but I just feel obligated because we are so close to where they are at, we know so much information of what they are doing. [So] I just take it upon myself to track these guys and follow what they are doing and help out the sites that have no clue that they are being compromised....

This incident showed some examples of the workings of communities. Security administrators from across the United States and Europe were in close collaboration. There was an ad hoc alliance among institutions that had been attacked. They shared knowledge of which machines were compromised, which accounts were being used, and which vulnerabilities were exploited. They shared ideas, tools, and techniques for detecting and tracing activities of the perpetrators. Joe spent significant time leading this collaboration, even though his formal job responsibilities were limited to issues arising at his own university. He even went out of his way to notify newly affected institutions when they became part of the Web of compromised machines. Yet, even in this ad hoc community of security administrators with well-known credentials and reputations, problems of trust surfaced (Kandogan & Haber, 2005; Werlinger, Hawkey & Beznosov, 2008). Some universities were not willing to share all they knew or to leave machines vulnerable to help the broader community. However, trust was never an issue within Joe's own team, as evidenced by the fact that they built and maintained an elaborate directory structure to share logs, scripts, and findings.

Beyond this particular incident and the specific groups of security administrators that got involved, Joe's team often leveraged the broader community to handle incidents and to learn about security-related issues. The security community was very active in collaborating and reporting new incident signatures to public Web sites to alert others. Joe's team relied on very comprehensive reports written by fellow security administrators, such as the OpenSSL exploit report Aaron found. However, collaboration within the broader community was not always easy. As Joe explained, security Web sites contained so much information that it was often difficult to find information on current incidents.

> **Joe**: So there is all kinds of things you try to do, but all these things take so much time and effort. Because, you know, a lot of these, packetstorm, that is a huge site that tons of tons of people use. [...] So it is like a needle in a haystack sometimes, and even a chance if it is in there.

The fundamental problem was really grounding the context of the current incident with a large body of incident reports and related information. For instance, it was often difficult to describe an incident—given many technical details, it may not be clear which ones were relevant. On the flip side, when donating information about an incident to a shared repository, such as online forums, specifying all technical details and anonymizing personal data in the logs might put a lot of burden on the contributor. So, often, neither the context of the incident nor the solutions were fully described, making grounding even more difficult.

At the broadest level, we saw Aaron using hacker Web sites to find examples of exploit tools to better understand how they worked. This was a case in which the interests of the attackers and security administrators overlapped, because both groups were concerned with learning how to attack machines. In this case, the resources for the attacker were obviously useful for the defender. Of course, the attackers knew this, and worked to separate their community from that of the defenders. Exploit code was often obfuscated, and Joe told us of some exploits that had been designed not to run within virtual machines to make it harder to analyze and protect against.

Without question, the job of the security administrators was difficult. Though personal satisfaction was great when a security incident got resolved, the work required extreme attention to detail. Unfortunately, their work was most noticed only when things went wrong and when compromised machines and accounts made news.

Sharing Tools Locally and Globally

On our second visit four months later, the worldwide security incident was still going on. Though the center itself had not been attacked for some time, Joe was still on the case. This time, we happened to visit on a relatively quiet week. Aaron reported that it was an unusual Monday, with no significant alerts or warnings from the weekend:

> **Aaron**: Today is a very quite day. Mondays are not like this...

That was a problem. In the world of a security administrator, even the absence of warnings could be a sign of an attack. Discussing the weekend with Tom, Aaron reported that the logs were bigger than usual, but no particular alerts were triggered:

> **Aaron**: Tom, I went through pretty much all the TCP dumps. It is mostly scans and internal traffic. So it looks fairly okay, right now. There are some SSH scans, but those are the typical ones. So I think we should be okay on this machine. [...] We wanted to see what exactly happened because we haven't seen any notification, nothing over the weekend. It has been a quiet weekend, so why?

In this, Aaron referred to logs generated by *honeypots,* bait systems designed to lure attackers into compromising them. They had installed honeypots on four machines, and monitored and logged all network traffic related to them. The four machines were not in actual use but were loaded with files and services to make them look like real systems in use, so that they might be of interest to attackers. By having a small number of computers that were vulnerable and closely monitored, Aaron's team could observe the tools and techniques attackers used, and they could prepare for attacks on real systems.

Aaron's honeypots made use of the resources at HoneyNet (www.honeynet.org), a community effort at creating and providing tools to set up honeypots and analyze the data they generated. HoneyNet also supported education in analyzing attacks by providing a "scan of the month," capturing some nefarious activity and offering a prize for the best solutions.

In fact, during our visit, we observed a meeting between Joe's team and one of the HoneyNet contributors discussing the available data-capture and analysis tools, and the needs and experiences of Joe's site.

When a honeypot indicated some activity, Aaron would investigate by looking at the Argus network logs, which recorded details for every network connection for every computer at the university. The Argus data included the time, type of network traffic, and source and destination addresses. With thousands of computers continually using the network, the logs contained millions of records such as:

```
01 Nov 04 00:00:24 F rtcp 111.111.192.16.4610 ->
123.123.100.5.25 O INT
```

Given the sheer volume of data, it was not practical to analyze the logs manually, so Aaron often created ad hoc command-line tools using text-processing commands like *grep* and *awk*. In these logs, it was difficult to trace a specific pattern of communication between two different systems, because these would appear as numerous entries at different places in the chronological log file. To automate that process, Aaron had written a shell script called "flows.sh" that produced several custom aggregations of the data. The script took the IP address of a single computer as input and produced statistics of traffic involving that computer, such as subnet count, number of external IP addresses and ports, number of internal IP addresses and ports, and detailed information on the top IP addresses and ports used. The script was fairly simple, not much more complex than the ad hoc processing he often did, but embedding the commands in a script was a big improvement:

> **Aaron**: I started working on this script, which basically translates all the flows into TCP flows…It is fairly difficult to find out machines, like I am tracking 111.111 to 123.123, so it goes this port to this port, so next time, I will have to go and see where is next, where is next, so…This thing [flows.sh] just linearizes everything and makes it very easy after that. This is just a bash shell script. It does grep. It is fairly straightforward grep'ing and awk'ing, but it makes a lot of difference. What I have done here is also try to find out some statistics, like, how many IP addresses are communicating, just in case a machine has a worm or virus and starts a…picks one

internal address and scans thousands others. I immediately see that. It is also adding the byte count and stuff like that, like how many ports, what are the...then it resolves the ports...So, it is pretty handy. I use it a lot of times.

Given the output of the script (Figure 7.4), he used command-line tools to further process and enhance the output, with commands like:

```
for a in `cat as.o' | awk '{print $2}' -; do echo $a;
host $a | awk '{print $5}' -; done
```

As we saw with other sysadmins, Aaron kept a series of cheat sheets with names such as "vi substitute commands," "performing Unix

```
Stage1: grep -v [I,D[ 111.111.192.160.o
Stage2: grep -w [I,D]
Stage 3: q S
Stage 4 q\* S
Stage 5: Now cat init & cleaning data
Stage 6: Computing Iniital Stats
[-] subnet count: 2
[-] # external IP addressL 2
[-] # external Ports in communication: 1
[-] # internal IP's in communication: 6
[-] # internal ports in communications: 4
Do you want to view detail statistics [ Top
10 subnets + IP address )?
[-] Top 10 subnets [ Count Subnet]:
1 239.255
1 209.132
[-] Top 10 IP address:
1 239.255.255.250
1. 209.132.177.100
[-] Internal IP Address:
2 123.123.100.5
1 123.123.96.107
1 123.123.41.154
2 123.123.100.6
1 123.123.100.4
1 123.123.100.3
[-] Top traffic IP Address:
5438 2592 209.142.177.100
4092 0 239.255.255.250
```

FIGURE 7.4. Output from Aarons "flows" script, showing statistics on network communication.

```
env
who
ps -efl
ifconfig -a
ifconfig -s
cat /etc/hosts
cat/etc/resolv.conf
cat /etc/passwd
cat /etc/shado
netstat -anp
lsof -P-i -n
lsof
cat /proc/meminfo
cat /proc/mounts
cat /proc/swaps
cat /etc/fstab
ls/proc |sort -n |grep -v [a-xA-Z] | while read PID
do
   echo "ProcessID $PID:"
   echo "/proc/$PID/cmdline:"
   cat /proc/$PID/cmdline
   echo
   echo
   echo "/proc/$PID/environ:"
   cat /proc/$PID/environ
```

FIGURE 7.5. Aaron's cheat sheet for performing Unix forensics.

forensics," "TripWire commands," "TCPDump commands," "running exploits," "Linux commands," "awk, argus commands," "installing AFS," and so on (Figure 7.5).

Aaron used his script and an assortment of ad hoc command-line tools to investigate the logs thoroughly, eventually deciding that the weekend really *had* been quiet, with no attacks going on. It appeared to us that the flows.sh script was very handy for Aaron. He used it several times and it helped improve his productivity because he no longer needed to navigate large network logs by hand. He designed the output of this script to have just the right kind of information. The script was in his site's shared repository, so others could use or improve it. Aaron also described plans to improve the script to do more proactive and real-time analysis on the network data to better monitor patterns as they occurred and to make it more widely useful. In its current state, however, the script was probably best suited to the particular needs of Aaron's group alone.

Using and Developing Community Tools

Joe's team put considerable effort into continuously scanning their systems for problems. They used a wide variety of open-source tools and community-developed plug-ins for publicly available software, including nmap (for network exploration and security auditing), Nessus (a vulnerability scanner, which later became a closed source), Bro (an automated intrusion detection system), and NfSen (a net flow data analysis and display tool, more general and richer than Aaron's script). These tools had been created by fellow security administrators and software engineers, and, thus, they were well aligned with the needs of Joe's team—and they were open source, so Joe and his colleagues could inspect the code to verify and understand exactly how they worked.

Joe's team used Nessus to scan computers on their network for open ports, software versions, and configurations to identify known and potential security problems. Nessus had a plug-in architecture that allowed users to create specific vulnerability checks. New plug-ins appeared almost every day as new vulnerabilities were discovered.

> **Aaron**: So what those guys [Nessus contributors] are doing are, like, whenever a new vulnerability comes in, they write plug-ins for it. So, every now and then I will go and update the plug-ins.

Because he found no signs of an ongoing attack so far that week, Aaron scanned the systems for potential vulnerabilities in commonly used software, such as SSH, MySQL, and BIND (DNS). Before performing the scans, Aaron sent e-mail to other administrators to let them know that he would be doing scans on the network. He identified which systems the scans would originate from so that other administrators could ignore any alerts that might be triggered as a result; such a scan would increase the load on scanned machines and could appear like an attack. At least they would know the source of increased activity on their systems.

Just before Aaron was about to launch the first scan, he got a message on the MOO from Jake, who had read Aaron's e-mail about the system-wide scan. Jake suggested that Aaron run nmap first, which performed a much less intensive scan. Aaron was particularly interested in SSH versions below a certain level, and nmap could pinpoint these more quickly. He could then run the more intrusive Nessus scan on a smaller set of machines which have the version of SSH they thought were vulnerable. Aaron told us that running Nessus could take five or six hours and it would generate a fairly detailed report that might be too much for their purposes, at least for the initial phase. Reducing the number of machines to scan was important not only because it would reduce Aaron's work, but also because of its impact on the network and on the systems being scanned. In the past, there had been a lot of complaints from users about this kind of broad scanning.

On one occasion, the complaint was not just that there was a significant performance impact but also that some of the plug-ins Aaron used in Nessus were dangerous. In fact, one of the plug-ins he used gained root access on vulnerable machines and changed host names. It was not a malicious plug-in, but one that apparently tested a potential vulnerability by literally exploiting it. So when Aaron asked Jake about whether he should run all the plug-ins, they recalled this, the so-called "mowgli incident."

```
Jake whispers to Aaron, "probably, I suppose it could
cause unexpected results. test it on a small subset of
systems sometime to see, or try it on any systems that
come back as vulnerable."
Aaron whispers to Jake, "yes, it might result in
something similar to mowgli incident. i will disable
dangerous plug-ins and then run them on the ones which
come out vulnerable."
```

Aaron devoted significant time and attention to choosing the plug-ins this time around. For some, he even examined the source code to see if there was anything unusual. Aaron had never written a plug-in, but he said he would if he had more time. Others in the community wrote plug-ins, which Aaron simply downloaded and installed on their Nessus system:

> **Aaron**: I just download them. I ran Nessus update and brings you plug-ins. I was reading about it but never decided to write it. There are a lot of them. There are 4,941 plug-ins, which is good but you do not know what exactly they are running.

This was a problem. There were just too many plug-ins written by too many people. How could Aaron know which ones to trust?

Past experience suggested that he should take care to examine them in advance. Fortunately, most plug-in scripts were easy to understand. Most plug-ins essentially did a pattern search on software version, configuration files, and the like. Referring to one, Aaron quickly identified what it did:

> **Aaron**: It is probably checking for version or something. And then, going and searching for this pattern, and then it is showing a warning. Once you determine what pattern or what particular signature could be used for an exploit you can go ahead and write plug-ins like that. Basically it is executing all these scripts one after another.

Other plug-ins were more complicated. He checked those before running them.

When the Nessus scan completed, Aaron wrote e-mails to others telling them that the reports had been copied to a shared directory. Though he had not gone through the reports in detail, he had already identified three machines that would require further investigation.

Though Joe's team was only a user of the Nessus tool, they contributed to other community tools. They created scripts for improving the output of Bro that had been included in the public release. They also created a number of other tools that were only shared with trusted members of the community. (Not surprisingly, if the attackers know what you use to monitor, they will try to work around it.) For the trusted community, Joe's team created and shared Bro policy files and incident data, NfSen modules for detecting certain network traffic patterns, and a user profiling tool to detect when attackers had taken over a user's account. It is clear that community-created tools were an indispensible part of Joe and Aaron's work, and they, in turn, gave back to the community. Unfortunately, trust could be a significant impediment in the evolution of tools, as evidenced by the mowgli incident. This was an important lesson for Aaron, which taught him to verify what he was running and not take just anything from the community.

System Administration across Communities

Communities operate at many levels in IT. At the lowest level, we saw Joe, Aaron, and their colleagues collaborating closely via the MOO and face-to-face on immediate problems, collecting and sharing information needed for evaluating alerts. Within the university as a whole, we saw more general discussions via the MOO on topics such as how machines had been infected by MyDoom. We also heard that the MOO could become extremely busy during university-wide incidents such as virus outbreaks, because security administrators from different parts of the university would coordinate their efforts at containing the problem. At a broader level, we saw a community of trusted colleagues across several institutions deal with ongoing attacks, sharing knowledge and tools via phone and e-mail. Finally, at the broadest level, we saw interaction through community-generated Web sites, discussion groups, and open-source projects.

Interactions and tasks were somewhat different at the different levels. Within Joe's group, interactions centered on problem solving and information sharing as part of tasks such as evaluating alerts or deciding the best way to scan for a certain vulnerability. Effective grounding was essential, but there was already much shared context among group members. In fact, members of Joe's group deliberately replicated one another's' work to make sure that nothing fell through the cracks. The group also engaged in a longer-term accumulation of knowledge in the form of a system for tracking attacks on their machines and better understanding longer term trends and patterns. Communication took place primarily in real-time, face-to-face, via phone or using the MOO. Tools shared within the team, such as Aaron's flows script, were relatively basic and specific to their particular tasks. Thus, grounding was less of an issue, because the team collectively shared a lot of context. This helped ease the burden on communication, particularly when deeply technical matters were discussed. The context also simplified tool use and development: Aaron used his cheat sheets as templates to build new commands by combining them in different ways, based on the current need, though this was not easily transferred beyond his own group, because the scripts and commands had a lot of their context built in.

At the scale of the university, the community was less concerned with immediate problem solving and more engaged in information sharing (e.g., "I'm starting a scan now," or, "how do you think the MyDoom worm is getting in?"). The examples we saw of longer-term accumulation of knowledge were in the form of policy documents, which changed relatively slowly, being updated every year or two. Communication for information sharing occurred primarily via the MOO, an excellent medium for ongoing discussion (given its recorded history of conversations).

We found the category of "trusted colleagues" to be unique to security administration: communities of administrators brought together by human adversaries from whom information must be withheld (Haber, Kandogan & Maglio, 2011). Trusted colleagues worked together to coordinate responses to the ongoing worldwide attack, sharing details of attacks and machines involved to trace the attackers and to patch the vulnerabilities. Joe's group also shared various intrusion detection tools only with their trusted colleagues because broader distribution would permit attackers to bypass detection. Sharing information about honeypots was also restricted to trusted colleagues because a honeypot only works when its true nature is hidden. We saw communication within the trusted community taking place by phone and encrypted e-mail.

At the broadest level, the community was oriented primarily toward sharing information and tools. Security e-mail lists and Web sites kept administrators abreast of the latest threats and provided samples of exploit code and vulnerability patches. Open source projects, such as Bro, and publicly available plug-ins for Nessus provided Joe's team with powerful tools. They also allowed Joe's team to contribute back to the community with scripts and refinements to help address new attacks and vulnerabilities. Communication at this level goes on at a slower pace, with requests and responses on a discussion Web site separated by hours or days, and with new tools released days or months apart. Equally slow was the evolution of tools. It took time to build community tools, particularly in security administration where trust is key, not only in contributions to community tools but also in use of community tools. Appropriate cautionary steps were taken before running such a tool, as evidenced by Aaron's careful examination of the plug-ins for Nessus.

It is clear that the community of practice surrounding security administration was a critical resource for Joe and his team. It provided the tools, knowledge, and coordination necessary to accomplish their tasks, both locally and globally. The same was true throughout the other stories in this book. Close collaboration among various specialists is needed to solve the problems that arise hour-by-hour, whereas the

> **Box 7.2 Observations for Design—Joe and Aaron**
>
> The story of Joe and Aaron shows both the importance of and the complexities inherent in community interactions. We saw sysadmins share knowledge and insight in groups, organizations, and worldwide communities of practice. For security administrators specifically, sharing was limited because they were engaged in a kind of information warfare: They need to share information with friends and keep information from enemies, and so trusted communities played an important role. Because of the high stakes—small attacks can spread quickly if they are not caught early—it was useful to have multiple team members doing the same work in parallel to help ensure nothing fell through the cracks. Though many automated tools were used to gather information for intrusion detection, it seems human judgment was still required to make the final decision about whether suspicious activity was in fact evidence of an attack.
>
> As in most of the stories in the book, we saw Joe and Aaron's team actively creating their own tools. We also saw them adopt, customize, and rely heavily on community-developed open-source tools. These tools were often designed and used by fellow sysadmins, supported by a community of practitioners, and they were available at no cost. Joe and Aaron described how many commercial security products were out of reach, given their limited university budget. The administrators we observed made few contributions back to open-source communities, probably because they lacked the time, resources, or skills required to create robust general tools.

broader community accumulates the knowledge and tools to manage systems for the longer term. The complexity and rapidly changing nature of IT systems means that there is a huge body of knowledge related to their management; when a system administrator sees an unfamiliar error message or a strange configuration issue, it is often necessary to consult the worldwide community to find an answer from someone who has dealt with it before. Similarly, effective and appropriate tools for system administration require considerable knowledge and effort to create. There is a big gap between one individual's script and a tool that can be used by many people at many sites. Community-developed tools can help bridge that gap, permitting individuals to make smaller contributions, with everybody benefiting from those who have the time and resources to build general tools.

8

Findings and Lessons

This book tells the story of IT management through first-hand observations of those who manage IT, the sysadmins and others on the front lines of IT service delivery. We started with people. Sysadmins play a key role in making IT work. They are knowledge workers, and IT management is knowledge work—configuring, troubleshooting, optimizing, and protecting computer systems—and requires individual skills and expertise. However, beyond technical knowledge, given massive scale, complexity, and risk, IT management requires communication and coordination of work among many individuals. Therefore, sysadmins must communicate and coordinate not only content—what they did and what they observed on the systems—but also process—who does the work, when, and how. They do this through grounding, the basic cognitive and social process whereby multiple parties establish mutual knowledge, understanding, and assumptions (Clark, 1996; Clark & Brennan, 1991; Klein et al, 2005). This process of grounding requires attending to and giving evidence of what others know and think second-by-second during a conversation. In this process, both the purpose—what people are trying to accomplish—and medium of communication—which mechanisms people use to communicate, for example, phone, face-to-face, and so forth—play a critical role in effective communication. The basic principles of grounding apply not only to communication among people but also between people and systems and between people and artifacts such as documents (Brennan, 1998; Clark, 1999), though the process is for the most part one-sided in that only people try to attend to what they think the system is doing, what they think the document is referring to, what assumptions were coded into the system, and so on. As with person-to-person interaction, people engage in a grounding process with systems as they test their understanding by interacting with systems and observing system output.

Organizations help facilitate coordination, transfer, and transformation of information and work. They help sysadmins establish common ground with their co-workers and with their systems. The goal is to provide a working IT infrastructure, and organizations must do this in a consistent manner for many customers, across many sysadmins in different groups, with different responsibilities, and working at different times. Practices are established within organizations to support grounding, ensuring that customer requirements are translated into an actionable form for front line workers, and that sysadmins have a common understanding of what is going on. Sometimes, common ground is formalized in agreements (e.g., SLAs), processes, practices, and tools, often using standardization to improve interoperability and consistency. Beyond organizations, communities of practice, loose collections of specialists working together, usually informally, solve problems and advance their craft (Orr, 1996; Wenger, 2000).

Information technology management work is also embedded in broader social, business, and technology contexts, and what we observed was not the result merely of tools and practices of a single individual but of organizations and communities, created, inherited, and evolved across time and space. Business and technology, both very dynamic, change and grow more complex, drive professional specialization of administrators, and in turn drive the need for better communication and grounding. Business and technology pressures over time demand changes to tools and practices, to the structure and processes of organizations, and to the grounding process itself. That is, as IT evolves, so too does its management.

We see the evolution of IT management as similar to the evolution of ideas and practices as memes (Dawkins, 1989), and of technology (Arthur, 2009). Technologies evolve combinatorially as new technologies inherit parts from older ones, combined in novel ways to create value, and new technologies themselves become parts of future technologies, in a kind of recursive cycle of innovation. New businesses emerge from new technologies, and businesses evolve in response to pressures from the technological environment. Likewise technologies evolve under pressure from the business environment and change over time. We observed this same sort of process in IT management tools and practices. Simply put, sysadmins frequently innovate, developing their own tools and practices adapted to their complex and idiosyncratic environments. They adapt their tools and practices to changes in the technical environment—what technologies are used, how they are deployed and managed—and to changes in the business environment—what uses and purposes exist for these technologies. Sysadmins combine existing tools and practices to fit new purposes. The tools and practices that work effectively survive, providing the basis for new generations of tools and practices. Organizations and communities help facilitate evolution of individual innovations into more broadly adopted tools, practices, processes, conventions, and standards.

Individuals, organizations, communities, tools, practices, processes, and standards all play critical roles in making IT systems work. In fact, it was impossible to understand many specific cases of IT management without taking account of how the distributed system of people and artifacts worked together to accomplish their tasks. Much of the time, understanding and the ability to act lay not within individuals but rather among individuals and artifacts in a distributed cognitive system (Hutchins, 1995, 1996; see also Klein et al, 2005; Maglio, et al., 2008; Wright et al., 2000). We showed how common ground was fragmented, how information moved through networks of people and technologies, and how appropriate action depended on the integrated operation of all involved.

What is the moral of the story? How does IT management actually work? Our observations describe highly complex, large-scale, and often-idiosyncratic environments in which people perform lengthy and risky operations given dynamic requirements and dynamic configurations. System administrators cope through specialization, innovation in tools and practices, and standardization. However, these coping strategies interact: (a) Technical complexity leads to specialization, which demands communication and coordination between individuals and teams, as workers and organizations spend considerable time establishing common ground with each other and with their systems. (b) Technical complexity, technical change, and idiosyncratic systems demand innovations from a variety of actors, with system administrators creating tools and practices optimized for their own environments, communities of practice developing broadly applicable tools and best practices, and organizations engaging in standardization. (c) IT management practices—tools, organizations, policies, standards—and information technologies co-evolve, driven by individual and organizational needs, incrementally adapting and institutionalizing those adaptations that enable effective management as technology and business changes. This has practical implications. One is that collaboration is critical. Another is that local innovation in tools and practices is necessary because of the idiosyncrasies of complex IT systems. There are more. In the rest of this chapter, we discuss the overall lessons we learned (summarized in Box 8.1).

> **Box 8.1 Observations for Design**
>
> Throughout the book, we pointed out a number of observations relevant to the design of tools and practices for sysadmins. Our stories also showed many existing tools that do a poor job supporting sysadmins' needs, and which required sysadmins to fill in the gaps. For one thing, sysadmins rely on the same communication tools as everybody else: e-mail, phone, and instant messaging. Yet these do a poor job helping to communicate the complexities of real-time system state. For another, error messages—and sometimes, success messages—all too frequently do a lousy job conveying information to the sysadmin. We saw many cases in which messages lacked sufficient detail or were reported too late. At other times, messages came in such volume that it was impossible to extract any meaning from them. For yet another, sysadmins commonly rehearse complex operations, but we saw no formal tooling support for this.
>
> Beyond specific tools and practices, we made a number of general observations about the nature of system administration work. Here, we summarize the most important of them. First, modern IT systems are complex aggregations of multiple components, which are often managed by different people in different organizations using different tools. In this context, it is often difficult for any one individual to develop an understanding of the system as a whole. Second, IT management is inherently collaborative.
>
> *(countinued)*

> Multiple teams work together to accomplish local goals, larger organizations direct broader work activities, and worldwide communities of practice influence activities at all levels through best practices and shared tools. Third, sysadmins frequently engage in lengthy, multistep operations requiring hours or days to complete. For this and other reasons, the work is risky, requiring sysadmins to develop and adopt many risk-mitigation practices. Fourth, tool building is ubiquitous among sysadmins. They often have to create their own methods for handling the volume, complexity, and risk of their work, and to maintain awareness of past and ongoing work, whether within organizations, across organizations, or with customers. Finally, although much sysadmin work depends on standards and best practices, human expertise is usually required to ensure that overall goals are met. Total automation cannot be the end goal for system administration.

System Administrators Depend on Collaboration

Information-technology management is complex technologically, organizationally, and socially. Technical complexity leads to specialization in expertise and ultimately to complex organizational structures. Establishment of common ground is critical, and so the key to effective IT management is effective collaboration and coordination of action among specialists and among organizations.

The story of George (chapter 2) demonstrated the need for collaboration and coordination. At the start, George's task was seemingly simple. All he needed to do was to create another instance of a Web server and connect it to other pieces of software—matching a working example he already had. However, his mental model of the system was wrong to begin with, and this flawed mental model affected both his interactions with systems (how he configured systems to accomplish his task) and his interactions with others (joint actions aimed at achieving mutual understanding). Of all the people he worked with, only his colleague Ted had direct access to the systems—Ted did not have to depend on

George to ground his understanding of system state—he could see what was happening first hand. This enabled him to find the problem, but he still needed to convince George. In the end, Ted relied on his personal relationship with George to shake up his mental model and establish a new common ground about the system's state.

We watched Dot (chapter 3) upgrade an existing Web application. She had to rely on two different sets of instructions, one from remote application developers and another from her local team. In this case, she had to ground her understanding of the process from two different and sometimes conflicting sources of information: one specific to the application at hand, yet created by developers working in a different environment; the other more general, but created specifically for her production environment. Like most people receiving conflicting instructions, Dot looked at both, chose one, and only switched when she ran into trouble. When error messages appeared, she needed to reconcile the two sets of instructions against the behavior of the system. We can imagine Dot was engaged in a process of grounding with the application developers (via application instructions), local administrators (via the local instructions), and her systems (via commands, output, and GUIs), to establish a mental model of the process (Brennan, 1998; Clark, 1999). The developers specified application-specific requirements; the local documentation provided site-specific requirements; the systems themselves embodied a model of the way they work; and the various interfaces, including their configuration settings, contained clues to that model.

In the story of the crit-sit (chapter 3), we saw continuous face-to-face, instant messaging and phone interactions among a large group of sysadmins located both in the war room and elsewhere. They all shared the goal of solving a critical but intermittent problem. Their approach was to work individually to determine the state of each system component, and then work closely together, joining their findings, ideas, and theories to form a collective sense of what was going on. At any point in the war room, there were several conversations as people developed theories, exchanged information about system state, and shared ideas for possible fixes. They were constantly seeking to develop common ground with one another and with their systems. As the system came close to the point of failure, we saw them generating and analyzing a seemingly endless stream of traces and log files looking for clues. Data from different components were pasted into the common chat room so everyone could look for patterns. When the system did fail, they investigated all the different components, trying to understand the state of each to see how it might be contributing to the failure. Having everybody together in a single room was the best way for them to develop, test, and verify their common understanding of the system.

In all these stories, grounding is the basic cognitive and social process (Clark, 1996). It is the basis of all human communication. It establishes shared beliefs, shared references, and ultimately mental models of other people and of the world. It is the most basic of coordinated activities, requiring joint action among multiple parties to establish shared understanding (Woods, 1988). We saw system administrators collaborating with other system administrators, either face-to-face or through a communications tool such as phone, e-mail, or instant messaging, or through artifacts created by system administrators, potentially distributed in time and space. System administrators coordinate and negotiate their understanding with one another and across organizations. We saw a number of patterns, including a single responsible hub with many independent collaborators (George in chapter 2, Dot in chapter 3, Amy in chapter 6, and Henry in chapter 6), a pair of responsible people at the hub of collaboration (Christine and Mike, in chapter 4), distributed responsibility and independent interactions (as seen in the crit-sit in chapter 3), a chain of independent interactions (storage allocation for Henry and Ryan in chapter 6), and parallel responsibility and repeated work (Joe and Aaron in chapter 7). Each of these structures has advantages and disadvantages in terms of cost, flexibility, and effectiveness for different tasks, yet in all cases, the underlying goal is to get the right information to those who need to manage specific parts of the IT infrastructure.

The lesson is that collaboration, coordination of action, and sense making are fundamental to system administration. Collaboration among individuals is often free form and improvisational, but it can be aided by appropriate tools for communication and situational awareness. Improved tools for easily visualizing and sharing system state and for collaboration and coordination between sysadmins would go a long way toward improving effectiveness and efficiency. The focus should be on tools to support what sysadmins actually do (Haber & Bailey, 2007; Haber, Kandogan, Cypher, Maglio & Barrett, 2005; Kandogan et al. 2005).

System Administrators Create and Adapt Tools and Practices

Everywhere we went, we saw sysadmins creating their own tools and practices. All too often the off-the-shelf tools were not up to the task of managing complex IT systems. This resulted from the idiosyncratic structure of IT systems: collections of numerous components supplied by various vendors. There are so many ways that a system can be put together that vendor-provided tools could not handle all the different ways each component might be used. Therefore, sysadmins have to innovate to fill the gaps, creating their own tools and practices and sharing them with others. These innovations may be broadly adopted and improved. Tools and practices evolve slowly through incremental changes made by sysadmins and others under continuous selection pressures in the technical and business environment, including pressure from many stakeholders, such as customers, developers, administrators, service providers, and end users.

The crit-sit (chapter 3) clearly demonstrated the complex technical and social environments sysadmins work in. In that story, the overall system was so complex and idiosyncratic—with several application servers, Web servers, databases, network load balancers, firewalls, and so forth—it was necessary to bring together a variety of experts in a single conference room for many weeks to debug a subtle problem. Though component vendors provided management tools, none provided a sufficiently detailed view of the entire system. No off-the-shelf tool was good enough to create a holistic view of the system. Diana faced a similar situation (chapter 5), having to write her own scripts for migrating data between two Hierarchical File Systems (HFSs); using a single HFS was uncommon, and using a system of multiple HFSs was extremely rare.

Sysadmins have no choice but to deal with this complexity themselves, because they usually have little say in what systems or vendors are chosen to implement a solution. As we heard from Henry (chapter 6): "They (customers) want to board an HP server, we don't tell them 'no.' They want to use VMWare, we say, 'fine.'" Organizations try to bring some order to this complexity by enforcing standards to improve consistency and to reduce costs, as we saw with Dot (chapter 3) and Patrick (chapter 4), but even then, there was significant flexibility in the way building blocks for Web applications might be configured. Shawn and his colleagues (chapter 5) were responsible for maintaining servers with the latest vendor patches, and because the vendor-provided automated tool did not meet customer requirements, they created their own patch database and Web site, a "living tool" that evolved over time to keep track of patch levels and monitor policy compliance. They also created patch depot servers to address local network and performance limitations, and they wrote their own scripts to automate patch deployment while following the geographic and process requirements of their site.

Christine (chapter 4) used a practice similar to extreme programming (Beck, 1999)—sitting side-by-side with Mike to take advantage of his knowledge and his second pair of eyes to spot mistakes. This practice had been informally adopted by the DBAs at her site as a means to reduce the risk of data loss and unscheduled database outages. Furthermore, she rehearsed the task on a series of test systems, a formally adopted practice for reducing risk. This practice could not have existed without organizational support, given the expensive infrastructure required. Another important tool for Christine was *crontab,* used to launch database backups. Crontab itself was simply a utility for executing system tasks at regular intervals. Christine's group had tailored it with a wide variety of commonly executed database commands, turning it from a simple utility into a kind of menu-based command-execution environment. This ensured that commands would be run with the precise settings required for the site, with the added benefit that execution could be delayed for a few minutes, allowing time to correct errors. These features gave her a level of comfort not available in vendor-provided database management tools.

We saw a range of tools and practices in terms of flexibility, adoption, and use. Some were personal and transient, used once and discarded. Some were reused many times by the individuals who created them and by others in the local organization. Some were very sophisticated with automation capabilities. Some were simple collections of commands and human-readable instructions, gathered over time by individuals and sometimes shared with others. Some tools and practices were included in guidelines and architecture designs, grew to become standards, and eventually established as processes. In some cases, adoption was informal. For example, Christine obtained a document with instructions from a repository, and as she applied it, she annotated and updated the instructions to provide the benefit of her experience to future system administrators, finally depositing her updated document back into the repository. There was no review process. By contrast, Patrick had an elaborate review process that governed the evolution of tools, practices, and guidelines of work. Some innovative practices occurred at the individual level, such as Christine suffixing log and script file names with her name. Some organizational practices were developed locally, such as Henry and Ryan's organizational structure. Others come from an outside group, such as GWA and GNA (chapter 4).

In all these activities, we see something like an evolutionary process governing the innovation, dissemination, and selection of tools and practices used in IT management. This makes sense, as technologies themselves evolve over time as combinations of simpler technologies (Arthur, 2009). As diversity increases, the practices and tools for managing IT become more complex, too. It seems to us that sysadmins follow Arthur's principle of innovation by combination in putting together what is at hand to create new tools and practices, which become instrumental in accomplishing their jobs. A script is literally a combination or sequence of discrete commands. An architectural standard describes a fixed way to combine technologies together into a system. An organizational structure is a combination of people and roles aimed at ensuring that work gets done effectively. A process is a set of discrete operations put together to successfully accomplish some goal.

The lesson is that organizations and sysadmins try to find the tools and practices they need. If the tools and practices they find are not good enough, they will create something that is. Sysadmins have to create and adapt their own tools and practices to manage idiosyncratic systems, changing technologies, and evolving customer requirements. It is not optional; it is not simply a good thing to do. Adapting tools and practices is necessary. The main management consequence is that tool adaptation—development— ought to be a supported and valued activity for sysadmins.

Organizations Orchestrate Information Flow and Work

Large scale IT management is organizationally complex. Systems are big, comprised of many different parts, and the management structure is the same. The scale and complexity of organizational structure serves a purpose: efficiently providing consistent IT services to many customers using sysadmins with different backgrounds and skills, working across different shifts and geographies. Organizational structures help ensure information is transmitted effectively and established processes and standards are followed (Meum, Monteiro & Ellingsen, 2011; Walsh, 1991).

In the story of Henry and Ryan (chapter 6) from MSS, we saw grounding at an organizational level. Different organizations exist because IT delivery has a number of distinct domains, each with its own specific tasks and necessary skills and expertise; for example, selling storage services is different from designing and provisioning systems, which is, in turn, different from allocating storage and day-to-day operations (Burgess, 2004). It makes sense to separate these domains into different organizations—yet the organizations must carefully coordinate their work to ensure correct and timely service delivery. Ryan's job was to take customer storage requests, determine how best to satisfy them, and transform those requests into a form that Henry's team in the operations center could implement. To reduce potential misunderstandings, Ryan and Henry's teams established standard spreadsheets to describe storage allocation designs, using conventions, such as a limited set of storage allocation sizes (LUN sizes) and the same port numbers on the red and green fabrics, a symmetry that made the design easier to understand and implement correctly. Henry's team also established standard practices, such as verifying the design before implementation to ensure that problems could be addressed while the designers were available, and developing an elaborate 4-week process to coordinate upgrades to ensure customers and operations were aligned about which changes would occur and when.

IT management involves extensive coordination between individuals and organizations. We saw organizations achieving common ground through standardized tools and practices, coordinating the flow of information and determining what, when, and how to do things. In a world of complex, interconnected systems, with specialized experts and distributed responsibility, grounding between people, organizations, and systems is a prerequisite for successful IT management. As systems become ever-more complex over time, tools and practices to support coordination and understanding will play an increasingly important role in IT management.

The lesson is that organizations can create and orchestrate the flow of information to enable efficient and effective system administration. System administration is not simply the responsibility of individual sysadmins, but results from a distributed cognitive process. Organizational structures, with well-defined roles and responsibilities for individuals, play a critical role in IT management—getting the organization right will help get the system management right.

System Administrators Depend on their Communities

The work we saw system administrators do was not simply the result of individuals but of a community of practice, inherited across time and space (Wenger, 2000). As sysadmins configure or troubleshoot systems, they directly or indirectly benefit from the collective work of all those in their profession. The practice of system administration has developed over years through shared problem solving, development of tools, and coordination of work—through messages posted to online forums, attendance at conferences or local gatherings, and contributions to open-source projects (Orr, 1996; Lave & Wenger, 1990).

In the story of Aaron and Joe (chapter 7), we saw Aaron benefiting greatly from the security community, which worked together to report new incidents and to resolve incidents collectively. Aaron monitored several Web sites and e-mail lists for new vulnerabilities and used information posted by others to contain and stop attacks. They shared knowledge and strategies. They shared tools, software, scripts, and plug-ins. They shared patterns of attacks, even complete reports of security attacks with highly detailed analyses. We saw Joe collaborating closely with a community of security administrators at several sites to develop a coordinated response to a large-scale attack. Although these ad hoc communities were critical to their work, there were challenges to collaboration when information needed to be exchanged beyond local organizations (Gibson & Cohen, 2003; Hertzum et al., 2002; Kramer, 1999). Joe paid close attention to what he was sharing with whom, and always encrypted his messages. Sometimes, lack of shared objectives and lack of trust impeded effective collaboration, as we saw in Joe's effort to extract information from other universities. In nearly all the stories in this book, we saw communities playing a critical role in the work of sysadmins, from searching the Web for an error code that often leads to forum posts by sysadmins, to using open-source software for system monitoring developed collectively by the community. However, we saw few contributions (only in the case of Aaron and Joe, security administrators at a university data center) back to the community because most sysadmins we observed were in service organizations in which hours needed to be charged to a customer account.

Throughout our studies, the innovations our participants created were limited mainly to personal or organizational use. Clearly, there is a high barrier to broad adoption. Sysadmins often share innovations with colleagues, and some might even be adopted as a local standard. Yet bringing a tool or practice to general use requires a level of robustness, documentation, and support that was often beyond the abilities and resources of those we observed. Our interviews and surveys showed that a minority of system administrators had a degree in computer science, and few had the skills required to create large-scale robust systems suitable for general use. Furthermore, the system administrators we observed worked under tremendous time pressure, and, thus, they lacked the time and resources to go beyond what is needed for immediate use. For example, one DBA at the same site as Christine and Mike had created a Web-based system for monitoring every database table space at the site, but he told us he did not have enough time to work on it, as every hour of his day had to be charged to a single customer; there was no way to charge for generally useful infrastructure changes. Though none of the innovations we observed evolved into broadly useful tools, the existence of open-source administration tools and community information sites suggest that there is a path for locally developed tools and practices to reach the broader world—for sysadmins with the resources and expertise required.

The lesson is that those with the best understanding of the problems—the sysadmins—are not always in the best position to create broadly useful solutions. Additional training, resources, and rewards might help change that. Considering the importance of communities in IT management, we ought to support these communities in developing the necessary mechanisms for sharing and evolving innovations, and put the appropriate reward mechanisms in place to foster active communities and productivity gains in IT management.

Automation Cannot Replace System Administrators

Given the high cost of human labor and the high cost of human error, automation is often seen as the best approach for improving IT management—for example, *autonomic computing* aimed to develop systems that configure, manage, and heal themselves, according to high-level guidance provided by system administrators. People were expected to set policies, high-level statements of the scope, condition, utility, and goal of desired system behavior, which were then to be interpreted by the system to configure components, discover and correct errors, monitor and optimize resources, and proactively identify and protect systems from attacks (Kephart & Chess, 2003). Such policies were expected to embody system complexity, thereby reducing the need for grounding among system administrators and the need for low-level interaction with systems. It would reduce labor and the chance for error.

Policies exist in one form or another across all aspects of IT management. In our studies, we came across policies given as standards, guidelines, and rules in instructions, documents, and architecture diagrams, implemented via tools and processes, and enforced by SLAs (Kandogan et al., 2011). Consider Shawn's SLA-mandated patch policy ensuring systems were up to date every 120 days (chapter 5), storage designer Ryan's standard request and design document formats and network-port-assignment procedures (chapter 6), and security administrator Aaron's rule-based intrusion detection systems and his manual efforts verifying potential alerts (chapter 7). In all these examples, parts of a policy were automated to some degree, yet other parts required human judgment to evaluate and execute. Shawn needed to negotiate with customers about when to apply patches so as not to interfere with their work. Ryan needed to verify requests, especially when there was insufficient information provided. Aaron needed to collect lots of contextual information to determine whether alerts were really evidence of an ongoing attack. In general, we found that policies were written for people to follow, and as a result, they often omitted details, relying on contextual information and human judgment to decide whether a policy applied and how to achieve or implement the result. Furthermore, policies often conflicted, requiring people to arbitrate among them. It seems to us that the value of existing policies is that they *do not* specify every last detail, allowing people to determine how best to achieve their high-level goals.

Of course, automation does have a place in improving system administration. Automation makes it possible for people to manage increasingly complex systems (Burgess, 1998; Frisch, 2002; Barrett et al., 2005). Consider Aaron's rule-based network monitoring intrusion detection system (chapter 7)—it would be impossible to monitor a modern university network without such a tool. Consider Jimmy's elaborate, handcrafted scripting environment for managing change in a large retail chain (chapter 5)—it certainly improved the practices and effectiveness of the team. Automation is a hot topic in system management, and there have been several recent advances, particularly in configuration management (Burgess, 2006; Walberg, 2008). Yet improvements in automation seem only to just keep pace with increases in system scale and complexity. As better technology is adopted, reduction in amount of work may not follow; for example, studies of housework and household technology show that labor-saving devices—dishwashers, washing machines, electric appliances—do not actually reduce labor, but instead increase expectations for household cleanliness, quality, and variety of cooking, and so on (Cowan, 1985). Technology, and in particular automation, may change what people do, but not how much people do. It moves people up the value chain, requiring more expertise—rather than less—over time (cf. Levy & Murnane, 2004).

The lesson is that automation cannot replace system administrators. Information technology exists to serve human purposes. Automation facilitates scale; enabling management of larger, more complex systems. It is important and necessary, but it does not take away the role for human system administrators: people are needed to gather contextual information, arbitrate among conflicting policies, and ensure that IT systems achieve their intended purposes (see Kandogan et al., 2011).

Conclusion

In this book, we told the story of IT management. Really, we told stories about system administrators—about how individuals, groups, organizations, and communities work to configure, troubleshoot, optimize, and protect the computer infrastructure that modern society depends on. These stories show that system administrators work in a socially and technically complex environment. With complexity comes specialization. Administration tasks often involve numerous steps and multiple people, and work must be coordinated among people of different skills and expertise.

The stories also show how individuals, organizations, and communities create, adopt, and evolve tools and practices over time in a never-ending quest to improve the effectiveness of the complex socio-technical systems they are part of. Information technology management is dynamic, both in the short and long terms. System workloads and configurations change in response to day-to-day demand fluctuations and to overall market conditions. Configurations and customer requirements change daily, and errors and problems occur all the time. System administrators must always be vigilant, ready to react. Over the longer term, pressures from evolving technology, business, regulations, and globalization affect system administrator roles, responsibilities, goals, and concerns.

We focused on the front lines of IT management: individual sysadmins and their interactions with one another and with their systems as they coordinated activities and built common ground. We saw many tools, processes, and organizational structures that had been created or adopted to make grounding easier and more effective. For example, system administrators were organized into teams with similar skills and expertise, making grounding among team members easy given their common backgrounds. For tasks requiring common ground between sysadmins from a variety of backgrounds, we saw grounding aided by common practices, such as file and server naming conventions and standard document formats.

People also created innovative tools, practices, and organizational structures to achieve productivity gains in their complex and varied environments. Sysadmins often had to innovate simply because appropriate tools did not exist for a particular system configuration. These innovations were sometimes shared, evolving as they were adopted across broader communities and becoming useful in different technical, social, and business contexts. We saw many instances of local repositories of scripts and instructions shared with a group or organization, and standard practices developed and adopted across organizations and enterprises. Furthermore, though we did not see most of our participants producing many globally adopted tools, the existence of lots of open-source administration tools indicates that some innovations are shared across worldwide communities. There are barriers to broader sharing, however, as environments vary, and creating tools that work robustly in a range of environments requires resources and skills not available to many system administrators.

Is it really efficient to have sysadmins at each site creating their own tools and processes? This runs counter to the ideas of reuse and standardization, but may be unavoidable because of the idiosyncrasies of each system configuration. Perhaps the true value to an organization is in the development of skills and knowledge as sysadmins build, adapt, and enhance tools and processes for their given contexts. In creating tools, sysadmins learn about the technology, configuration, and specific customer requirements. More generally, they learn principles, approaches, and conventions that may be transferable to new situations. This learning makes them more adaptable, knowledgeable, and valuable to their organization. After all, IT service is knowledge-intensive, and knowledge is the key differentiator. The process of developing scripts, tools, and processes is an effective way of learning, creating, and distributing knowledge. So the real value is in *developing the people*, enhancing their knowledge and skills, which, in turn, allows them to deal more effectively with change. So local innovation is valuable not just for the short term benefits of the resulting artifacts, which help improve efficiency, effectiveness, and overall quality of service, but also for its longer-term benefit of building and leveraging institutional knowledge, growing new and valuable skills for individuals who can make the overall system of machines and people more resilient and adaptable to change.

We studied IT management mainly in the context of IT service delivery. In almost all cases, sysadmins and their organizations managed and ran IT infrastructure and applications for others. As such, our system administrators were embedded in complex service systems, arrangements of resources including people, technologies, organizations, and information that create value across organizational boundaries (Maglio, Srinivasan, Kreulen & Spohrer, 2006). Of course, people are *the* key resources, responsible for—well—everything! The capabilities and productivity of knowledge workers—those who can adapt to changing circumstances and interact effectively with others—separates winning firms from losing firms (Johnson, Manyika & Lee, 2005). Sysadmins are prototypical knowledge workers, standing between different organizations, negotiating day-to-day. They work hard to ground their understanding with their systems and their colleagues. They work hard to improve their environments, developing tools and organizations. They have a stake in their broader communities, aiming to improve not only their own situations but their colleagues' situations as well.

We were on an expedition. It took us back and forth across the United States many times over many years. We interviewed, surveyed, and observed sysadmins in many different settings. We found that fundamentally, they are knowledge workers, critical actors within their complex social and technical systems. They cope as best as they can with the complexity they face, improving themselves and their environments given the resources at hand. More precisely, across different types of sysadmins and different contexts of work, we found that (a) systems are complex, administration roles are specialized, and system administrators are always involved in a process of grounding to achieve a common understanding of the state of their systems; (b) IT systems are idiosyncratic combinations of many interacting components, meaning appropriate tools for managing whole systems are often not available and require sysadmins to innovate and create their own tools, practices, and organizational structures to support grounding and improve productivity; and (c) automation is a critical tool for helping sysadmins manage the ever-increasing complexity of IT systems, but sysadmins are needed to ensure that IT systems achieve human ends.

Epilogue: Where Are They Now?

The stories in this book come from a series of observations and interviews in data centers done between 2002 and 2007. Our participants were real people, doing real work in support of large IT infrastructures. In 2009 and 2010, we looked them up and found many working in the same organizations. Quite a few were willing to spend time with us to discuss how their work had changed since we first met. Throughout, we showed how communication, collaboration, change, and the evolution of tools and practices are important aspects of system administration work. These follow-up interviews show many specific changes, some good and some not so good.

Our follow-up interviews included George the Web administrator (chapter 2), Dot and one of her colleagues, both Web administrators (chapter 3), Diana the storage administrator (chapter 5), Ryan the storage architect (chapter 6), Amy the transition manager (chapter 6), and Joe and Aaron the security administrators (chapter 7).

George, Web Administrator

We began the book with the story of George—he was having a very bad day (chapter 2). At the time, George worked in "applications middleware support and delivery," part of a team located entirely at a single site. By 2009, he was part of a globally distributed "advanced architecture" team that supported high profile projects for internal and external customers. His work still involved the same kinds of Web applications, but he told us that operations had improved significantly:

> **George**: I am working with all those technologies still, very similar there. We do work in a bit of a different environment in

that the hosting infrastructure that we work in now is multisite, continuously available infrastructure. Basically, it's three-sited. Each site runs at 50 percent capacity. It kind of makes things nice because realistically speaking we can run off two sites and still be running at 100 percent capacity. This gives us the ability to bring sites down in the middle of the day, for instance, do our maintenance work, then bring it back up when we're done.

This multisite architecture significantly reduced the need for night and weekend changes. When night changes were required, having a globally distributed team meant that some part of the team could work on changes during regular business hours. Even more importantly, they developed and adopted a standard architecture across all projects to improve reliability and consistency:

> **George**: One of the first tasks that I remember being involved in when I joined the team was establishing a solid foundation for application architecture, and we developed reference architecture. That reference architecture that we thought up still exists today, and we do our best to abide by it for all our customers. That was the groundwork for the standardization effort, and I continue to work in the efforts related to standardization. It went as deep as simple file system and directory naming conventions. How do we ensure that we maintain that standardization and do things repeatedly in compliance with that standard? The obvious answer to that was automation. Scripts automate the tasks, so we know it's going to put this certain file in the appropriate directory, or it's going to configure the WebSphere global security to use the appropriate directory server for logins, or things like that.

George described having an active role in the standardization effort from its beginning. The resulting standards sounded extremely detailed, specifying everything from software versions to file-system-level details, yet this configuration consistency allowed them to automate processes, leading to operational consistency. It had to be kept up as tools and environments evolved over time:

> **George**:…an important thing to note that when you develop these tools, they're dynamic, they need to change

as the products change, and be upgraded as the products are upgraded.

Keeping scripts up to date was sometimes done by those who created the scripts, but that effort was also spread across the organization to help keep everybody familiar with the tools and technologies, and to train new people:

> **George:** In some cases we took these changes as a way we could train and educate people that weren't so familiar with scripting or the various products that we're working with. So we almost forced it upon others to get involved with these things, so it became an educational tool, we would say, "Let's give it to some one who doesn't know about it and let it be a learning experience."

We see George's organization had struck on two of the powerful forces we discussed: skills and standardization. It is critical to ensure that sysadmins know what they are doing, and keeping skills up through everyday work is a very effective way of training. Similarly, it is critical for costs to be kept low, and adopting consistent and standard IT practices is very effective way of doing this.

The tooling George relied on had evolved, too. When we first watched him, most tools had native Java-based console GUIs, which required additional effort to access over networks and through firewalls. George reported that now all those GUIs were Web-based, and considerably easier to access, yet he still preferred the command line:

> **George:** I tend to lean toward the command-line tools, because with our automation effort, it's obviously a lot more effective. Because we're working in a multisite environment, everything needs to be done on three sites, so rather than to click through and perform a process three times for each node and every site, we'll simply automate it and use tools like DSH, which will distribute a command to various nodes at the same time and execute it across all three sites.

George's organization had improved their tooling for collaboration and communication, both within his team, and also with customers.

For real-time communication and awareness, they had adopted Internet Relay Chat (IRC) (Oikarinen & Reed, 1993; see also Johri, 2011), and they used wikis (Leuf & Cunningham, 2001) for longer-term planning and coordination:

> **George**: Our primary communications tool is IRC, which is just a chat tool. What we have is multiple rooms: we have a main team room that everybody joins, and we have a main room for pages. So all our monitoring systems send alerts to a bot in that room, which displays any paging alerts related to systems that we're monitoring, display the alert in that page. In addition to that, we have specialized rooms related to customers. In some cases we even have customers that join our rooms. It's a pretty effective tool because you can literally monitor 6, 10, 12 different things going on in one screen. We also do use some wiki tools, mainly for calendaring, planning, things like that. A lot of our project managers put together wiki calendars and we share that with our customers, this helps us plan for upcoming deployments.

Here, we see George and his organization using improved tools and practices compared to our earlier observations. IRC improves on the previous instant messaging system in that IRC conversations persist, can be organized by topic, and be shared with customers and others outside the firewall. This made sense for Joe and Aaron (chapter 7), and it makes sense for George, too.

When we first observed George, he was relatively junior, and was having considerable trouble with the ad hoc configuration of a Web application. As his career matured, so did his environment, with improved communication and standard architectures, practices, and automation making his systems more manageable and enabling his group to work together more effectively.

Dot and Nora, Web Administrators

When we first observed Dot and her colleagues (chapter 3), she was a Web administrator, deploying and maintaining Web applications. Seven years later, she had moved to an architecture group because the Web administration group had been moved offshore. Most of her colleagues, such as Nora, moved to different companies,

> **Dot:** I would say that the majority of the people who are doing that kind of work are now in South America and India and China.

Dot's new architecture role was still related to Web applications, but her work focused on an earlier stage of the development process. She ensured that the developers followed all appropriate guidelines, used shared resources to the extent possible, used standard versions of the software, and so on.

Dot was part of a team of 20–30 architects, each working on 7–15 application projects at a time. Each project typically stretched over several months, resulting in an architecture diagram, a standardized document that showed how systems interact with each other, their physical locations as well as network locations, firewall configuration, and so on. Dot would then represent the development team in the architecture review board for final approval. Once approved, it would be implemented by the developers and deployed by offshore administrators.

We later learned that Dot's architecture team had been moved offshore as well. By contrast, Nora moved to a different company that had a government contract and was mandated to keep Web system administration onshore. Nora described her offshore counterparts, and of problems with turnover and organizational memory (Dignan 2010; Rai 2005):

> **Nora:** I worked with them extensively, all over the world, really…there's a lot of opportunity there, so these guys move from positions.…A lot of [institutional memory] is lost.

Nora described her new job as more flexible, particularly with respect to tools. They relied heavily on freeware tools that cost nothing and suited her work quite well:

> **Nora:** …we're using a bunch of freeware tools that cost nothing, that I think do the job twice as good. Let me give you an example. We're using a tool that's a freeware product out there called Puppet…I can have all my middleware installed. It's like less than 5 minutes. I've seen them give me a whole virtual machine in

20 seconds. It just kind of goes and picks the modules out of Puppet that I want, and bam, almost instantaneous gratification.

In Dot and Nora's updates, we see a different side of change than we saw in George's. For both, globally distributed teams are transforming the very nature of Web administration work. George noted improved practices and increased responsibilities. Dot and Nora noted jobs moving offshore, high turnover rates, and reduced organizational memory—changes that ultimately led them to new roles and new employers.

Diana, Storage Administrator

When we first met Diana, she was maintaining one of two huge HSM systems at a large government laboratory. Six years later, she was doing similar work, but her responsibilities had changed in unexpected ways, mostly the result of cost constraints. In addition to her regular system administration duties, she also occasionally had to do operator work, such as moving tapes from here to there. Likewise, for cost reasons, they had consolidated on a single HSM, in the process eliminating test systems, which had a negative impact on their practices:

> **Diana:** Back when we were running SAM, we had a nice large system, and it was configured to begin with a test system, and we tested everything before we did anything on the production system. And since we've moved to SGI,…the focus is on compute, and the archive is seen as plumbing, and it just hasn't been given the resources. We desperately need a test system. We've had many attempted upgrades that we had to revert because they didn't go as planned, and if we'd only had a test system, we probably would have figured out a lot of that. In a way we've gone backwards, as far as that is concerned.

One big problem was that Diana and her colleagues had made access to the huge tape-based data repository too transparent, and many users no longer appreciated the resources they were using:

> **Diana:** …there's a lot of our users who don't even realize that we have a mass storage system here because, on this SGI system, we

have allowed NFS [Network File System] access to the storage. The mass storage file systems are just NFS mounted to the compute server, and you just write there. They just run their jobs and they let the output go directly to the archive, without realizing that this is a mass storage system. There's all sorts of garbage that gets written there. In the old days, under SAM, we were ftp-only, or sftp only, where a user had to deliberately store stuff, and if they were doing that, they would consciously make a decision about what they were going to store.

Perhaps partly because of this transparency, the focus of the users shifted to computation rather than data storage:

> **Diana:** At this point, the focus of our computing center is much more on the compute rather than the data, so it sometimes means that we have to shout to make ourselves heard, "We really need this now! We need to buy this!" And sometimes we get it, and sometimes we can't. Because everybody's looking much more at, "Well, do we need more CPUs on the compute side?" It's an attitude that we're noticing.

This is a fascinating problem. Previously, users had to explicitly transfer files to and from the HSM. To make things easier for them, Diana's team made the HSM look like just another disk connected to their computers, and users started treating the HSM as an inexhaustible data store, filling it up with things they may or may not need. Of course, it is usually good to try to make things easier for users, but it can become a problem if it leads the users to squander resources and misunderstand how those resources actually work.

When we first observed Diana, she described her work practices as "living and breathing scripts," as scripting was core to her work. After the HSM consolidation was completed, she only occasionally wrote scripts, as the system became mature:

> **Diana:** When we first converged to this new SGI system, I wrote a zillion scripts to read the logs each night, and characterize what was going on, but once those were in place, that was the bulk of it. After that I started writing scripts when I saw that certain things just needed to be automated, and so I started writing a script to

detect if there was a read-child that was hanging out there and needed to be restarted. I haven't written any of those recently, I think because we haven't changed much recently with regard to what we have going on here. When I see a need, I certainly write another, but it's no longer a regular occurrence.

For communication, Diana's site had adopted the chat-room tool Jabber, which she saw as a great advance, because she could communicate virtually with her colleagues all the time:

Diana: I live and die by Jabber. Jabber is an excellent way to have everybody in on the same conversation at the same time. It's like having a meeting all day long without taking you away from your work.

In the end, Diana still found her work to be challenging, and that kept her going. Like others, Diana's situation had changed considerably. Her technical environment had been consolidated. Some changes were for the better, such as improved communication tools, whereas others were not, such as the removal of the test environment, the direct file system access to the HSM, and the change in focus from storage to computation.

Ryan, Storage Architect

When we first observed Ryan (chapter 6), he was a storage architect in MSS, spending time setting up connections on the storage area network (SAN) and "carving storage," that is, allocating storage volumes on the huge storage subsystems that the SAN connects to customer computers. In the follow-up interview, we found his work had changed substantially.

Overall, MSS was moving toward a model of service delivery that was standardized globally. Furthermore, they now also managed existing customer storage systems—so-called strategic outsourcing or SO accounts—in addition to providing standardized storage services on MSS systems:

Ryan: In the beginning, it was strictly, "I have a need, gimme." It progressed into people having their own equipment, a lot of times it was [our] equipment, thankfully, and sometimes it wasn't. So we started down that road, taking over accounts, but they were still MSS accounts, instead of SO [Strategic Outsourcing] accounts. And now with the GDF [Global Delivery Framework], we're handling SO accounts like [customer names], it's quite a few. So the business is growing right now in that direction, where it wasn't before. It was pretty much in MSS, "Here's how we do it, here's how we want it done, here's the type of equipment you will use, and here's the rules, and we can give it to you for a good price, rent-a-Gig."

Taking on SO accounts meant more business, but it also meant a more heterogeneous environment had to be managed. The scale and complexity had grown, but Ryan's responsibilities had narrowed. He now focused primarily on designing and maintaining the SAN, with storage design details handled by the operations team:

Ryan: At this point now, the business has changed where we don't send designs down anymore, for the most part, unless they're new, or if they are in a transition state. We'll do that as SAN designers. So the [operations team] now is doing some of the designs themselves and then executing, so they have a pretty good force down there.

Some of the tooling was the same: Ryan mentioned that they still were using the locally developed "capture database" that automatically collected status and configuration information from systems. The move toward a globally standard organization, however, had brought more standardized tools, such as a customer-facing Web interface for making requests rather than the prior practice of e-mailing spreadsheets around:

Ryan: The customer can get on the Web with this tool, and say, "O.K., here's what I want" and they'll design [...] It used to be that you had to send an e-mail, and say, "O.K. this is my server, this is that,...and I want x, y, z," and it was all done manually. And now that's been loaded into a database. If it's a current customer, a steady-state customer, then his information is added in there, so when they go to do these designs, they can look at and they know the WWPN number is correct. [...] That was a big step, because when it was a manual thing, or even when we had the capture database going on, quite often you would step on each other.

In our studies, we watched Ryan spend lots of time verifying data entries in customer request spreadsheets, so having the specification and verification processes automated sounded like a big advance. It seemed that they resolved most of the friction they used to have between the operations and design teams. This new tool also helped coordinate the work among many admins. Ryan mentioned that there was now a dedicated team responsible for building tools like the new Web tool.

The distributed nature of the new organization created new problems, however, as Ryan described interactions with other teams:

Ryan: Not very well, because they keep moving it to different countries. As far as the SAN fabric stuff, that's pretty much sacred, thankfully. But service stuff has all been off-shored, and these people, while they do a very good job, cannot be proactive. They have to be reactive, that's the way this has been structured, overall. So the guy that's been working on server A may not see that again for two months. He's working on X, Y, and Z tomorrow, and E, F, and G the day after, so they're basically being directed to do PTFs [Program Temporary Fix] or fix something that might have run amok. And it doesn't help that we don't know who these people are, generally, unless we call some 800 number or you have a contact some place.

We see multiple forces at work in the structural and operational changes Ryan and his organization went through. Not only was there globalization, but also standardization, as well as deliberate tooling support. However, coordinating activities and grounding understanding—both among people and between people and systems—seemed as difficult as ever, given the distributed nature of the work and the shifting of responsibility from known individuals to groups (Carroll, Convertine, Ganoe & Rosson, 2008; Kraut et al., 2002; Hertzum et al., 2002).

Amy, Transition Manager

When we first met Amy, she was a "transition manager" in the On Demand Data Center Services (ODCS) organization, having responsibility for getting computer systems for new accounts up and running (chapter 6). By the time of our follow-up interview, she had finished a masters degree, completed a project-management certification, and moved up the ranks to become "an overall transition manager" with much broader responsibilities. The rhythm of the work, however, was the same: procuring, provisioning, putting systems together, and handing them off to the steady-state team, then repeating it with the next project. The teams had become more spread out geographically: Whereas previously the team she worked with was all co-located, by 2009 the team was distributed around the world. Consequently, they had communication and coordination challenges, though tools helped to some degree:

> **Amy:**...if you work with some people out of the country, maybe in a different time zone so your hours have stretched...I know that's been a problem for years but this is something that you have to work around. There are now some folks that I've worked with out of India, so there's communication issues at times, people may not understand, if they're over the phone, especially when in conference calls. [...] When you have folks who are outside the country, and if I have a hard time understanding, or if the phone's not so good, I really like e-mail, and use [a screen sharing tool] quite a bit.

The biggest change was the adoption of consistent standard practices across the organization:

> **Amy:**...[management] has been better at establishing and following through with a repeatable model process....regardless of what type of projects we do, we've got standardized templates and flows and "here's where you go for this information..." It keeps maturing, and getting better, and it's definitely been a huge help...especially when you get your very large projects.

In Amy's case, the standardization effort was supported by the whole management chain, and it matured over time with feedback from all involved. Amy described how this was a big improvement over the way things were before, as it provided consistency across the organization:

> **Amy**: There are process documents, [and] also work flows, helping meet our curve, and actual word document templates that we use, they're literally templates, so you can take things out, or morph the words as appropriate for your account or for your piece of the project. [...] We were all doing things differently, across different platforms. It wasn't easily integrateable. With my project plan, some people didn't even use Microsoft Project. So there were too many inconsistencies, if you were moved from one account to another it was hard to pick up what was done.

Not everything was standardized, however. Amy had to deal with "a multitude" of ticketing systems, as each customer demanded a different system. On the whole, however, Amy was happy with the direction things were going. Her management had engaged in standardization and had established consistency across projects:

> **Amy**: It was frustrating, because I kept trying to bring in, "Hey, what about using this?"…So it's nice to finally see that someone, they heard us, they're acting on it, and they're establishing more consistency, so I'm happy to see things finally coming to fruition and improving my job.

Amy's environment improved with standardization on a global scale, just as Ryan's had. She echoed some of the same issues as Ryan concerning coordination across globally distributed teams. Key to Amy's positive view seems to be a feeling of empowerment—that her specific concerns and suggestions regarding standards and tools had been taken up (Ellingsen, Monteiro & Munkvold, 2007). She felt partly responsible for bringing effective changes to her organization.

Aaron and Joe, Security Administrators

Of all our follow-up interviewees, Aaron and Joe's roles and responsibilities (chapter 7) had changed the least in five years. They worked in the same group, and only one member of the team had changed. Aaron's central practice of continually checking e-mail for alerts from intrusion detection systems was also similar, though his scope had expanded:

> **Aaron:** So I still spend a lot of time looking at my e-mail, and looking at alerts coming up and deciding if it's worth investigating further. What has changed since then is that the alert mechanism has gotten a lot more refined in certain aspects, and it has gotten a lot more diverse in certain aspects also. So we are monitoring a lot more activities on the network now.

Aaron's manager, Joe, added that the types of attacks had changed over the years:

> **Joe:** A lot of things have evolved: the types of attacks, and even the mentality of the attackers. We've seen just a huge escalation of computer crime. So you don't see a lot of the same types of hackers who would just do it for glory, you'll see most computer intrusions that are going on now are for some form of crime. They want to make money, they can see that, "Not only can I do this for fun I can actually do this and make money." So you actually see crime syndicates getting really sophisticated in the online crime that they do.

New technologies such as virtual machines were also having an impact on their work. Virtual machines were considered disposable resources, and as such, users (and system administrators who create such machines) were not being as careful as they would be with regular computer systems:

> **Joe:** Yeah, virtual machines, I'd say they've created more problems for us, only because the administrators in their minds see them as consumable machines, if they're compromised, "Oh well, I'll just

take them down and put up a new virtual machine. No big deal." And so it's created more security issues for us because they're not as concerned. They don't view it as a real machine.

Given evolving attacks and evolving target computer systems, Aaron and his team had increased the scope and detail of their intrusion detection work using both custom and open-source tools. They made extensions to open-source tools, built databases to keep track of events, and wrote scripts that automatically triggered when events correlated:

> **Aaron:** We are doing a lot more extensive monitoring on who is logging in, from where they are logging, what they are doing, how long they have been inactive before they logged in now, are they doing something nasty or malicious, are they downloading something, is a particular IP address used by multiple users to log on to [our] system? So there was off-the-shelf software that was full-event correlator. It's a Perl script that does a really good job of correlation. It's open source. But we modified SSH […] so that we can actually see a few more things which were not enabled by default. So we implemented that part. Another area is that we actually wrote ourselves a lot of scripts including database design, and these scripts are triggered when the event correlator finds a correlation and actually triggers this script which goes and looks at all the data back in the database.

Though they had considered alternatives to e-mail notifications, they decided that e-mail was still the best means for disseminating possible alerts. But now they put more contextual data into e-mail so that they could make decisions on the spot, reducing the need for additional research and analysis. By receiving alerts in e-mail, multiple team members could examine each alert, ensuring that nothing fell through the cracks:

> **Aaron:** I may look at an alert and I just don't see anything, and I say, "It looks normal, I don't see anything." Somebody else may look at it and say, "You know, there's something about that, I remembered six months ago seeing something, and I'm going to look into this." And sure enough it's an alert, it's actually an actionable item, an incident. So I feel like if everybody gets the e-mail, you get more eyes looking at the alerts.

This was the same sort of redundancy built into the practices of Christine and Mike (chapter 4), who sat side-by-side keeping an eye on each other's actions.

A big driver for locally created tools was cost. As a public university, they simply could not afford to pay a hefty price for many commercial tools.

> **Joe:** Many sites are moving from trying to utilize open source, homegrown things, to buying appliances. We just have really not had the money to do that kind of stuff, but I know sites that have dropped a $150 thousand on buying this box that you can just throw all your logs at. [...] So actually a lot of sites have moved to that kind of thing, we just don't have the money to do that here. That's why we still mostly use open source tools.

Thus, they focused on using and contributing to open-source software, and on developing homegrown tools. Open-source, however, had its own problems, as Joe explained:

> **Joe:** The problem that they run into now is that, is funding issues, that particular project's funding has ended, they open sourced the software for that. It's out there on Source Forge. Nobody's really picked it up. We're still running it, but if we have any problems...there's no adequate development on it yet, [not] right now.

On the positive side, because of their association with the university, they were also experimenting with tools coming from several research groups. They were promising, but so far none had been "able to handle the amount of data that we have."

One major change they made was to improve the infrastructure for tracking security incidents, helping share information about what is going on within the team and also with management. Previously, they dumped all their logs and reports in a shared file system. Now, they used wikis to track incidents in a standard manner.

> **Joe:** We have a standard format. Here's a new incident: There's a template for this incident that has all the fields, [and] these are the things that you should fill out, with information from Bro,

maybe nmap, what's going on, any alerts that had triggered this particular incident, solutions as to what happened when things [were] finally over with….As soon as the wiki came, everything has become quite automatic. […] So now, my managers have access to that wiki, so when we have an incident, I can just tell them, "here, go to this wiki, look at the latest incident page."

In the end, Aaron said that he continued to enjoy his work, "it's fun; every day there is something always new that is happening. We discuss a lot of ideas, and there is a lot more to be done."

The Journey Continues

This book tells the stories of computer sysadmins—through observations and interviews done during a particular period. However, the people and their stories are ongoing, for the work is ongoing. Change is the rule—new technologies, organizational changes, resource constraints, and outsourcing are met with improved practices, tooling, communications, automation, and standards. Technology sets the stage, and then people rely on creativity, judgment, and hard work to understand, design, deploy, maintain, and troubleshoot ever-changing and ever-growing IT systems. Despite the years and the changes, it seems the same basic processes are at work: (a) people still work hard to ground their understanding with others and with systems, and in many cases it may be harder because of globally distributed teams and increased system complexity; (b) change and innovation go hand-in-hand, as people must adapt to maintain understanding and control of systems; and (c) tools, practices, and organizations evolve incrementally, often toward standards, as a result of pressures such as cost and complexity.

A number of years ago, we started on an expedition, a journey into the world of system administration to learn how sysadmins worked and what we could do to make their work easier and more effective. This book is the result. Now, our journey is over. Their journey continues.

References

Ackerman, M. S., Wulf, V., & Pipek, V. (2002). *Sharing expertise: Beyond knowledge management*. Cambridge. MA: MIT Press.

Arthur, W. B. (2009). *The nature of technology: What it is and how it evolves*. New York: Free Press.

Bailey, J., Etgen, M., & Freeman, K. (2003). Situation awareness and system administration. *Proceedings of the Conference on Human Factors in Computing Systems*. Presented at Workshop on System Administrators Are Users, Too: Designing Workspaces for Managing Internet-Scale Systems, Ft Lauderdale, FL.

Bailey J., Kandogan E., Maglio, P. P., & Haber E. (2007). Activity-based management of IT service delivery. *Proceedings of the ACM Symposium on Computer Human Interaction for the Management of Information Technology*. New York: ACM Press.

Barley, S. R. & Kunda, G. (2004). *Gurus, hired guns and warm bodies: Itinerant experts in a knowledge economy*. Princeton, NJ: Princeton University Press.

Barley, S. R. & Orr, J. (Eds.) (1997). *Between craft and science: Technical work in the United States*. Ithaca, NY: ILR Press.

Barrett, R. (2004). People and policies: Transforming the human-computer partnership. *Proceedings of the 5th IEEE International Workshop on Policies for Distributed Systems and Networks* (Policy 2004) (pp. 111–114). Los Alamitos, CA: IEEE Computer Society.

Barrett, R., Chen, M., & Maglio, P. P. (2003). System administrators are users too: Designing workspaces for internet-scale systems. *Proceedings of the SIGCHI Conference Extended Abstracts on Human Factors in Computing Systems* (pp. 1068–1069). New York: ACM Press.

Barrett, R., Kandogan, E., Maglio, P. P., Haber, E. M., Prabaker, M., & Takayama, L. A. (2004). Field studies of computer system administrators: Analysis of system management tools and practices. *Proceedings of the Conference on Computer-Supported Collaborative Work* (pp. 388–395). New York: ACM Press.

Barrett, R., Maglio, P. P., Kandogan, E., & Bailey, J. (2005). Usable autonomic computing systems: The systems administrator's perspective. *Advanced engineering informatics, 19*(3), 213–221.

Beck, K. (1999). Embracing change with extreme programming. *Computer, 32*(10), 70–77.

Becker, G. S., & Murphy, K. M. (1992). The division of labor, coordination costs, and knowledge. *Quarterly Journal of Economics, 107*(4), 1137–1160.

Bernard, H. R. (1998). *Handbook of methods in cultural anthropology.* Walnut Creek, CA: Altamira Press.

Bernstein, M., van Kleek, M., Karger, D., & Schraefel, M. C. (2008). Information scraps: How and why information eludes our personal information management tools. *ACM Transations on Information Systems, 26*(4), 1–46.

Bettenhausen, K. (1991). Five years of groups research: What we have learned and what needs to be addressed. *Journal of Management, 17*(2), 345–381.

Birnholtz, J. P., Finholt, T. A., Horn, D. B., & Bae, S. J. (2005). Grounding needs: Achieving common ground via lightweight chat in large, distributed, ad-hoc groups. *Proceedings of the SIGCHI Conference on Human Factors in Computing Systems* (pp. 21–30). New York: ACM Press.

Botta, D., Werlinger, R., Gagné, A., Beznosov, K., Iverson, L., Fels, S., et al. (2007). Towards understanding IT security professionals and their tools. *Proceedings of the Symposium on Usable Privacy and Security* (pp. 100–111). New York: ACM Press.

Bozman, J. S. & Perry, R. (2010). The business value of large-scale server consolidation. IDC Whitepaper. Retrieved from http://www05.ibm.com/innovation/uk/leadership/meter/capabilities_support/documents/IDC_White_paper.pdf

Brennan, S. E. (1998). The grounding problem in communication with and through computers. In S. R. Fussell & R. J. Kreuz (Eds.), *Social and cognitive psychological approaches to interpersonal communication* (pp. 201–225). Hillsdale NJ: Erlbaum.

Brown, A. B., & Hellerstein, J. L. (2005). Reducing the cost of IT operations: Is automation always the answer? *Proceedings of the 10th Conference on Hot Topics in Operating Systems, 10.* Berkeley, CA: USENIX.

Brown, A. B. & Patterson, D. A. (2003). *Undo for operators: Building an undoable e-mail store.* Paper presented at the Annual Conference on USENIX Annual Technical Conference, San Antonio, TX.

Brown, J. S. & Duguid, P. (1991). Organizational learning and communities-of-Practice: Toward a unified view of working, learning, and innovation [Special issue] Organizational Learning: Papers in Honor of (and by) James G. March, *Organization Science, 2*(1) 40–57

Brunsson, N., & Jacobsson, B. (2000). *A world of standards.* Oxford, England: Oxford University Press.

Burgess, M. (2006, April). A control theory perspective on configuration management and Cfengine. *ACM SIGBED Review, 3*(2), 12–16.

Burgess, M. (1998). Automated system administration with feedback regulation. *Software-Practice and Experience, 28,* 1519–1530.

Burgess, M. (2004). *Analytical network and system administration. Managing human-computer networks.* West Sussex, England: Wiley.

Bystrom, K., & Jarvelin, K. (1995). Task complexity affects information seeking and use. *Information Processing and Management, 31*(2), 191–213.

Campbell, C., & Maglio, P. (2003). Supporting notable information in office work. *Proceedings of the SIGCHI Conference Extended Abstracts on Human Factors in Computing Systems* (pp. 902–903). New York: ACM Press.

Cappuccio, D., Keyworth, B., & Kirwin, W. (2002). Total cost of ownership: The impact of system management tools. Technical Report, The Gartner Group.

Cargill, C. (1999). Consortia and the evolution of information technology standardization. In K. Jakobs & R. Williams (Eds.), *SIIT '99 Proceedings* (pp. 37–42). Piscataway, NJ: IEEE.

Carlile, P. R. (2002). A pragmatic view of knowledge and boundaries: Boundary objects in new product development. *Organization Science, 13*(4), 442–455.

Carroll, J. M., Convertino, G., Ganoe, C., & Rosson, M. B. (2008). Toward a conceptual model of common ground in teamwork. In M. Letsky, N. Warner, S. Fiore, & C. Smith (Eds.), *Macrocognition in teams: Understanding the mental processes that underlie collaborative team activity* (pp. 87–105). Hampshire, UK: Ashgate.

Cavusoglu, H., Cavusoglu, H., & Zhang, J. (2008). Security patch management: Share the burden or share the damage? *Management Science, 54*(4), 657–670.

Clark H. H. (1996). *Using language*. Cambridge, England: Cambridge University Press.

Clark, H. H. (1999). *How do real people communicate with virtual partners?* Paper presented at AAAI Fall Symposium on Psychological Models of Communication in Collaborative Systems, North Falmouth, MA.

Clark, H. H. & Brennan, S. E. (1991). Grounding in communication. In L. B. Resnick, J. M. Levine, & J. S. D. Teasley (Eds.), *Perspectives on socially shared cognition* (pp. 127–149). Washington, DC: American Psychological Association.

Clark, H. H., & Wilkes-Gibbs, D. (1986). Referring as a collaborative process. *Cognition, 22,* 1–39

Connell, J. B., Mendelsohn, G. A., Robins, R. W., & Canny, J. (2001). Effects of communication medium on interpersonal perceptions. *Proceedings of the 2001 International ACM SIGGROUP Conference on Supporting Group Work* (GROUP '01) (pp. 117–124). New York: ACM.

Cowan, R. S. (1985). *More work for mother: The ironies of household technology from the open hearth to the microwave*. New York: Basic Books.

Cramton, C. D. (2001). The mutual knowledge problem and its consequences for dispersed collaboration. *Organization Science, 12*(3), 346–371.

Crow, G. B. & Muthuswamy, B. (2003). International outsourcing in the information technology industry: Trends and Implications. *Communications of the International Information Management Association, 3*(1), 25–34.

Czerwinski, M., Horvitz, E., & Wilhite, S. (2004). A diary study of task switching and interruptions. *Proceedings of the SIGCHI conference on Human factors in computing systems* (pp. 175–182). New York, ACM Press.

Dawkins, R. (1989). *The Selfish Gene* (2nd ed.). New York: Oxford University Press.

Deetz, S. A. & Kersten, A. (1983). Critical models of interpretive research. In L. Putnam, & M. E. Pacanowsky (Eds.), *Communication and organizations: An interpretive approach* (pp. 147–172). Beverly Hills, CA: Sage.

Deloitte (2006). Deloitte 2006 Global Security Survey (2006). *Deloitte.* Retrieved from http://www.deloitte.com/dtt/cda/doc/content/dtt_fsi_2006%20Global%20%20Survey_2006-06-13.pdf

Dewar, R., Hage, J. (1978). Size, technology, complexity, and structural differentiation: toward a theoretical synthesis. *Administrative Science Quarterly, 23*(1), 111–136.

Dignan, L. (2010, July 13). Infosys wrestles with India IT worker turnover. *ZDNet.* Retrieved from http://www.zdnet.com/blog/btl/infosys-wrestles-with-india-it-worker-turnover/36652

Dossani, R., & Kenney, M. (2003). Lift and shift: Moving the back office to India. *Information Technologies and International Development, 1*(2), 21–37.

Drury, J. L., Beaton, E., Boiney, L., Duncan, M. O., GreenPope, R., Howland, M. D., et al. (2010). Collaboration research for crisis management teams. *Foundations and Trends in Human-Computer Interaction, 3*(3), 139–212.

Edmondson, W. H., & Beale, R. (2008). Projected cognition—extending distributed cognition for the study of human interaction with computers. *Interactive Computing, 20*(1), 128–140.

Egyedi, T. M., & Dahanayake, A. (2003). Difficulties implementing standards. In T. M. Egyedi, K. Krechmer, & K. Jakobs (Eds.), *Proceedings of the 3rd IEEE conference on standardization and innovation in information technology* (pp. 75–84). Delft, the Netherlands. Piscataway, NJ: IEEE Press.

Ellingsen, G., Monteiro, E., & Munkvold, G. (2007). Standardization of work: Co-constructed practice. *Information Society, 23*(5), 309–326.

Emery, F., & Trist, E. (1965). The causal texture of organizational environments. *Human Relations, 18*(1), 21–32.

Emery, F., & Trist, E. (1972). *Toward a social ecology.* London: Plenum Press.

Endsley, M. R. (1995). Toward a theory of situation awareness in dynamic systems. *Human Factors: The Journal of the Human Factors and Ergonomics Society, 37*(1) 32–64.

Engardio, P., Arndt, M. & Foust, D. The future of outsourcing. (2006, January 30) *BusinessWeek.* Retrieved from http://www.businessweek.com/magazine/content/06_05/b3969401.htm

Evard, R. (1993). Collaborative networked communication: MUDS as sytems tools. *Proceedings of the Seventh Systems Administration Conference* (pp. 1–8). Berkeley, CA: USENIX.

Fetterman, D. M. (1998). *Ethnography: Step by step* (2nd ed). Thousand Oaks, CA: Sage.

Fitzgerald, B. (2006). The transformation of open source software. *MIS Quarterly, 30*(3), 587–598.

Fox, K. (2004). MOO-Cows FAQ. Retrieved from http://www.moo.mud.org/moo-faq/

Frisch, A. (2002). *Essential system administration.* Sebastopol, CA: O'Reilly Media.

Fussell, S. R., Kraut, R. E., Lerch, F. J., Scherlis, W. L., McNally, M. M., & Cadiz, J. J. 1998. Coordination, overload and team performance: Effects of team communication strategies. *Proceedings of the 1998 ACM Conference on Computer supported cooperative work* (pp. 275–284). New York: ACM.

Gartner Group/Dataquest. (1999, May). Server Storage and RAID Worldwide. Retrieved from http://www.gartner.com

Gartner Group/Dataquest. (2007, August). IT services forecast, worldwide, 2004–2011. Retrieved from http://www.gartner.com/DisplayDocument?=512914&ref=g_sitelink

Geertz, C. (1973). Thick description: Toward an interpretive theory of culture. In *The interpretation of cultures: Selected essays* (pp. 3–30). New York: Basic Books.

Giacomazzi, F., Panella, C., Pernici, B., & Sansoni, M. (1997). Information systems integration in mergers and acquisitions: A normative model. *Information & Management, 32*(6), 289–302.

Gibson, C. B., & Cohen, S. G. (2003). *Virtual teams that work: Creating conditions for virtual collaboration effectiveness.* San Francisco: Jossey-Bass.

Gibson, J. L., Ivancevich, J. M., & Donnelly, J. H. (2002). *Organizations: Behavior, structure, processes.* New York: McGraw-Hill/Irwin.

Goh, S. C. (2002). Managing effective knowledge transfer: An integrative framework and some practice implications. *Journal of Knowledge Management, 6*(1), 23–30.

Grow, B., Epstein, K., & Tschang, C. -C. (April 21, 2008). The New E-spionage Threat. *Businessweek,* 32–41.

Gupta, B., Iyer, L. S., & Aronson, J. E. (2000). Knowledge management: Practices and challenges. *Industrial Management & Data Systems, 100*(1), 17–21.

Haber, E., Kandogan, E., & Maglio, P. P (2011). Collaboration in system administration. *Communications of the ACM, 54*(1), 46–53.

Haber, E. M., & Bailey, J. (2007). Design guidelines for system administration tools developed through ethnographic field studies. *Proceedings of the 2007 Symposium on Computer Human Interaction for the Management of Information Technology.* New York: ACM Press.

Haber, E. M., Kandogan, E., Cypher, A., Maglio, P. P., & Barrett, R. (2005). A1: Spreadsheet-based scripting for developing web tools. *Proceedings of the 19th Conference on Large Installation System Administration Conference.* Berkeley, CA: USENIX.

Halverson, C. A., & Ackerman, M. S. (2008). The birth of an organizational resource: The surprising life of a cheat sheet. In M. S. Ackerman, C. A. Halverson, T. Erickson, & W. A. Kellogg (Eds.), *Resources, co-evolution and artifacts* (pp. 9–35). London: Springer-Verlag.

Heath, C., & Luff, P. (1992). Collaboration and control: Crisis management and multimedia technology in London underground line control rooms. *Journal of Computer Supported Cooperative Work, 1*(1), 24–48.

Hertzum, M. (2008). Collaborative information seeking: The combined activity of information seeking and collaborative grounding. *Information Processing and Management, 44*(2), 957–962.

Hertzum, M., Andersen, H. H. K., Andersen, V., & Hansen, C. B. (2002). Trust in information sources: Seeking information from people, documents, and virtual agents. *Interacting with computers, 14,* 575–599.

Hinds, P. J. & Kiesler, S. (2002). *Distributed work,* Cambridge, MA: MIT Press.

Hinds, P. J. & Weisband, S. P. (2003). Knowledge sharing and shared understanding in virtual teams. In *Virtual teams that work: Creating conditions for virtual team effectiveness* (pp. 21–36). San Francisco: Jossey-Bass.

Hirschheim, R. (2009). Offshoring and the new world order. *Communications of the ACM, 52*(11), 132–135.

Holland J. H. (1992). *Adaptation in natural and artificial Systems.* Ann Arbor, MI: University of Michigan Press.

HP (2009). *HP adaptive infrastructure maturity model.* Retrieved from www.hp.com/go/aimm

Hrebec, D. G., Stiber, M. (2001). A survey of system administrator mental models and situation awareness. *Proceedings of the ACM Conference on Computer Personnel Research* (pp. 166–172). New York: ACM.

Hudson, J. M., Christensen, J., Kellogg, W. A., & Erickson. T. (2002). "I'd be overwhelmed, but it's just one more thing to do": Availability and interruption in research management. *Proceedings of the SIGCHI Conference on Human Factors in Computing Systems: Changing Our World, Changing Ourselves* (pp. 97–104). New York: ACM.

Hutchins, E. (1995). How a cockpit remembers its speeds. *Cognitive Science, 19,* 265–288.

Hutchins, E. (1996). *Cognition in the wild.* Cambridge, MA: MIT Press.

Hutchins, E. L., Hollan, J. D., & Norman, D. A (1986). Direct manipulation interfaces. In D. A. Norman & S. W. Draper (Eds.), *User centered system design* (pp. 87–124). Hillsdale, NJ: Erlbaum.

IBM. (2001). *Autonomic Computing: IBM's Perspective on the State of Information Technology.* Retrieved from http://www.research.ibm.com/autonomic/manifesto/autonomic_computing.pdf, 2001

Isaacs, E., Walendowski, A., Whittaker, S., Schiano, D. J., & Kamm, C. (2002). The character, functions, and styles of instant messaging in the workplace. *Proceedings of the 2002 ACM Conference on Computer Supported Cooperative Work* (pp. 11–20). New York: ACM.

ITCentrix. (2001). *Storage on tap: Understanding the business value of storage service providers. ITCentrix.* Retrieved from http://www.itcentrix.com, 2001.

Jarvenpaa, S. L., Knoll, K., & Leidner, D. (1998). Is anybody out there? The antecedents of trust in global virtual teams. *Journal of Management Information Systems, 14*(4), 29–64.

Jarvenpaa, S. L., & Leidner, D. E. (1999). Communication and trust in global virtual teams. *Organizational Science, 10*(6), 791–815.

Johnson, B. C., Manyika, J. M., & Yee, L. A. (2005). The next revolution in interactions. *The McKinsey Quarterly, 4,* 20–33.

Johri, A. (2011). Look ma, no email! Blogs and IRC as primary and preferred communication tools in a distributed firm. *Proceedings of the ACM 2011 Conference on Computer Supported Cooperative Work* (pp. 305–308). New York: ACM.

Jones, P. M. (1995). Cooperative work in mission operations: analysis and implications for computer support. *Computer Supported Cooperative Work, 3,* 103–145.

Kamsin, A. (2004, June). Management of information technology: The study on strategy, planning and policies. *Proceedings of the 2004 International Symposium on Information and Communication Technologies* (pp. 152–157). *ACM International Conference Proceeding Series, 90, Trinity College Dublin.* New York: ACM Press.

Kanawattanachai, P., & Yoo, Y. (2002). Dynamic nature of trust in virtual teams. *Journal of Strategic Information Systems, 11(3–4),* 187–213.

Kandogan, E, Bailey, J., Maglio, P. P., & Haber, E. (2008). Policy-based IT automation: The role of human judgment. *Proceedings of the Second ACM Symposium on Computer Human Interaction for the Management of Information Technology.*

Kandogan, E., Haber, E., Barrett, R., Cypher, A., Maglio, P., & Zhao, H. (2005). A1: End-user programming for web-based system administration. *Proceedings of the 18th Annual ACM Symposium on User Interface Software and Technology* (pp. 211–220). New York: ACM.

Kandogan, E., & Haber, E. M. (2005) Security administration tools and practices. In L. Faith Cranor and S. Garfinkel (Eds.), *Security and usability: Designing secure systems that people can use* (pp. 357–378). Sebastopol, CA: O'Reilly Media.

Kandogan, E., Haber, E. M., Bailey, J. H., & Maglio, P. P. (2009). Studying reactive, risky, complex, long-spanning, and collaborative work: The case of IT service delivery. In J. A. Jacko (Ed.), *Proceedings of the 13th International Conference on Human-Computer Interaction. Part IV: Interacting in Various Application Domains* (pp. 504–513). Berlin, Heidelberg, Germany: Springer-Verlag.

Kandogan, E, Maglio, P. P., Bailey, J., & Haber, E. (2009). Scripting practices in complex system management. *Proceedings of the Third ACM Symposium on Computer Human Interaction for the Management of Information Technology).* New York: ACM Press.

Kandogan, E., Maglio, P. P., Haber, E., & Bailey, J. (2011). On the roles of policies in computer system management. *International Journal of Human-Computer Studies, 69(4),* 351–361.

Kanellos, M. (2004, July 26). MyDoom variant slams mailboxes, search engines. *ZDNet.* Retrieved from http://www.zdnet.com/news/mydoom-variant-slams-mailboxes-search-engines/137392

Kauffman, R. J., & Walden, E. A. (2001). Economics and electronic commerce: Survey and directions for research. *International Journal on Electronic Commerce, 5(4),* 5–116.

Kephart, J. O., & Chess, D. M. (2003). The vision of autonomic computing, *IEEE Computer, 36(1),* 41–51.

Klein, G., Feltovich, P. J., Bradshaw, J. M., & Woods, D. D. (2005). Common ground and coordination in joint activity. In W. R. Rouse & K. B. Boff (Eds.), *Organizational simulation* (pp. 139–184). New York: Wiley.

Knittel, C. R., & Stango, V. (2010). *The productivity benefits of IT outsourcing.* Working Paper. Retrieved from http://web.mit.edu/knittel/www/papers/CUproduct_latest.pdf.

Kolstad, R. (2001–2006). *SAGE salary survey results.* Retrieved from http://www.sage.org/salsurv.

Kramer, R. M. (1999). Trust and distrust in organizations: Emerging perspectives, enduring questions. *Annual Review of Psychology, 50,* 569–598.

Kraut, R. E., Fussell, S. R., Brennan, S. E., & Siegel, J. (2002). Understanding effects of proximity on collaboration: Implications for technologies to support remote collaborative work. In P. Hinds & S. Kiesler (Eds.), *Distributed work* (pp. 137–162). Cambridge, MA: MIT Press.

Kumar, R. L. (2004). A framework for assessing the business value of information technology infrastructures. *Journal of Management Information Systems, 21*(2), 11–32.

Lackow, H. M. (2001). Information technology outsourcing trends. *The Conference Board.* Retrieved from http://www.conference-board.org/publications/.cfm?publicationid=462

Landsdale, M. W. (1988). The psychology of personal information management. *Applied Ergonomics, 19,* 55–66.

Larsson, A. (2003). Making sense of collaboration: The challenge of thinking together in global design teams. *Proceedings of the 2003 International ACM SIGGROUP Conference on Supporting Group Work* (pp. 153–160). New York: ACM Press.

Lave, J. (1988). *Cognition in practice: Mind, mathematics and culture in everyday life.* Cambridge, MA: Cambridge University Press.

Lave, J., & Wenger, E. (1990). *Situated learning: Legitimate peripheral participation.* Institute for Research on Learning, Palo Alto, CA

Lave, J., & Wenger, E. (1991). *Situated learning: Legitimate peripheral participation.* Cambridge, England: Cambridge University Press.

Lawrence, P., & Lorsch, J. (1967). Differentiation and integration in complex organizations. *Administrative Science Quarterly, 12,* 1–30.

Leidner, R. (1993). *Fast food, fast talk: Service work and the routinization of everyday life.* Berkeley, CA: University of California Press.

Leuf, B., & Cunningham, W. (2001). *The wiki way: Quick collaboration on the web.* Boston, MA: Addison-Wesley Professional.

Levy, F., & Murnane, R. J. (2004). *The new division of labor: How computers are creating the next job market.* Princeton, NJ: Princeton University Press.

Limoncelli, T., Hogan, C. J., & Chalup, S. R. (2007). *The practice of system and network administration.* Upper Saddle River, NJ: Addison-Wesley Professional.

Maglio, P. P., & Kandogan, E. (2004). Error messages: What's the problem? *ACM Queue, 2*(8), 50–55.

Maglio, P. P., Kandogan, E., & Haber, E. (2008). Distributed cognition and joint activity in computer-system administration. M. S. Ackerman, C. Halverson,

T. Erickson, & W. A. Kellogg (Eds.), *Resources, co-evolution, and artifacts: Theory in CSCW* (pp. 145–166). New York: Springer.

Maglio, P. P., Srinivasan, S., Kreulen, J. T., & Spohrer, J. (2006). Service systems, service scientists, SSME, and innovation. *Communications of the ACM, 49*(7), 81–85.

Malone, T. W. (1983). How do people organize their desks?: Implications for the design of office information systems. *ACM Transaction on Information Systems, 1*(1), 99–112.

Malone, T. W. (1990). Organizing information processing systems: parallels between organizations and computer systems. In W. Zachary, S. Robertson, & J. Black (Eds.), *Cognition, computation, and cooperation* (pp. 56–83). Norwood, NJ: Ablex.

Malone, T. W., & Crowston, K. (1994). The interdisciplinary study of coordination. *ACM Computing Surveys, 26*(1), 87–119.

Malone, T. W., Crowston, K., Lee, J., Pentland, B., Dellarocas, C., Wyner, G., et al. (1999). Tools for inventing organization: Towards a handbook of organizational processes. *Management Science, 45*(3), 425–443.

Manion M., & Evan, W. M., (2000). The Y2K problem and professional responsibility: A retrospective analysis. *Technology in Society, 22*(3), 361–387.

March, J. G., & Olsen, J. P. (1989). *Rediscovering institutions. The organizational basis of politics.* London: Macmillan.

March, J. G., & Simon H. A. (1958). *Organizations.* New York: Wiley.

Mark, G. (2002). Extreme collaboration. *Communications of the ACM, 45*(6), 89–93.

Mark, G., González, V. M., & Harris, J. (2005). No task left behind?: Examining the nature of fragmented work. *Proceedings of the SIGCHI Conference on Human Factors in Computing Systems* (pp. 312–330). New York: ACM.

McAllister, D. J. (1995). Affect and cognition-based trust as foundations for interpersonal cooperation in organizations. *Academy of Management Journal, 38*(1), 24–59.

Menascé, D. A., Almeida, V. A. F., & Dowdy, L. W. 1994. *Capacity planning and performance modeling: From mainframes to client-server systems.* Upper Saddle River, NJ: Prentice-Hall.

Meum, T., Monteiro, E., & Ellingsen, G. (2011). The pendulum of standardization. *Proceedings of the 12th European Conference on Computer Supported Cooperative Work* (pp. 101–120). Aahus, Denmark: Springer.

Nardi, B. A., Whittaker, S., & Bradner, E. (2000). Interaction and outeraction: Instant messaging in action. *Proceedings of the 2000 ACM Conference on Computer Supported Cooperative Work* (pp. 79–88). New York: ACM.

O'Dell, C., & Grayson, C. J. (1998). If only we knew what we know: Identification and transfer of internal best practices. *California Management Review, 40*(3), 154–174.

Office of Government Commerce. (2000). Service support. *IT Infrastructure Library (ITIL) Series.* UK: Stationery Office.

Office of Government Commerce (2001). Service delivery. *IT Infrastructure Library (ITIL) Series*. UK: Stationery Office.

Office of Government Commerce (2002). Application management. *IT Infrastructure Library (ITIL) Series*. UK: Stationery Office.

Office of Government Commerce (2002). ICT infrastructure management. *IT Infrastructure Library (ITIL) Series*. UK: Stationery Office.

Office of Government Commerce (2002). Planning to implement service management. *IT Infrastructure Library (ITIL) Series*. UK: Stationery Office.

Office of Government Commerce (2005). ITIL small scale implementation. *IT Infrastructure Library (ITIL) Series*. UK: Stationery Office.

Office of Government Commerce (2005). The business perspective. In *IT Infrastructure Library (ITIL) Series*. UK: Stationery Office.

Oleson, C., Hagan, M., & DeMoss, C. (2009). *Achieving IT service quality: The opposite of luck*. Austin, TX: Synergy Books.

Oppenheimer, D., Ganapathi, A., & Patterson, D. A. (2003, March). Why do Internet services fail, and what can be done about it? *Proceedings of the 4th USENIX Symposium on Internet Technologies and Systems*. Berkely, CA: USENIX.

Orikarinen, J., & Reed, D. (1993). *Internet relay chat protocol*. IETF RFC 1459. Retrieved from http://tools.ietf.org/html/rfc1459

Orlikowski, W. A. (2002). Knowing in practice: enacting a collective capability in distributed organizing. *Organization Science, 13*(3), 249–273.

Orlikowski, W. J., & Baroudi, J. (1991). Studying information technology in organizations: Research approaches and assumptions. *Information Systems Research, 2*(1), 1–28.

Orr, J. (1986). Narratives at work: storytelling as cooperative diagnostic activity. *Proceedings of the Conference on Computer Supported Cooperative Work* (pp. 62–72). New York: ACM.

Orr, J. E. (1996). *Talking about machines: An ethnography of a modern job*. Ithaca, NY: Cornell University Press.

Paepcke, A. (1996). Information needs in technical work settings and their implications for the design of computer tools. *Computer Supported Cooperative Work: The Journal of Collaborative Computing, 5*(1), 63–92.

Parasuraman, R., Sheridan, T. B., & Wickens, C. D. (2000). A model of types and levels of human interaction with automation. *IEEE Transactions on Systems, Man and Cybernetics, 30*, 286–297.

Paxson, V. (1999). Bro: A system for detecting network intruders in real-time. *Computer networks, 31*(23–24), 2435–2463.

Preece, J., Rogers, Y., & Sharp, H. (2002). *Interaction Design*. New York: Wiley.

QoSient. (2011). *Argus FAQ*. Retrieved from http://www.qosient.com/argus/faq.shtml.

Quiggin, J. (2005). The Y2K scare: Causes, costs and cures. *Australian Journal of Public Administration, 64*(3), 46–55.

Rada, R. (2000). Consensus versus speed. In K. Jakobs (Ed.), *IT standards and standardization: A global perspective* (pp. 19–34). London: Idea Group Publishing.

Rai, S. (2005, November 2). Outsources in India fight for skilled labor. *The New York Times*. Retrieved from http://www.nytimes.com/2005/11/01/business/worldbusiness/01iht-outsource.t.html.

Rasmussen J. (1986). *Information processing and human-machine interaction*. New York: North Holland.

Rogers, Y. (1992). Ghosts in the network: Distributed troubleshooting in a shared working environment. *Proceedings of the 1992 ACM Conference on Computer-Supported Cooperative Work* (pp. 346–355). New York: ACM.

Rogers, Y., Ellis, J. (1994). Distributed cognition: an alternative framework for analysing and explaining collaborative working. *Journal of Information Technology*, 9(2), 119–128.

Roschelle, J. & Teasley S. D. (1995) The construction of shared knowledge in collaborative problem solving. In C. E. O'Malley (Ed), *Computer-supported collaborative learning* (pp. 69–197). Berlin: Springer-Verlag.

Sandusky, R. J. (1997). Infrastructure management as cooperative Work: implications for systems design, *Proceedings of the International ACM SIGGROUP Conference on Supporting Group Work: The Integration Challenge* (pp. 91–100). New York: ACM.

Sarter, N. B. & Woods, D. D. (1991). Situation awareness: A critical but ill-defined phenomenon. *International Journal of Aviation Psychology, 1*, 45–57.

Schein, E. H. (1990). Organizational culture. *American Psychologist, 45*(2), 109–119.

Schmidt, S. K, & Werle, R. (1998). *Coordinating technology. Studies in the international standardization of telecommunications*. Cambridge, MA: MIT Press.

Serenity Systems (2005). Managed client impact on the cost of computing. Houston, TX: Author. Retrieved from http://www.serenity-systems.com.

Sharrock, W. W., Anderson, B., & Anderson, R. J. (1986). *The ethnomethodologists*. London: Taylor & Francis.

Sheridan, T. (2002). *Humans and automation: System design and research Issues*. Hoboken, NJ: Wiley.

Sonnenwald, D. H., Maglaughlin, K. L., & Whitton, M. C. (2004). Designing to support situation awareness across distances: an example from a scientific collaboratory. *Information Processing & Management, 40*(6), 989–1011.

Spohrer, J., & Riecken, D. (2006, July). Introduction. *Communications of the ACM, 49*(7), 30–32.

Spool, J. M. & Snyder, C. (1995). Designing for complex products. *Conference companion on human factors in computing systems* (pp. 395–396). New York: ACM Press.

Star, S. L. (1989). The structure of ill-structured solutions: boundary objects and heterogeneous distributed problem solving. In L. Gasser and M. N. Huhns, (Eds.), *Distributed artificial intelligence* (Vol. 2, pp. 37–54). San Mateo, CA: Morgan Kaufman.

Star, S. L. (1995). The politics of formal representations: wizards, gurus, and organizational complexity. In S. L. Star (Ed.), *Ecologies of knowledge: Work and politics in science and technology* (pp. 88–118). Albany, NY: SUNY Press.

Stone, B. (2008, July 6). As web traffic grows crashes take bigger toll. *New York Times*. Retrieved from http://www.nytimes.com/2008/07/06/technology/06outage.html.

Stylianou, A. C., Jeffries, C. J., & Robbins, S. S. (1996). Corporate mergers and the problems of IS integration. *Information & Management, 31*(4), 203–213.

Takayama, L., & Kandogan, E. (2006). Trust as an underlying factor of system administrator interface choice. *CHI '06 extended abstracts on human factors in computing systems* (pp. 1391–1396). New York: ACM.

Teasley, S., Covi, L., Krishnan, M. S., Olson, J. S. (2000). How does radical collocation help a team succeed? *Proceedings of the 2000 ACM conference on computer supported cooperative work* (pp. 339–346). New York: ACM.

Tyler, T. R., & Kramer, R. M. (1996). Whither trust. In R. M. Kramer, T. R. Tyler, (Eds.), *Trust in organizations: Frontiers of theory and research* (pp. 1–15). Thousand Oaks, CA: Sage.

Velasquez, N. F., & Durcikova, A. (2008). Sysadmins and the need for verification information. *Proceedings of the 2nd ACM Symposium on Computer Human Interaction for Management of Information Technology*. New York: ACM.

Velasquez, N. F., & Weisband, S. P. (2008). Work practices of system administrators: implications for tool design. *Proceedings of the 2nd ACM Symposium on Computer Human Interaction for Management of Information Technology*, New York: ACM.

Velasquez, N. F., & Weisband, S. P. (2009). System administrators as broker technicians. *Proceedings of the Symposium on Computer Human Interaction for the Management of Information Technology*. New York: ACM.

Verdoes, J. A. (1997). In search of a complete and scalable systems administration suite. *Proceedings of the Large Scale System Administration of Windows NT*. Berkeley, CA: USENIX.

Vinck, D. (2003). *Everyday engineering: An ethnography of design and innovation*. Cambridge, MA: MIT Press.

Voida, A., Mynatt, E. D., Erickson, T., & Kellogg, W. A. (2004). Interviewing over instant messaging. *CHI '04 Extended Abstracts on Human Factors in Computing Systems* (pp. 1344–1347). New York: ACM.

Vygotsky, L. S. (1979). *Thought and language*. Cambridge, MA: MIT Press. (First published 1934.)

Walberg, S. (2008). Automate system administration tasks with puppet. *Linux Journal, 176*. Retrieved from http://www.linuxjournal.com/article/10046.

Walsh, J. P. (1991). Organizational memory. *Academy of management review, 16*(1), 57–91.

Weimer, W., & Necula, G. C. (2004). Finding and preventing run-time error handling mistakes. *Proceedings of the 19th Annual ACM SIGPLAN Conference on Object-Oriented Programming, Systems, Languages, and Applications* (pp. 419–431). New York: ACM.

Wenger, E. (2000). Communities of practice and social learning systems. *Organization, 7*(2), 225–246.

Wenger, E. (2001). *Supporting communities of practice.* Retrieved from http://www.ewenger.com/tech/.

Wenger, E. (2006). *Communities of practice, a brief introduction.* Retrieved from http://www.ewenger.com/theory/.

Wenger, E., Snyder, W. M. (2000). Communities of practice: The organizational frontier. *Harvard Business Review, 78*(1), 139–145.

Werlinger, R., Hawkey, K., & Beznosov, K. (2008). Security practitioners in context: their activities and interactions. *CHI '08 Extended Abstracts on Human Factors in Computing Systems* (pp. 3789–3794). New York: ACM.

Whalley, P., & Barley, S. R. (1997). Technical work in the division of labor: Stalking the Wily anomaly. In S. R. Barley and J. E. Orr (Eds.), *Between craft and science* (pp. 23–52). Ithaca, NY: Cornell University Press.

White, K. F., & Lutters, W. G. (2007). Midweight collaborative remembering: Wikis in the workplace. *Proceedings of the 2007 Symposium on Computer Human Interaction for the Management of Information Technology.* New York: ACM.

Whittaker, S., Frohlich, D., & Daly-Jones, O. (1994). Informal workplace communication: What is it like and how might we support it? *Proceedings of the SIGCHI Conference on Human Factors in Computing Systems: Celebrating Interdependence* (pp. 131–137). New York: ACM.

Wilkes, J., Hoover, C., Keer, B., Mehra, P., & Veitch, A. (2008). *Storage, data, and information system* (5th ed.). Palo Alto, CA: HP Laboratories.

Williams, L., & Kessler, R. (2002). *Pair programming illuminated.* Boston, MA: Addison-Wesley Longman.

Woods, D. D. (1988). Coping with complexity: The psychology of human behavior in complex systems. In H. B. Goodstein & S. E. Olsen (Eds.), *Tasks, errors, and mental models* (pp. 128–148). London: Taylor & Francis, 128–148.

Woods, D. D. (1996). Decomposing automation: Apparent simplicity, real complexity. In R. Parasuraman & M. Mouloua (Eds.), *Automation and human performance-theory and applications* (pp. 3–17). Mahwah, NJ: Erlbaum.

Woods, D. D., & Roth, E. M., (1988). Cognitive engineering: Human problem solving with tools. *Human Factors, 30*(4), 415–430.

Wright, P. C., Fields, R. E., & Harrison, M. D. (2000). Analyzing human-computer interaction as distributed cognition: The resources model. *Human Computer Interaction, 15*(1), 1–41.

Yates, J. (1989). *Control through communication: The rise of system in American management.* Baltimore, MD: Johns Hopkins University Press.

Author Index

Ackerman, M. S., 105, 126, 155, 157
Almeida, V. A. F., 117
Andersen, H. H. K., 51, 240, 256
Andersen, V., 51, 240, 256
Anderson, B., 2
Anderson, R. J., 2
Arndt, M., 3
Arthur, W. B., 14, 230, 238

Bae, S. J., 57
Bailey, J., 8, 11, 156, 158, 235, 242, 243
Barley, S. R., 8, 52
Baroudi, J., 2
Barrett, R., x, 2, 8, 10, 11, 13, 19, 52, 129, 235, 236, 243
Beale, R., 52
Beaton, E., 84
Beck, K., 237
Becker, G. S., 52
Bernard, H. R., 1
Bernstein, M., 194
Bettenhausen, K., 13
Beznosov, K., 154, 215
Birnholtz, J. P., 57

Boiney, L., 84
Botta, D., 154
Bozman, J. S., 3, 5
Bradner, E., 37, 99
Bradshaw, J. M., 12, 20, 229, 231
Brennan, S. E., 12, 13, 20, 32, 52, 57, 59, 85, 114, 229, 234, 256
Brown, A. B., 3, 95
Brown, J. S., 124, 127
Brunsson, N. B., 117
Burgess, M., 239, 243
Bystrom, K., 86

Cadiz, J. J., 52
Campbell, C., 194
Canny, J., 37, 41
Cappuccio, D., 3
Cargill, C., 87, 123
Carlile, P. R., 64, 105, 126
Carroll, J. M., 256
Cavusoglu, H., 144
Chalup, S. R., 53
Chen, M, x, 8
Chess, D. M, ix, 7, 242

277

Christensen, J., 48
Clark, H. H., 12, 13, 20, 52, 57, 59, 85, 229, 234, 235
Cohen, S. G., 13, 20, 240
Connell, J. B., 37, 41
Convertino, G., 256
Covi, L., 52
Cowan, R. S., 243
Cramton, C. D., 20, 32
Crow, G. B., 183
Crowston, K, 14
Cunningham, W., 250
Cypher, A., 235, 236
Czerwinski, M, 48

Dahanayake, A., 127
Daly-Jones, O., 99
Dawkins, R., 230
Deetz, S. A., 127
Dellarocas, C., 14
Deloitte 2006 Global Security Survey, 5
DeMoss, C., 65
Dewar, R., 52
Dignan, L., 251
Donnelly, J. H., 159
Dossani, R., 183
Dowdy, L. W., 117
Drury, J. L., 84
Duguid, P., 124, 127
Duncan, M. O., 84
Durcikova, A., 114, 126

Edmondsen, W. H., 52
Egyedi, T. M., 127
Ellingsen, G., 123, 126, 239, 258

Ellis, J., 52
Emery, F., 7
Endsley, M. R., 144
Engardio, P., 3
Epstein, K., 200
Erickson, T., 37, 48
Etgen, M., 156
Evan, W. M., 2
Evard, R., 199

Fels, S., 154
Feltovich, P. J., 12, 20, 229, 231
Fetterman, D. M., 1
Fields, R. E., 13
Finholt, T. A., 57
Fitzgerald, B., 14
Foust, D., 3
Fox, K., 199
Freeman, K., 156
Frisch, A., 53, 243
Frohlich, D., 99
Fussell, S. R., 20, 32, 52, 256

Gagné, A., 154
Ganapathi, A., 6
Ganoe, C., 256
Gartner Group/Dataquest, 3, 5
Geertz, C., 1
Giacomazzi, F., 151
Gibson, C. B., 13, 20, 240
Gibson, J. L., 159
Goh, S. C., 87
González, V. M., 48, 184
Grayson, C. J., 14
GreenPope, R., 84
Grow, B., 200

Haber, E., 8, 11, 13, 19, 39, 44, 52, 65, 129, 158, 215, 225, 235, 236, 242, 243
Hagan, M., 65
Hage, J., 52
Halverson, C. A., 126, 155, 157
Hansen, C. B., 51, 240, 256
Harris, J., 48, 184
Harrison, M. D., 13
Hawkey, K., 215
Heath, C., 52
Hellerstein, J.L., 3
Hertzum, M., 20, 51, 57, 240, 256
Hinds, P. J., 13, 20
Hirschheim, R., 5
Hogan, C. J., 53
Hollan, J. D., 20, 59
Holland, J. H., 14
Hoover, C., 163
Horn, D. B., 57
Horvitz, E., 48
Howland, M. D., 84
HP, 7
Hrebec, D. G., 155, 156
Hudson, J. M, 48
Hutchins, E., 13, 20, 44, 47, 181, 231
Hutchins, E. I., 59

IBM, 3
Isaacs, E., 37, 99
ITCentrix, 3
ITCentrix (2001), 5
Ivancevich, J. M., 159
Iverson, L., 154

Jacobsson, B., 117
Jarvelin, K., 86
Jarvenpaa, S. L., 20
Jeffries, C. J., 151
Johnson, B. C., 246
Johri, A., 250
Jones, P. M., 13

Kamm, C., 37, 99
Kamsin, A., 124
Kanawattanachai, P., 20
Kandogan, E., 8, 10, 11, 13, 19, 39, 44, 47, 52, 65, 85, 129, 154, 158, 215, 225, 235, 236, 242, 243
Kanellos, M., 205
Karger, D., 194
Kauffman, R. J., 124
Keer, B., 163
Kellogg, W. A., 37, 48
Kenney, M., 183
Kephart, J.O., ix, 7, 242
Kersten, A., 127
Kessler, R., 105
Keyworth, B., 3
Kiesler, S., 20
Kirwin, W., 3
Klein, G., 12, 20, 229, 231
Knittel, C.R., 5
Knoll, K., 20
Kolstad, R., 157
Kramer, R. M., 20, 240
Kraut, R. E., 20, 32, 52, 256
Kreulen, J.T., 245
Krishnan, M.S., 52
Kumar, R. L., 124
Kunda, G., 8

Lackow, H. M., 183
Landsdale, M. W., 194
Larrson, A., 32
Lave, J., 13, 14, 197, 240
Lawrence, P., 52
Lee, J., 14
Leidner, D., 20, 117
Lerch, F. J., 52
Leuf, B., 250
Levy, F., 243
Limoncelli, T., 53
Lorsch, J., 52
Luff, P., 52

Maglaughlin, K. L., 156
Maglio, P. P., 8, 11, 13, 19, 39, 44, 47, 52, 65, 85, 129, 158, 194, 225, 235, 236, 242, 243, 245
Malone, T. W., 13, 14, 194
Manion, M., 2
Manyika, J. M., 246
March, J. G., 14, 88, 123, 159
Mark, G., 48, 52, 65, 184
McAllister, D. J., 20
McNally, M. M., 52
Mehra, P., 163
Menascé, D. A., 117
Mendelsohn, G. A., 37, 41
Meum, T., 123, 126, 239
Monteiro, E., 123, 126, 239, 258
Munkvold, G., 258
Murnami, R. J., 243
Murphy, K. M., 52
Muthuswamy, B., 183
Mynatt, E. D., 37

Nardi, B. A., 37, 99

Necula, G. C., 95
Norman, D. A., 20, 59

O'Dell, C., 14
Office of Government Commerce, 6, 123
Oleson, C., 65
Olsen, J. P., 14, 88, 123
Olson, J. S., 52
Oppenheimer, D., 6
Orikainen, J., 250
Orlikowski, W. J., 2, 84
Orr, J., 8, 230, 240

Paepcke, A., 64
Panella, C., 151
Parasuraman, R., 51
Patterson, D. A., 6, 95
Paxson, V., 203
Pentland, B., 14
Pernici, B., 151
Perry, R., 3, 5
Pipek, V., 105
Prabaker, M., 19, 129
Preece, J., 10

Qosient, 206
Quiggin, J., 2

Rada, R., 88, 123
Rai, S., 251
Rasmussen, J., 13, 83
Reed, D., 250
Riecken, D., 124
Robbins, S. S., 151
Robins, R. W., 37, 41
Rogers, Y., 10, 52

Roschelle, J., 52
Rosson, M. B., 256
Roth, E. M., 13

Sandusky, R. J., 84, 157
Sansoni, M., 151
Sarter, N. B., 144
Schein, E. H., 126
Scherlis, W. I., 52
Schiano, D. J., 37, 99
Schmidt, S. K., 117, 127
Scraefel, M. C., 194
Serenity Systems, 3
Sharp, H., 10
Sharrock, W. W., 2
Sheridan, T., 51
Sheridan, T. B., 51
Siegel, J., 20, 32, 256
Simon, H. A., 159
Snyder, C., 51
Snyder, W. M., 14
Sonnenwald, D. H., 156
Spohrer, J., 124, 245
Spool, J. M., 51
Srinivasan, S., 245
Stango, V., 5
Star, S. L., 64, 126
Stiber, M., 155, 156
Stone, B., 2
Stylianou, A. C., 151

Takayama, L., 10, 19, 129, 154
Teasley, S., 52
Teasley, S. D., 52
Trist, E., 7
Tschang, C., 200
Tyler, T. R., 20

van Kleek, M., 194
Veitch, A., 163
Velasquez, N. F., 85, 114, 126, 182, 194
Verdoes, J. A., 85
Vinck, D., 8
Voida, A., 37
Vygotsky, L. S., 13

Walberg, S., 243
Walden, E. A., 124
Walendowski, A., 37, 99
Walsh, J. P., 239
Weimer, W., 95
Weisband, S. P., 13, 85, 182, 194
Wenger, E., 14, 197, 230, 240
Werle, R., 117, 127
Werlinger, R., 154, 215
Whalley, P., 52
Whittaker, S., 37, 99
Whitton, M. C., 156
Wickens, C. D., 51
Wilhite, S., 48
Wilkes, J., 163
Wilkes-Gibb, D., 12
Williams, L., 105
Woods, D. D., 12, 13, 20, 48, 51, 52, 65, 83, 144, 229, 231, 235
Wright, P. C., 13
Wulf, V., 105
Wyner, G., 14

Yates, J., 191
Yee, I. A., 246
Yoo, Y., 20

Zhang, J., 144
Zhao, H., 236

Subject Index

Activity hubs, system administrators as, 188–191
Adaptation of tools and methods, 3, 12, 13, 14, 17–18, 123, 152–153, 166, 231–232, 236–238
Allocating assignment
 ad hoc, 165
 for client updates, 169–171
 division of labor, 192
 dynamic reallocation, 162, 193
 for On Demand Data Center Services, 184
 practices of system administrators, 159–161
Architectural standards, defined, 238
Architecture, multi-site, 247–248
Architecture development, 250–251
Asset managers, 188
Assets, client, 4
Automation
 balancing with customization, 131–136
 benefits of, 148–150, 243

developing tools for, 129–158
 observations for design, 146, 151
 overview of, 242–243
 of patches, 144–146
 scripts for, 145
 for standardization, 248–249
 trade-offs, 51, 130, 131–136
 trends in, 3, 7–8
 verification processes, 256
Autonomic computing, trends in, 7–8, 242
Availability managers, 98

Back-up operations, 108–109, 110, 111
Best practices, 95
Billing practices
 claim codes, 187–188
 effect on communities of practice, 241
Book chapters, roadmap to, 15–18
"Build sheets" for new servers, 185–187
Build teams, 186–187
 fixing vs. building, 190–191

283

Built-in capacity overhead, 186
Business trends
　creating and adapting tools, 236–238
　in information technology management, 3–5
　and need for grounding, 230

Capacity allocation
　expected *vs.* actual values, 121–122
　innovation *vs.* standard practices for, 118–121, 122–124
　observations for design, 124
　overhead ratios, 186
Capacity planning
　See also Capacity allocation
　demands of, 117–118
　descriptive episode, 117–124
　innovation for, 121–124
　observations for design, 124
"Capture database," 177, 255
Change managers, 91, 97
Change windows, 53, 89
"Cheat sheets"
　defined, 155
　for performing infrequent tasks, 184
　for security administration, 219–220
Checklists, for software upgrade, 170
Claim codes, 187–188
Client assets, 4, 188
Client perspectives on IT delivery, 168
Cognitive processes
　distributed cognitive system, 13
　grounding, 12–13
　and system administration, 231

Collaboration, 19–49, 226, 233–236
　allocation of resources, 164–165
　"build sheets" for new servers, 185–187
　change-tracking database, 174
　in complex environment, 85
　consensus building, 38–45
　creating mental models, 235
　descriptive episode of, 20–44
　detecting errors, 25–30
　global responses to global security concerns, 209–217
　MOO text-based chat system, 199, 208–209
　obstacles to, 33–38
　online repositories of information, 166
　posting warnings online, 135
　recent changes in, 247–262
　reducing friction between organizations, 166–168
　regarding security threats, 200, 207, 224–225
　remote troubleshooting, 30–33
　script development, 157–158
　security community *vs.* broader community, 216
　sharing tools locally and globally, 217–221
　storage architects, 175
　synchronizing work across the organization, 174–180
　system administration as, 45–49
　in technical environment, 21–25
　using and developing community tools, 221–223

Commands
    cutting and pasting *vs.* typing, 96
Communication
    of both content and process, 229
    change-tracking database, 174
    for effective security administration, 224–225
    flowchart for client upgrades, 172–173
    global responses to global security concerns, 209–217
    grounding as basis of, 235
    managing information flow, 191–195
    methods of, 229
    MOO text-based chat system, 199, 208–209
    and outsourcing, 257
    with previous clients, 187
    recent changes in, 247–262
    reducing friction between organizations, 166–168
    regarding security threats, 207
    security community *vs.* broader community, 216
    and situational awareness, 144
    sorting out chaotic situations, 75–82
    standard practices regarding, 242–243
    summarizing system states, 72–75
    system administrators as information hubs, 185–188
    in technical environments, 45, 47–49

Communities of practice
    computer security, significance of, 200
    global responses to global security concerns, 209–217
    MOO text-based chat system, 199, 208–209
    overlapping interests of attackers and administrators, 216
    overview of, 240–241
    role of human judgment in assessing security threats, 202–205
    security community *vs.* broader community, 216
    sharing tools globally and locally, 217–221
    supporting and nurturing, 241
    system administration across communities, 223–227
    and trust, 197–227
    use of multiple different channels, 33, 45, 154, 190
    using and developing community tools, 221–223
    working with local communities, 205–209
Community tools, using and developing, 221–223
Complexity,
organizational, 159–196
social, 7, 19–50
technical, 6, 51–86, 226
Computer crime, recent changes in, 259
Computer networks, characteristics of, 23–24

286 Subject Index

Computer security, significance of, 200
Computers, increasing complexity of, 6
Configuration changes, tracking, 144
Consolidation servers, 90
Conventions
    information layout, 174–180
    system names, 31, 180
Coordinating information
    balancing developer and on-site instructions, 60–62, 64, 234
    "build sheets" for new servers, 185–187
    flowchart for client upgrades, 172–173
    managing information flow, 191–195
    regarding patches, 144–146
    sorting out chaotic situations, 75–82
    synchronizing work across the organization, 174–180
    system administrators as information hubs, 185–188
    in troubleshooting, 54–57
    updates and client schedules, 162
Core dumps, system, 79
Costs, labor
    and automation, 242, 249
    trends in addressing, 3, 5–7
Critical situations ("crit-sit")
    configuration of, 66
    descriptive episode, 65–84
    observations for design, 83
    overview of, 234–235
    sorting out chaotic situations, 75–82
    summarizing system state, 72–75
    transient problems in, 69–72
    using product technical support, 67–68
Crontab utility
    defined, 109
    repurposing of, 113–114
    scheduling backup with, 110–112
    screenshot of file, 110
    tailoring of, 237
Customization
    balancing with automation, 131–136
    building one-of-a-kind tools, 150
    patches, 144–146
    security tools, 203, 205
    spreadsheets and databases, 187
    tools and practices, 178, 194–195, 230–231

Database administration
    database management systems defined, 26–27
    descriptive episode, 88–117, 150–154
    organizational support for administrators, 97–101
    responsibilities of administrators, 89
    staging operations, 91–97
    testing operations, 89–90
Databases
    "capture database," 177, 255
    change-tracking database, 174
    significance of, 89
    verifying, 178
Depot servers, for patches, 132, 237

Descriptive episodes, 11–12
  capacity planning, 117–124
  critical situations ("crit-sit"), 65–84
  database administration, 88–117, 150–154
  On Demand Data Center Services (ODCS), 182–191
  security administration, 198–223
  storage administration, 146–150, 161–182
  tool creation, 131–146
  transition management, 182–191
  of Web administrator, 20–22, 24–25, 27, 29–44, 52–65
Designing systems, schedule for, 193
Development servers, 90
Distributed cognition, 13, 15, 18, 44, 47, 181, 193–194, 231–235
Division of labor, 192

E-mail, managing, 185, 194
E-mail, security alerts, 199, 201–202, 260
Education servers, 90
Enterprise storage architecture, 164
Errors
  administrative practices to minimize, 90, 91–97, 105, 114–115, 115
  ambiguity of messages, 29, 30, 46, 47, 51
  assessing severity of, 96
  collaborating with colleagues to detect, 25–30
  cutting and pasting commands *vs.* typing, 96
  handling in complex environment, 85
  insufficient information regarding, 64
  notification of, 58–59
  solving, 34, 59–62
Evolutionary processes, of technology development, 14–15, 223–231, 238

Files
  configuration, 31, 39, 55, 58
  log, 31, 42, 59, 68, 112, 201, 206
  "read-me", 135, 145
Firewalls, defined, 24
Firmware, updating, 162
Flowchart for client upgrades, 172–173, 192–193

Global responses to global security concerns, 209–217, 217–221
Grounding
  barriers to, 32–33
  basic principles of, 229–230
  change-tracking database, 174
  cognitive process of, 12–13
  in communication, 235
  in complex environments, 84–86
  defined, 229
  for effective security administration, 224
  formalizing concepts, 230
  human-computer interaction, 59
  past and future client work, 169–174
  standard practices to encourage, 192–193
  in system state, 57–60, 74–75

Hardware, as client asset, 4
Hierarchical Storage Managers (HSMs), 147–148

Honeypots, 217–218, 225
Human judgment, role in security administration, 202–205
Humor and collaboration with colleagues, 34

Information flow, among organizations, 159–195
  "build sheets" for new servers, 185–187
  customized spreadsheets and databases, 187
  descriptive episode, storage administration, 161–182
  grounding past and future client work, 169–174
  optimizing within an organization, 162–166
  orchestrating information flow, 181–182
  orchestrating organizations, 191–195
  overview of, 238–240
  reducing friction between organizations, 166–168
  synchronizing work across the organization, 174–180
  system administrators as information hubs, 185–188
Information technology, 2, 6–7
Information technology infrastructure library (ITIL), 6–7
Innovation
  see Standard practices and individual innovation
Instant messaging
  as back-channel communication, 190
  limits of, 37, 41

Institutional knowledge
  building and leveraging, 245
  effect of outsourcing, 251, 256
Interviews, with system administrators, 10
Intrusion detection
  software, 198, 202
Investigation-phase teams (I-phase), 165
IP address, defined, 23
ITIL
  See Information technology infrastructure library

Joint activity, 13, 59, 62, 85–86, 233, 235

Labor
  costs and automation, 242, 249
  divisions of, 192
  shifting responsibilities, 254–257
  trends in addressing cost, 3, 5–7
LUN size, 176

Malware, defined, 200
Managed Storage Services (MSS), 160, 161
Manual interactions in technically complex environment, 60–62
Mental models
  establishing, 234, 235
  importance in problem solving, 233–234
  of system states, 74–75
Mentoring employees, 193
MOO text-based chat system, 199, 208–209
MSS
  See Managed Storage Services

Multitasking
  during back-up operations, 109
  during long-running tasks, 108, 109
  need for focus during, 98, 99
  by system administrators, 48
  on transition teams, 189

Naturalistic observation, as research method, 10
Network partitioning and Web application deployment, 54, 60
Network ports, defined, 24
Networking equipment, as client asset, 4

Observations for design
  automation, 151
  capacity planning and allocation, 124
  change windows, 63
  conflicting requirements, 63
  coordinating administrative work, 181
  creating tools, 146
  the critical situation ("crit-sit"), 83
  grounding and collaboration, 46
  overview of, 232–233
  risk management, 116
  security administration, 226
On Demand Data Center Services (ODCS)
  descriptive episode, 182–191
  phases of, 183
Operating system administration
  descriptive episode, 131–146
  schedule for, 193
Orchestrating organizations, 191–195

Organizational awareness, 105–108
Organizational knowledge
  compiling, 105
Organizational structure
  defined, 238
  significance of, 238–239
Organizations, and information flow
  See Information flow, among ogranizations
Outsourcing
  and communication, 257
  of infrastructure and service delivery, 2, 5
  and institutional knowledge, 251, 256
  reasons, challenges, 2, 4–5, 183, 250–252
Overhead/utilization ratio, 186

Patch management
  coordinating with client, 141–144
  customizing, automating, and coordinating, 144–146
  descriptive episode, 131–146
  homemade tools for, 136–141
  innovation and deployment of, 237
  patch database, image of, 138
  progressively testing patches, 141
Patches
  defined, 131
  instruction for, 133
  posting warnings online, 135
  "read-me" files for, 135–136
  recommended clusters, 140
  to repair security breaches, 200
  types of, 137

290 Subject Index

Peer support
  during database operations, 88, 101
Personnel, development of, 245
Phone consultation
  vs. instant messaging, 37, 41
Plugins
  for vulnerability scanner software, 221–223
  risks of using public plugins, 221–223
Policy
  compliance, 126, 136, 156, 165, 237
  exceptions, 130, 137–140
Ports, network, 24
Prioritization
  of customer requests, 162–163
  fixing *vs.* building, 190–191
  of technical problems, 4
Problem ticket
  initiating, 4
Product technical support
  balancing developer and on-site instructions, 60–62, 64
  collaboration with, 33–38
  during troubleshooting, 55–57
  use by Web administrators, 67–68
Production machines
  used to test database operations, 90
Project managers
  on transition teams, 190
Provisioning storage, 162

Quality-assurance servers, 90

Redundancy, inherent
  for avoiding outages and downtime, 169

Rehearsal
  of database operations, 87–88, 101–105
  organizational support for, 237
  of table move, 91–97
Repositories of information, 166, 220, 238
Research
  methods and motivation for, 1–18
Research-phase teams (R-phase), 165
Resource allocation
  for On Demand Data Center Services, 184
  spreadsheet to track storage allocation, 176–177
  and storage administration, 164–165
Resources, for system administrators
  "best practices," 7, 88
  communities of practice, 225–226
  creating tools for system administration, 154–158
  development of, 129–130
  personnel, 245
  responses to security threats, 199–202
Risk, managing, 108–115
  in database operations, 115–117
  managing individual innovation, 124–127
  observations for design, 116
  standard practices *vs.* individual innovations, 116–117
  validation of test results, 126–127
Roadmap to book chapters, 15–18
Roles, system administrator
  architect, 166, 174, 251

Subject Index   291

bridge, 17, 159, 182
coordinator of activity, 188–191
coordinator of information,
    185–188
emotional support, 45, 101
focal, 131, 144, 162, 168
liaison, 168, 174, 192
management, 47, 72, 91, 160
technical support, 20, 33–38
team lead, 160, 164

Sales phase, of On Demand Data
    Center Services (ODCS), 183
Sandbox servers, 90
SANs
    See Storage Area Networks
Scripts
    for automation and analysis, 145,
        152–154
    "cheat sheets" for, 155
    collaboration with colleagues,
        157–158
    defined, 238
    examples of, 94, 102, 148–149
    for rehearsing procedures, 101–105
    shell scripts, 154
    standardizing and modifying, 95
    vs. other job demands, 155
Security administration, 197–227
    "cheat sheets" for, 219–220
    collaboration with colleagues,
        224–225
    computer security, significance of,
        200
    descriptive episode, 198–223
    e-mail alerts, 199, 201–202, 260

global responses to global security
    concerns, 209–217
grounding for, 224
MOO text-based chat system, 199,
    208–209
observations for design, 226
overlapping interests of attackers
    and administrators, 216
recent changes in, 259–262
role of human judgment in
    assessing security threats, 202–205
sharing tools globally and locally,
    217–221
system administration across
    communities, 223–227
using and developing community
    tools, 221–223
working with local community of
    practice, 205–209
Servers, computer
    allocation of, 122–124
    "build sheets" for, 185–187
    consolidation, 90, 96, 125
    defined, 23
    fixing *vs.* building servers, 190–191
    patch depot servers, 132
    production, 90, 104, 125, 141, 190
    sandbox, 90
    staging, 54, 84, 119,
    testing, 54, 90, 157
    types used in database operations, 90
Service delivery
    fixing *vs.* building servers, 190–191
    service-level agreements, 4
    specialized, 6
    trends in, 3

Service-level agreement (SLA), 4
  availability, 4
  costs, penalties, 3, 183, 190
  fixing *vs.* building servers, 190–191
  and grounding, 230
SHARK
  chart to explain storage system, 179
  port assignments, 180
  and provisioning storage, 162
  subsets of Manage Storage Services, 161
Shell scripts, 154, 218–219
Shift schedules
  coordinating, 165
  operating *vs.* design teams, 193
  recent changes in, 248, 257
Situational awareness
  importance of, 144
  and resource allocation, 164
Skills, updating, 249
SOC
  See Storage Operations Center
Social environments
  among system administrators, 7
  and cognitive process of grounding, 12–13
  communicating both content and process, 229
  formulating process for client upgrades, 169–171
  reducing friction between organizations, 166–168
  and risk management, 117
  system administration as collaboration, 45, 47–49
Specialization, in response to complexity, 231–232

Staging operations, 90, 91–97
Standard practices and individual innovation, 87–127
  advantages and disadvantages of each, 88, 127
  automation for standardization, 248–249
  capacity planning and allocation, 117–124
  compiling organizational knowledge, 105
  customizing work tools, 178
  descriptive episode, database management, 88–117
  documenting innovation, 125–126
  established policies, 242–243
  evolution of standard practices, 120–121, 194–195
  formal agreements to standardize practices, 230
  managing risk, 108–115, 115–117, 124–127
  observations for design, 146
  organizational awareness, 105–108
  organizational interaction, 160
  recent changes in, 247–262
  staging operations, 91–97
  standardization on a global scale, 257–258
  standardizing and modifying scripts, 95
  tracking storage allocation, 177
Steady-state operations team, 160–161
Steady-state phase, 183
Storage administration
  descriptive episode, 146–150, 161–182

Subject Index

enterprise storage architecture, 164
investigation-phase and
 research-phase teams, 165
optimizing with organization,
 162–166
overview of, 239
provisioning storage, 162
recent changes in, 252–254,
 254–257
spreadsheet to track storage
 allocation, 176–177
Storage Area Networks, 163
Storage architects, 174–180
Storage Area Networks (SANs), 161,
 163
Storage devices, as client asset, 4
Storage Operations Center (SOC)
 investigation-phase and
  research-phase teams, 165
 work by team leaders, 160
Study methods used for this book,
 8–15
Summarizing system states, 72–75
Summary of this book, 18
Synchronizing work, 174–180
System administration
 across communities, 223–227
 balancing human and computer
  interaction, 82–84
 build teams, 186–187
 capacity planning and allocation,
  117–124, 122–124
 claim codes, 187–188
 and cognitive processes, 231
 as collaboration, 45, 47–49
 computer security, significance of,
  200

conclusions drawn, 245–246
creating and collecting custom
 tools, 154–158, 155–157
critical situation response
 ("crit-sit"), 65–84
database administrators, 87–128
database administrative practices,
 115
descriptive episode, capacity
 planning, 117–124
descriptive episode, database
 administration, 150–154
descriptive episode, database
 management, 88–117
descriptive episode, On Demand
 Data Center Services, 182–191
descriptive episode, security
 administration, 198–223
descriptive episode, storage
 administration, 146–150, 161–182
descriptive episode, transition
 management, 182–191
descriptive episode, Web
 administration, 52–65
descriptive episodes, introduction
 to, 11–12
dynamic nature of work, 244
global responses to global security
 concerns, 209–217
Hierarchical Storage Managers,
 147–148
inadequate tools for, 46, 63, 129,
 155–157, 236
managing information flow, 191–195
methods for researching, 9–10
observations for design, coordinating work, 181

System administration (*conti.*)
  observations for design, security administration, 226
  overlapping interests of attackers and security administrators, 216
  patterns of, 235
  risk management, 108–115
  role of human judgment in assessing security threats, 202–205
  scripts for automation and analysis, 145
  shift schedules, coordinating, 165
  summary of findings, 229–246
  time-management practices, 183–184, 193–194
  using "cheat sheets," 155, 184, 219–220
System administrators
  as activity hubs, 188–191
  allocating assignments, 159–161, 169–171, 184, 192
  allocating resources, 164–165
  attention, distraction, 68, 38–44
  automation and, 242–243
  availability managers, 98
  balancing human and computer interaction, 82–84
  "best practice" resources for, 7, 88
  build teams, 186–187
  and cognitive process of grounding, 12–13
  collaboration with colleagues, 19–49
  communication with past clients, 187
  communities of practice, 240–241
  consensus building with colleagues, 38–45
  coordinating information, 64, 115
  database administrators, 87–128
  embodying "best practices" within scripts, 95
  errors attributed to, 5, 90, 125, 144
  guiding automation, 7–8
  human judgment, 96, 105, 127, 162, 201, 202–205
  human-computer interaction, 59
  individual adaptation of tools and methods, 3, 12, 13, 14, 17
  as information hubs, 185–188
  instant messaging by, 190
  as knowledge workers, 229, 245–246
  managing e-mail, 185, 194
  mental model, 20, 30, 39, 49, 74–75
  mentoring, 91, 108, 175, 193
  multitasking by, 48, 189
  observation and interviews, 10
  operating system administrators, 129–158
  as organizational bridges, 182, 194
  organizational support for, 97–101
  overlapping interests of attackers and security administrators, 216
  security administrators, 197–228
  situational awareness among, 144, 164
  social environments among, 7
  specializations among, 6
  staging database operations, 91–97
  stress, 19
  storage administrators, 129–158, 159–196
  storage architects, 174–180
  as system designers, 150

time-management practices,
  183–184, 193–194
 time pressures felt by, 241
 tools, customized, 129–131, 155–157
 tools and practices used by, 46, 63
 transition managers, 160–161,
  182–191
 trust, 198, 215
 Web administrators, 19–50, 51–86
System configurations
 problems encountered, 25, 27–30
 for Web access, 23, 28, 43

Table move
 instructions for, 92–93
 rehearsal of, 91–97
 script for, 94
Table space, defined, 89
Technical environment
 communication in, 47–49, 48–49, 229
 moves to specialization, 231–232
 problem solving in, 21–22, 24–25, 27–30
 remote troubleshooting, 30–33
 risk management, 117
 technical product support, 33–38
 technical solutions to organizational friction, 167
Technologies, increasing complexity of, 51–86
 computers, increasing complexity of, 6
 coordinating information, 54–57, 231–232
 critical situations ("crit-sit"), 65–84
 grounding, need for, 230

 grounding in complex environments, 84–86
 grounding system state, 57–60
 manual interactions with automated systems, 60–62
 navigating body of knowledge, 226–227
 problem-solving, 63–65
 rehearsing database operations, 87–88
 sorting out chaotic situations, 75–82
 specialization, need for, 243
 summarizing system states, 72–75
 using tool collections to address, 51–86
 virtual machines, 259–260
Technology
 evolutionary processes of development, 14–15
Test machines
 used to test database operations, 90
Time-management practices, 183–184
 managing e-mail, 185, 194
Tools
 building one-of-a-kind, 150
 creating system administration tools, 154–158
 crontab utility, 109, 110–112
 customization of security tools, 203, 205
 development across communities, 227
 evolving as organizations evolve, 194–195, 230–231
 individual development of, 129–158

overview of creation and
    adaptation, 236–238, 237–238
reasons for creating and collecting
    custom tools, 155–157
recent changes in, 247–262
sharing globally and locally,
    217–221
using and developing community
    tools, 221–223
for Web administrators, 21–22,
    24–25
wiki tools, 250, 261

Total cost of ownership, ix
Transient problems in critical
    situations ("crit-sit"), 69–72
Transition management
    descriptive episode, 182–191
    recent changes in, 257–259
    transition managers, 160–161
Transition phase, of On Demand
    Data Center Services (ODCS),
    182–183
Trends
    in automation, 7–8
    creating and adapting tools,
        236–238
    in information technology man-
        agement, 3–8
    labor, 5–7
Troubleshooting
    balancing human and computer
        interaction, 82–84
    in chaotic situations, 75–82
    coordinating information for,
        54–57

remote troubleshooting, 30–33
transient problems in Web
    applications, 69–72
"Trusted colleagues" in security
    administration, 225

Updating skills, 249
Upgrades
    coordinating, 239
    flowchart for, 172–173
    formulating schedule for, 169–171
    orchestrating, 192–193
Utilization/overhead ratio, 186

Validation of test results, 105, 126–127
Values, expected *vs.* actual, 121–122
Verification
    automated, 256
    of configuration file updates, 134
    of databases, 178
    as method of avoiding errors,
        114–115
Virtual machines, 259–260
Viruses
    defined, 200
Vulnerability
    scanner software, 221

Web administrators
    collaboration among, 233–234
    descriptive episode, 20–22, 24–25,
        27, 29–44
    recent changes for, 247–250,
        250–252
    use of product technical support,
        67–68

Web applications
  configuration of, 70
  deployment, 54–62
  grounding system state, 57–60
  testing and using, 53–54
  wizards for, 61–62
Wiki tools, 250, 261

Wizards for configuring Web applications, 61–62
World Wide Web, defined, 26
Worms
  defined, 200
  responding to variants, 206

Y2K phenomenon, 2

About the Authors

Eser Kandogan is a research staff member at IBM Research-Almaden and manages a group conducting research on visual interfaces to data. He served as the general chair and program chair for ACM CHIMIT symposium and was a member of the program committee for several conferences, including ACM CHI, USENIX LISA, and IEEE Policy. He holds a B.Sc. degree in computer engineering and information sciences from Bilkent University, Turkey, and a Ph.D. degree from University of Maryland, Computer Science Department. Dr. Kandogan has over 50 publications in areas such as human-computer interaction and information visualization.

Paul P. Maglio is a research staff member at IBM Research-Almaden, and a Professor of Technology Management at the University of California, Merced. He holds a bachelor's degree in computer science and engineering from MIT and a Ph.D. in cognitive science from the University of California, San Diego. One of the founders of the field of service science, Dr. Maglio serves on the editorial boards of the Journal of Service Research and of Service Science, and was lead editor of the Handbook of Service Science. Dr. Maglio has published more than 100 papers in computer science, cognitive science, and service science.

Eben Haber is a research staff member at IBM Research-Almaden, where he has worked on topics including IT System Administration (including studies of sysadmins, developing prototype administration tools, and designing new features for middleware management products), as well as research on end-user programming and information visualization. He holds an A.B. in computer science/physics from Dartmouth College, and an M.S. and Ph.D. in computer science from the University of Wisconsin-Madison. As the only person on earth so named, a wealth of additional information about him can be found using any web search engine.

John Bailey is a Director of Product Design at CA Technologies, where he creates leading-edge product user experiences for the management of information technology. Previously, Dr. Bailey was a research scientist at IBM Research-Almaden, where he did research on service systems, specializing in human factors in information technology service engagement and delivery, and prior to that, he was the Lead User Experience Architect for IBM WebSphere Application Server and manager for user-centered design. He holds a Ph.D. in human factors psychology from the University of Central Florida, and has published in the areas of virtual reality, human-computer interaction, automation, simulation and training, systems administration, and service science.